To Michael.

RATIONING
EARTH

ECONOMIC STRATEGY BY DESIGN

Great Photos

HERB BENTZ

Herb Bentz

◆ FriesenPress

Suite 300 - 990 Fort St
Victoria, BC, V8V 3K2
Canada

www.friesenpress.com

ISBN
978-1-4602-8095-9 (Hardcover)
978-1-4602-8096-6 (Paperback)
978-1-4602-8097-3 (eBook)

1. BUSINESS & ECONOMICS, ENVIRONMENTAL ECONOMICS

Distributed to the trade by The Ingram Book Company

To my wife Jackie, our children Julie and Simon, and Chris and Julie's children Crosby and Norah. I hope that our grandchildren's future will be brighter because of our actions today.

CONTENTS

PREFACE

From 1976 to 1979, I studied industrial design at the Royal College of Art in London, England while Bruce Archer was head of the Design Research Department there. Archer believed that "there exists a designerly way of thinking and communicating that is both different from scientific and scholarly ways of thinking and communicating, and as powerful as scientific and scholarly methods of enquiry when applied to its own kinds of problems." He was arguably the first author to use the now common phrase "design thinking."

Archer was also concerned with designers' place in society, especially in education. He noted the three Rs—reading, writing, and 'rithmetic—with reading and writing both referring to language, betray a prejudice against the doing and making professions. He claimed a great-aunt always said that the three Rs originally referred to *reading* and writing (language), *reckoning* and figuring (numbers), and *wroughting* and wrighting (the ability to make something)[1]. Archer was convinced that design should stand equal against the sciences and the humanities. He wrote prophetically in 1979, "modern society is faced with problems such as the ecological problem, the environmental problem, the quality-of-urban-life problem ... which demand ... competence in something else besides literacy and numeracy ... a level of awareness of the issues of the material culture."[2] These problems of the material culture—including economics and the environment—are problems that require a design perspective.

Design thinking, instead of a category of thought, is often presented as a special technique invented by designers that will lead to innovations if used as directed, leading to justified criticisms that design is not the only profession capable of thinking.[3] Critical musings of mathematicians, ruminations of engineers, or the quiet contemplation of anthropologists could be brought to bear on the world's problems. Design is not an artificial method, but a natural process used routinely by everyone to solve most everyday problems. What designers bring to the table is a specialization in design thinking, honed with years of experience and augmented with an ability to generate models and prototypes to evaluate solutions.

----

1   This was included in a speech by Sir William Curtis MP in c1825. It is possible that this was later shortened to reading, wrighting and 'rithmetic, which was then mistakenly transformed to the modern form of reading, writing, and 'rithmetic.

2   Bruce Archer, "Whatever Became of Design Methodology and The Three Rs," *Design Studies*, Vol. 1, No. 1, July 1979.

3   Stanford University, for example, presents the steps in a design thinking process: understand, observe, define, ideate, prototype, and test. While typical of how designers work, I do not believe a methodology can define a mode of thought, only a systematic way of proceeding.

Design is a method of problem solving distinct from the scientific method. Scientific analysis leads logically to a single solution. For the designer, this single solution is just the starting point that must be elaborated on according to detailed requirements of a specific context. Nigel Cross, another British design researcher, in a series of articles about "designerly ways of knowing," argues that we are all capable of designing; "… design thinking is something inherent within human cognition; it is a key part of what makes us human."

The difference between scientific analysis and design thinking is not so much a difference in the method used, but in the type of problem solved and in what constitutes a solution. Horst Rittel, a mathematician, design theorist, and university professor at the Ulm School of Design in Germany, suggested that most of the problems addressed by designers are "wicked problems"—those poorly defined and intertwined with solutions. In other words, a wicked problem cannot be understood completely without at the same time considering a possible solution. Solutions cannot be true or false; they can only be good or bad. There is no ultimate solution; every solution suggests a new understanding of the problem and this new understanding leads to a better solution. Another characteristic of wicked problems is that it is not possible to identify a single solution applicable to many similar problems. Instead, an infinity of solutions exists that are each good or bad, but not wrong. This solution focus means that the designer, in addressing a problem, continuously oscillates between trying to understand the problem and suggesting a solution.

What we gain with design thinking are possible concrete solutions before there is full understanding of the problem. We incorporate technology and scientific analysis in design thinking, but usually a leap of faith ignores some information and extrapolates other data—a "short circuit" of analysis that presents a concept for an actual solution that is possibly wrong, but leads more efficiently to one that is right. The premise in design thinking is that any action is sometimes better than no action because, as Thomas Edison believed, there are no failures, just many successes of finding different ways for something not to work. The major difference between scientific analysis and design thinking is that understanding of the problem is never complete with design. Whereas scientific analysis fails when the model fails to represent reality, design uses models and prototypes—representing a future reality—to optimize many variables through successive approximations to solutions.

Philippe Starck, the famous French industrial designer, tells how a "vision of a squid-like lemon squeezer" suddenly came to him while sitting in a restaurant, leading to the iconic product by Alessi.[4] But design thinking—the flash of insight that results from seeing the problem from a different angle—is not restricted to designers. Albert Einstein solved a problem of relativity—how the speed of light can be constant even though different sources of light are moving at different velocities—by realizing that the rate of time passing is what must vary.[5] Instead of the constant speed of light being the problem, it was our perception of time.

4   Nigel Cross, *Design Thinking: Understanding how Designers Think and Work*, (Oxford, New York: Berg, 2011), 6.
5   From a talk given by Einstein in Kyoto, Japan on 14 December 1922, reported in *Physics Today*, August, 1982, 45-47.

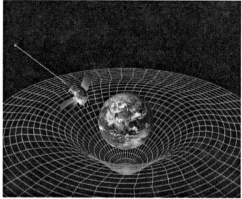

Figure 1: *Left: Philippe Starck's "Juicy Salif" lemon squeezer for Alessi; Right: artist's conception of four dimensional space-time around Earth.*[6]

Einstein also wryly observed that we can't solve problems by using the same kind of thinking we used when we created them. Design is a form of thinking and the complement to scientific analysis. The scientist believes that by thoroughly understanding the problem, the solution will be obvious. The designer searches for practical solutions without understanding the problem completely.

The belief that the economy is determined by a scientific theory and therefore does not have to be modified to suit changing contexts—of resource depletion including peak oil, technological change, and new competition from developing countries—not only explains the failure of mainstream economists to predict the

---

6   Photo of lemon squeezer by Niklas Morberg [CC BY-SA 2.0 (http:// creativecommons.org/licenses/by-sa/2.0)], via Wikimedia Commons, Space-time photo from NASA.

2008 crisis, but likely contributed to its occurrence. Of the failure, Paul Krugman maintained that economists "mistook beauty for truth."[7] James Galbraith responds in a recent book that such an admission is damaging to the profession and places doubt as to the "place of economics among the sciences."[8]

What should be designed and what should be allowed to ebb and flow naturally, like water in a stream, is a matter of practicality. The thinking that I would prefer to call design thinking is common to all doing and making professions, and design is simply the act of finding a solution to a poorly defined or "wicked" problem. Design emerges out of necessity. Cities can evolve naturally but at some point the random sprawl becomes unmanageable. The economy has also evolved randomly under the guidance of various scientific theories. Eventually society must decide, specifically, what type of economy it needs or wants. In this book, I argue that point is now.

---

7   Paul Krugman, "How Did Economists Get It So Wrong," *The New York Times*, 2009.

8   James K. Galbraith, *The End of Normal: The Great Crisis and the Future of Growth*, (New York, London, Toronto, Sydney, New Delhi: Simon & Schuster, 2015), 66.

INTRODUCTION

To be, or not to be, that is the question:[9]

—William Shakespeare

How can an economy that requires the momentum of continuous growth be reconciled with the new realities of a limited environment? Consumption is encouraged by business leaders, while environmentalists urge us to reduce, reuse, and recycle. Our already large population of over seven billion people will become nine or ten billion by the end of the century, stretching the earth's resources severely. Pollution, including the now apparent threat of global warming caused by greenhouse gases, threatens to restrict the impressive growth of our economy. These challenges alone would overwhelm our political decision making processes, but

---

9   William Shakespeare, *Hamlet,* the soliloquy of Act 3, Scene 1.

even if there could be ongoing economic growth, there may still be rising unemployment caused by technological advancement and continued automation of production and services.[10]

There is no compelling reason to believe our civilization, now encompassing the whole planet, will not collapse like the Mayas, the Romans, or the Rapanui of Easter Island. This is true even though our economy is more advanced and productive than ever.

Our problems are not difficult to solve. We have a great deal of insight and understanding about our predicament. We have solved many technological hurdles, but what remains is a complex puzzle of economic, cultural, and political factors that threaten a long crisis. To begin to solve the puzzle, we need to address a number of questions. What is blocking timely action on pressing environmental problems? Why is there still poverty, even in the richest economies? Why has ongoing economic growth failed to create economic security? Why is there political resistance, even when there appear to be obvious solutions?

Partial answers are well documented in numerous books. There are many expositions concerning the sad state of the earth. Jared Diamond's *Collapse* provides a revealing account of how civilizations have failed when they do not account for the limitations of their environment. *The Limits to Growth* by Meadows, Randers, and Meadows, written in 1972 and updated in 2004, has shown that these limitations now apply to us. Other writers, such as Joseph E. Stiglitz,

---

10   This point is made in numerous books such as Martin Ford, *The Lights in the Tunnel: Automation, Accelerating Technology and the Economy of the Future,* (Acculant Publishing, 2009) and Eric Brynjolfsson and Andrew McAfee, *Race Against the Machine: How the Digital Revolution is Accelerating Innovation, Driving Productivity, and Irreversibly Transforming Employment and the Economy,* (Lexington, Massachusetts: Digital Frontier Press, 2011).

winner of the Nobel Prize in economics, in *The Price of Inequality: How Today's Divided Society Endangers Our Future*; Paul Krugman, another Nobel Prize winner and frequent contributor to the New York Times in *End This Depression Now*; Jeffrey D. Sachs in *The Price of Civilization* and other books, and Robert H. Frank in *The Darwin Economy: Liberty, Competition, and the Common Good* describe the economic problems we face and how solutions are limited because of political and sociological barriers. Other writers complain that our economic system and the requirement for continuous economic growth are at odds with required solutions to the problems of the environment.[11] These tend to challenge the views of mainstream economics. Their proposed solution that economic growth must stop seems to ignore the financial and sociological implications of recession and mass unemployment.

In *Rationing Earth*, I present a case for environmental rather than economic austerity. With appropriate limits on resource consumption, we do not have to limit the resources that are in abundant supply. The world has a large production capacity, including vast amounts of underused labour. There is no limit to knowledge, and there is no reason to stop funding research for the development of new technology or for higher education. Economic growth has one positive effect: it creates jobs and a

---

11   These include Richard Douthwaite, *The Growth Illusion: How Economic Growth has enriched the few, impoverished the many and endangered the Planet*, (Gabriola Island: New Society Publishers, 1992, 1999); Richard Heinberg, *The End of Growth: Adapting to Our New Economic Reality*, (Gabriola Island: New Society Publishers, 2011); Herman E. Daly, *Beyond Growth: The Economics of Sustainable Development*, (Boston: Beacon Press, 1996); Brian Czech, *Supply Shock: Economic Growth at the Crossroads and the Steady State Solution*, (Gabriola Island, New Society Publishers, 2013).

strong economy. I argue that cutting wasteful consumption will not stop the economy from growing.

The expanding population means there is no possibility of regressing our economy back to some ideal agrarian form. We are stuck with a need for ongoing technological progress. I believe we can create the technological advances to solve environmental problems that face us. In fact, existing technology would suffice if directed appropriately and developed with sufficient investment. I also think that people will make sacrifices, given the right motivation. We only lack a coherent plan of action and a sense of urgency. This means we must ration our consumption, but not our economic dynamism or our will to work and solve problems. In this book, I argue that we can limit overall and long-term consumption without sacrificing prosperity, but at the same time grow the industries that produce innovations for more efficient use of resources, products that are more durable and repairable, and infrastructure that will lead to lower consumption but better quality of service.

Economic austerity has resulted in the proliferation of poor quality products made ever cheaper and less durable to satisfy an increasingly cash-strapped consumer. These products, underused or quickly worn out, fill our landfills and cause excess pollution. We need to have an economy in which there is an incentive to work hard, to innovate, and find better solutions, but at the same time, to be more frugal in our consumption habits. *Rationing Earth* proposes a radical strategy to bring consumption in line with available resources. It is about how our economy functions, how it must change, and how to reduce our consumption and impact on the planet without a significant sacrifice to our prosperity.

William Stanley Jevons, a nineteenth century economist, observed that improvements in the efficiency of coal production often led to increased consumption because of reduced prices. As with coal production, technological advancements also allow us to produce other things with greater efficiency, yet our levels of consumption continue to increase. Rationing is the only way to prevent this so-called Jevons paradox.

Rationing may seem like a drastic response that is associated with stressful conditions, such as wartime and major economic depressions, but we already ration many things in our economy. We ration money through austerity measures, and many public services through financial and bureaucratic hurdles. At the same time, economic growth represents an extravagant and reckless consumption of resources—mainly for products and services that we do not really need.

The rationing I have in mind is not oppressive, because we will never have to have less than we had before. Improvements in efficiency will allow us to have more, but with less impact—if our overall consumption is rationed appropriately. We will gain from the benefits of an improved environment, improved infrastructure, better service, and higher quality products.

As consumption declines, the focus of economic growth will shift from production to developing new technologies and infrastructures for low carbon industry, transportation, and housing. This will allow us to supplement ongoing increases in economic efficiency with even further increases in technological efficiency. People in poor countries will eventually meet our level of consumption, by both using and contributing to our advances in economic and technological efficiency. Rich countries have always lived with an affluence to which poor countries aspire in terms of quality of life and the availability of consumables. That is why it is critically important to learn how to maintain or increase prosperity, even with a significant reduction in consumption.

There should not be any attempt to end economic growth. It will only harm the economy and make technological development less likely. Poor countries need to grow in order to converge with the levels of prosperity enjoyed in wealthier nations. The economy can continue to grow despite reduced consumption, because our prosperity will increase, the quality of the things we produce will improve, and we will have to pay more for what we do buy. An example of this is the urbanization process. As people move into cities and density increases, land and property become more valuable. People pay more for privileges and efficiencies gained, while reducing impact on the environment.[12]

We must redefine political and economic systems, and technology, according to increasingly constrained requirements of efficiency, social justice, and human rights. We no longer have unlimited resources. Technology has costs as well as benefits and the economy must be designed to match these new requirements. Limited resources combined with rising populations point to efficiency as a major problem, and rationing as a potential solution.

ORGANIZATION OF THE BOOK AND KEY POINTS

Rationing Earth is structured in four parts—overconsumption, unemployment, distribution, and external costs—to address the fundamental problems of our economy.

Prince Hamlet, the titular character from Shakespeare's play, will lead us on our journey through these four parts. In his famous speech in Act 3, Scene 1, Hamlet contemplates suicide. My

---

12   Very densely populated cities have a much lower impact on the environment than those composed of suburban sprawl. Los Angeles generates about three times the greenhouse gas emissions per capita as New York City. See Jeffrey D Sachs, *The Age of Sustainable Development*, (New York: Columbia University Press, 2015), 366-368.

modernized version of his speech reflects on our present inaction on the environmental crisis as Hamlet considers the moral impasse we all face, and the possible death of our civilization.

I have divided the speech into four sections, each forming an introduction to the four parts of the book. Part One, "Overconsumption," raises a fundamental question about whether to respect ecological limits, do something about the environmental crisis, or take no action and enjoy the present by sacrificing the future.

> To be, or not to be, that is the question:
> Whether 'tis nobler in the mind to suffer
> The hurricanes and floods of global warming,
> And to take many long distance vacations,
> Or by opposing end them. To not buy—to consume,
> No more; but without consuming say we end
> The economic growth and thousand useful products
> Our world is blessed with: 'tis a consummation
> Sincerely to avoid. To buy, to consume;
> To consume, to forget the future—ay, there's the rub:
> For in that consumption what future may come,
> When we have gotten rid of all resources,
> Must give us pause—[13]

Hamlet tries to decide whether it is better to respect the limits to growth and make the required changes for an uncertain future, or just to continue on the pleasant path of increasing consumption, to our eventual demise. He questions economic growth and asks what will be the result of getting rid of all resources.

---

13   This passage and other similar ones are adapted by the author from William Shakespeare, *Hamlet*, the soliloquy of Act 3, Scene 1.

The developed world has many of the characteristics of a stagnating economy, including persistent underemployment,[14] declining quality of infrastructure, high poverty rates, and stagnant wage levels. What has superficially appeared to be economic growth we can now reinterpret as a simple dysfunction of the market mechanism. It includes the inflation of house prices and other assets, inflation of rewards for a few participants, and unproductive gambling in the financial sector. The wealth supposedly created now sits as abstract value in a few isolated bank accounts rather than becoming a real increase in the capital stock of the nation. Although life is much better than it was in the 1930s, it does not conform to the statistics of economic growth. Problems with the environment are becoming serious and financial security for most people is lower. The promises of a constantly improving quality of life and increasing leisure time now seem in doubt. To me, a practising industrial designer, the mechanical workings of the economy are wrong. It is like a poorly designed machine that works, but not well. The total reliance on the market mechanism to solve the problems of society is ineffective and increasingly inappropriate.

My parents lived through the Great Depression and World War II. For them, the economy improved enormously until the early 1970s, when cracks started appearing. This period, often called the golden years, refers to North America and the Western European countries that experienced a beneficial economic restructuring after the war. Since this period, the economy has

---

14   See "Youth unemployment: Generation jobless," *The Economist*, April 27, 2013. I use the term underemployment instead of unemployment throughout because statistics on unemployment understate the magnitude of the problem.

grown. Total consumption of resources, and resources consumed per capita, have risen. Technology has advanced impressively and we can rejoice that the failed experiments of totally planned economies in the Soviet Union and China have ended. At the same time, the economic structure of the developed countries of the world has either regressed or failed to evolve to deal with present problems.

I present the case that the size of the economy indicated by the Gross Domestic Product (GDP) is not an appropriate measure of prosperity, or a reliable indicator of environmental harm. It is true that environmental impact is highly correlated with economic growth, but it is not necessarily caused by it. GDP increases only by 1 or 2 percent per year and by far the largest proportion of economic transactions: growth in wealth and growth in income have no value in resource terms. The need to funnel huge amounts of money into the economy to keep it fluid results in increasing disparities of wealth. This inequality places miserly restrictions on poor people and has no effect on the consumption habits of the rich. The price of most goods we buy is going down. External costs representing damage to the environment are not included in GDP at all. However, consumption of resources has increased along with the nominal economic growth. Consumption is increasing, I maintain, not because of economic growth but because clever marketing, lack of government regulation, and our extravagant lifestyles encourage it.

In our modern economy, we define efficiency in terms of productivity: the production of more per unit of labour is said to be more efficient. Conversely in nature, every organism consumes according to its needs, efficiently reusing waste. Our industries inefficiently produce more than necessary and create unusable waste and pollution. Abundant food is produced, but inefficiently, with copious amounts of non-renewable energy derived from fossil fuels. Transportation is efficient only in terms of its accessibility and speed, not in the resources it uses. The industrial efficiency of our economy is more about increasing quantity of production and a great deal that is not necessary. Instead, we need the long-term efficiency that results from effective design that increases the quality of what we produce. By eliminating wasteful and unnecessary consumption, by increasing quality of manufacture, and by improving design, I believe we can increase prosperity while reducing environmental impact.

Hamlet's speech continues in Part Two, "Unemployment." If we accept the restrictions of the environmental movement, who will bear the burden of more work with less pay?

> ... there's the problem
> With the environmental movement.
> For who would bear the recycling and conservation,
> The reusable shopping bag, the carbon tax,
> The pangs of a despised Gaia theory, Kyoto's protocol,
> The insolence of eco-friendly products
> That the climate change denier takes,
> When he himself might his SUV drive
> With air conditioning? Who will bear the burden,
> To grunt and sweat with no more fossil fuels,...

Increasing efficiency of production (or productivity) by reducing labour inputs introduces the social problem of unemployment. Industrialization often increases throughput at the expense of resource efficiency—the impressive productivity of agriculture made possible with energy derived from fossil fuels. Or it merely shifts paid labour to unpaid labour, as is the case with bank machines and automated checkouts. Overall, it is inefficient and ineffective not to utilize all labour.

Part Two concerns labour and capital, describing how economic growth is about the growth of capital, and how the economy must shift to one based on the preservation of resources. Unemployment is a persistent problem of industrialization caused by the more efficient use of labour for a given level of production. This is not a new problem, however. Since the beginning of agriculture, technology has displaced labour towards other functions not related to survival, such as religion, science, the fine arts, and politics. The threat of machines doing all work will not be the end of human labour, but the start of a new era of personal, social, and cultural development. Changes in the economy are required to make this transition possible. The economy, instead of being built on work that earns a salary, has to provide for needs more directly, allowing for the freer application of labour for the benefit of the self and society.

In Part Three, "Distribution," Hamlet reminds us, though our future is unconfirmed, our past must be our guide. We must not be complacent because of present comforts.

> But for the dread of environmental collapse,
> The unconfirmed future of computer simulation
> No time traveller attests, puzzles the will,
> And makes us rather accept the way the world is
> Than consider others that we know not of?
> Past failures thus make cowards of us all,...

The limitation of the resources of the earth is absolute. If resources are limited, a degree of austerity is justified. When a government runs out of money, it is because it has chosen, for political reasons, to do so. As this happens, a relative poverty in our social institutions prompts a private response of excessive and environmentally destructive consumption. We can increase prosperity by addressing the imbalances in our economy through more funding for social programs, more progressive taxation, and higher minimum wages. When these systems are stronger, rationing limited resources will seem fair and inevitable for an overcrowded world.

Conventional wisdom is that markets are the most efficient way to allocate the right amount of goods and services to those that need them. But this is only true for goods and services that are optional. For those products and services that are universally required, governments can often be more efficient for distribution. A well-funded and effective government can improve the quality of the universally required goods and services we receive.

In Part Three, I discuss the philosophical underpinnings of our economy, the reasons changes are required to save our planet and, in summary, what these changes should be. We don't need to abandon capitalism, but we do need to abandon neoliberalism and get back to the type of capitalism originally advocated by Adam Smith—an economy based on self-interest, but limited by a strict morality and effective regulation. There must be fairer distribution of wealth and adequate funding of social programs. I have a lot to say about our aberrant form of capitalism, along with suggestions for how it has to change to do what we need it to do, which is to allocate resources in an equitable manner, and reduce environmental impact in such a way that we end up with more, not less, prosperity.

The stresses of industrialization in the last century led to unfortunate political movements like communism and fascism, and to major world wars. The argument is that the welfare state and the mixed economy that emerged were what mitigated these stresses and paved the way for recent prosperity. I describe the growth of the welfare state in Chapter Seven and conclude it has been a necessary development because of industrialization, and a spontaneous evolution from the city-state that emerged with the agricultural revolution.

Lack of regulation in the economy has caused a severe economic crisis and has made the coordination and changes required to address the problems of the environment more difficult. The market economy, based as it is on self-interest alone, cannot work without a moral framework and proper regulation. This becomes more important as the economy not only requires individual effort but cooperative sacrifice.

In Part Four, "External Costs," Prince Hamlet, shaken by the arguments of the first three parts, has a sudden churning of conscience, a regret of missed opportunities, and a desire to ask for forgiveness and make amends.

> And thus the quest to end global warming
> Is tainted with selfish individualism,
> And green enterprises of great importance
> With this regard their currents turn awry
> And lose the name of action. Soft you now,
> Sweet Gaia! Mother Earth, hear our prayers;
> Please forgive us all our sins.

Governments can also address the final problem, of external costs, with taxation and regulation. However, the problem is not that environmental costs are external to the market pricing mechanism; the problem is that they lie on an entirely different dimension of value. In the market economy, increasing cost indicates increasing value. A Lamborghini costs more than a Toyota. However, a carbon tax added to the cost of a product does the opposite. A product with a high carbon footprint should be less valuable and less desirable. There are really two independent dimensions of value. The problem is that our one-dimensional currencies only measure the value of desirability, and not the underlying cost of resource scarcity. Adding a second dimension of value increases market efficiency by not interfering with the usual parameters of supply and demand.

Free markets are associated with a capital-based industrial economy and are key to its proper functioning because such an economy is dependent upon orchestrated individual effort. I argue that we can no longer rely exclusively on the market to solve our problems. The market economy is productive but less effective for rationing scarce resources. Ideally, market value would reflect the real cost of goods including all external costs. In the real world, market value is often subsidized and external costs are not included. The relative scarcity of many of the goods and services we buy requires that we often have to pay a high rent for their use above the underlying resource cost. These rents do not provide an indication of environmental harm. Instead, they distort and trivialize the cost of the resources we use. The rationing of impact suggests we adopt a new value system that is perpendicular to the current market based values. Unlike the carbon tax that further distorts the economic value we place on manufactured goods, I suggest that our economic system of value should become two-dimensional. I introduce the concept of a two-dimensional currency (TDC) in Chapter Eleven to give the consumer two dimensions of value. One dimension is the value in conventional terms according to supply and demand, the other measures the damage to the environment and the scarcity of the resources used according to costs normally external to market value. One dimension rations and limits overall consumption while preserving choice, whereas the other dimension maintains the exclusionary principle of the market for the optional qualities of products.

Most would agree that our rate of resource consumption on the planet is too high. Proposals to limit consumption or the emission of greenhouse gases or even pollution have so far not resulted in any significant agreements. Protests, no matter how well organized, are impotent against huge global inertia. Even if stopping economic growth is the right strategy, it is not clear we should stop economic growth now. Growth may be desirable for constructing infrastructure, fighting wars, ending poverty, developing a new technology, or meeting the challenge of global warming.

While technology has created many of our problems, it has also made it possible for the world's seven billion people to survive. Industrialization has increased food production and provided the infrastructure to allow the concentration of many people into densely populated cities. Other technologies are now required to improve the efficiency of production in resource terms with far less impact on the environment. Unfortunately, our economy and most research and development are geared towards producing goods more efficiently and finding ways to sell more products. A lot must change politically and culturally for the right investments to be made to improve production efficiency in terms of resources instead of labour.

Prince Hamlet approaches.

To be, or not to be, that is the question:
Whether 'tis nobler in the mind to suffer
The slings and arrows of outrageous fortune,
Or to take arms against a sea of troubles
And by opposing end them. To die—to sleep,
No more; and by a sleep to say we end
The heart-ache and the thousand natural shocks
That flesh is heir to: 'tis a consummation
Devoutly to be wish'd. To die, to sleep;
To sleep, perchance to dream—ay, there's the rub:
For in that sleep of death what dreams may come,
When we have shuffled off this mortal coil,
Must give us pause—

—William Shakespeare, Hamlet

PART ONE OVERCONSUMPTION

To be, or not to be, that is the question:
Whether 'tis nobler in the mind to suffer
The hurricanes and floods of global warming,
And to take many long distance vacations,
Or by opposing end them. To not buy—to consume,
No more; but without consuming say we end
The economic growth and thousand useful products
Our world is blessed with: 'tis a consummation
Sincerely to avoid. To buy, to consume;
To consume, to forget the future—ay, there's the rub:
For in that consumption what future may come,
When we have gotten rid of all resources,
Must give us pause—

ONE THE RISE OF CIVILIZATION AND ITS COLLAPSE

In the year 1600, Rapa Nui (Easter Island), a remote island in the South Pacific, was not suffering from a depression. In fact, the economy was booming. They were producing statues, faster and bigger than ever. Productivity was improving. Artisans learned new techniques and could make bigger statues faster and with less labour. There were a few complaints about degradation of the environment and resources required to move the enormous pieces of stone from the quarries where they were made. "Shouldn't we cut down the number of statues we are making?" cried the local environmental groups. But making fewer statues would cause massive layoffs and high unemployment. So the people of Easter Island continued to make more statues, each one bigger than the last. Finally, the economy collapsed. There were no trees left, even to make a boat. The last statues were erected around 1620. After the peak of their economy, collapse proceeded quickly.

> The economy of Easter Island, like our own, was dependent on economic growth. Work was highly specialized, with increasing numbers of food producers supporting growing number of workers who created the statues. Competing clans organized workers to create monuments of increasing size until the resources required led to an ecological collapse.[15] In this context, there was no point in producing another statue smaller or even the same size as the one before. Eventually, the absurdity of their economy caught up with them. The same will happen to us. The world economy cannot continue to grow forever.

Civilization has developed in a series of jumps like the discrete energy levels of atoms, from the early Paleolithic economy, to the agrarian, to the feudal, and finally to the industrial. Within each level, population increased to an unsustainable degree and then crashed, only to rise again from the ashes. The first technologies, invented before civilization during the Paleolithic age, included the tools of hunting—bows and arrows, spears, and the use of fire. Before hunting technology, humans competed with other animals for food, gathering what they could from the local ecology and scavenging meat left behind by other animals.

The development of weapons, techniques for hunting, and harnessing the energies of fire allowed humans to live in any climate and placed humankind apart from nature. These new techniques worked so well that the world became a rich store of food, and

---

15   Mathematical models have been used to demonstrate that unsustainable use of resources for monument building likely led to Easter Island's collapse. John Flenley and Paul Bahn, *The Enigmas of Easter Island: Island on the Edge*, (Oxford: Oxford University Press, 2002), 191-192; 195-205.

populations increased and spread around the globe. There was plenty of food, time for cultural growth, and painting on cave walls. As this vast food resource dwindled with the extinction of the last stock of huge mammals, scarcity and the normal balance of nature once again set in.

Hunting, less required for killing large animals, evolved into new techniques for hunting the human animal. Control of larger populations required brutal techniques. As command systems grew, humans were often killed or beaten, treated like animals, and subjected to forced labour. Techniques of warfare allowed civilization to expand by swallowing smaller groups on neighbouring land, but their ability to transport food and other necessities from neighbouring lands ultimately limited their size. As resources became limited, the invention of techniques of plant domestication and animal husbandry exploited the soil as another vast resource.

We continue to depend on agriculture for our livelihood, but technology gives us access to large amounts of energy that allow for a more efficient and faster exploitation of resources. Capital, rather than labour, is the ultimate limitation of production and our ability to extract resources that were previously inaccessible is now the basis of the economy.

The fall of the Roman Empire led to a decentralization of command in Europe. The system that developed, later called feudalism, was not limited to a central governing body. It allowed civilization to grow simultaneously in several locales. Local manors, towns, city-states, and countries developed, linked by networks of decentralized authority, allowing the rise of a strong network of affiliations. Conditions during much of the medieval period were bleak, most notably during the Bubonic Plague, the Black Death, which decimated the population of Europe by a third. But new techniques in agriculture led to an even greater expansion of populations. Feudalism, new techniques of agriculture, trade across Asia and Europe, and a slow industrialisation in western and eastern cultures represented the pinnacle of human culture. Increasing poverty, the failure of local ecologies, and the collapse of whole civilizations could well have been the result.

Instead, as in modern science fiction novels, explorers went out and discovered a whole new world, conveniently solving the problem of population expansion. North America, a world fully developed and easily conquered by Europeans, aided by the spread of infectious diseases such as smallpox, provided new land for cultivation, new agricultural crops and, most importantly, a place to export people. This sudden and unexpected windfall allowed European civilization, the underdogs at the time, to thrive, develop, and fully industrialize.[16]

Inventions and innovations spontaneously multiplied, like the creation of stars and galaxies in the early universe. Along with fire and the techniques of hunting and agriculture, the exploitation of a vast untapped resource of fossil fuels has become the last and arguably the most important engine of population growth. During the Industrial Revolution, we learned to exploit a previously untapped resource that still feeds our vast culture. We are

---

16   Ronald Wright, *What is America? A Short History of the New World Order*, (Toronto: Alfred A. Knopf, 2008), 41-46. Because of new foods introduced from the Americas, the population of Europe increased. There was a surplus of workers for factories and many moved on to North America and Australia. African populations also increased because of the introduction of these new foods by slave traders. This provided an abundant source of slaves for work in American plantations. At the time, Europe was far less developed compared to Eastern civilizations.

now also rich, because we have learned to use a resource that has seemed endlessly abundant and adaptable to our needs. Fossil fuels provide energy for transportation, faster than at any time in history, from anywhere on the planet. This means that food can be grown anywhere and transported to where it is needed. The use of artificial fertilizers and insecticides expanded agriculture. It is now conceivable to feed up to ten billion people. Just as feudalism was far more effective than the centralized tribute economy because it created a vast network of control that a central blow could not disrupt, capitalism is even more decentralized and based on a wide, almost uniform distribution of power in a vast global network. It has proved extraordinarily resilient to disruption, powerfully motivating, and nearly unstoppable as an engine of growth.[17]

In 1972, the Club of Rome published *The Limits to Growth* by Meadows et al., which presented a dire warning to the world that a limit to growth would be reached in the twenty-first century. The study made various assumptions about available resources and used a computer model to show that the present course of exponential economic growth could lead to economic collapse. Rising price of oil in the same year coincided with the prediction, made by Marion King Hubbert, of reaching domestic peak

---

17   For more information see Rondo Cameron, *A Concise Economic History of the World: From Paleolithic Times to the Present*, (New York, Oxford: Oxford University Press, 1997); David Christian, *Maps of Time: An Introduction to Big History*, (Berkeley, Los Angeles, London: University of California Press, 2004); Francis Fukuyama, *The Origins of Political Order: From Prehuman Times to the French Revolution*, (New York: Farrar, Straus and Giroux, 2011); Ronald Wright, *A Short History of Progress* (Toronto: House of Anansi Press, 2004).

oil production. The Organization of Arab Petroleum Exporting Countries (OAPEC) stopped shipment of petroleum to the United States soon after, in 1973, for political reasons. No such embargo could have occurred ten years earlier because other countries would have easily replaced the missing production. *Small is Beautiful* by E. F. Schumacher, also published in 1973, criticized notions that "growth is good" and "bigger is better." In 1987, the report of the World Commission on Environment and Development used the term "sustainable development" and defined it as "meeting the needs of the present without compromising the ability of future generations to meet their own needs." In short, there was a growing consensus that unrestrained economic growth could not continue.

A follow-up book called *Beyond the Limits to Growth*, written in 1992, by Meadows et al., argued that we were already beyond the carrying capacity of the earth. The possibility of a controlled reduction of the rate of growth towards a sustainable economy had been lost. We had already overshot: "… rain forests were being cut at unsustainable rates; there was speculation that grain production could no longer keep up with population growth; some thought that the climate was warming; and there was concern about the recent appearance of a stratospheric ozone hole."[18] By the year 2000, the ecological footprint of humanity had reached 1.2 times the carrying capacity of the earth.[19] Researchers realized that the problem was massive.

The term "eco-efficiency" was used to mean the supplying of goods more efficiently in ecological terms. A growing part of the

18   Donella Meadows, Jorgen Randers, Dennis Meadows, *The Limits to Growth: The 30-Year Update* (London: Earthscan Ltd., 2005), xii-xiii.
19   Ibid xv. Currently, our ecological footprint is up to 1.4 planet earths.

population believed that the world economy should stop expanding. People were encouraged to use less and recycle. Many corporations started to at least appear "green." In 1994, a company called InterfaceFLOR made a commitment to eliminate all impact on the environment by 2020. They took back used carpet tiles from their customers and incorporated the waste into their production process through the concept of "waste equals food." Although consumerism was still rampant, there was a growing consensus to buy less and to use less. At the same time, various stimuli ensured that economic growth and consumption continued unchecked.

The conditions needed for an unlimited capital-based economy—free and unlimited resources—are ending. Growth is essential for this version of capitalism to function effectively, just as a certain momentum, explosion after explosion, is required for the pistons in an internal combustion engine to keep moving. Capitalism is an engine that burns through a lot of resources to improve living standards dramatically. Sustainability requires putting the brakes on the machine, like adding a regulator to an internal combustion engine, so that resources are not burned too fast, and so we can decelerate, accelerate, and sometimes just idle.

In North America since the 1950s, the size of the economy in terms of gross domestic product has grown by a factor of about four, but financial security has declined for about 80 percent of the population. Since the 1970s, North America has experienced a shrinking middle class, increasing poverty, and a deteriorating natural environment. The nominal growth of the economy did not bring about increased wealth for most people. Real wages did not increase at all from 1973 to 1980 and then only increased about 0.7 percent per year to the year 2000. During this time, single income families have had to become double income, and work hours have increased along with work-associated stress. With a four-fold increase in the size of the economy since 1950, why is there still poverty? Why cannot most people afford the slightest reduction in income? Why are there still shortages of basic essentials such as healthcare, food, and shelter? The economy seems to create more and more while life satisfaction and security seems to deteriorate. Despite the outstanding growth and overproduction of some goods and services—consumer goods, for example—there is a deficiency of other goods and services such as healthcare, education, community service, police protection, housing, and even food for some people. There is an irrational bias of the economy towards producing optional items of luxury for rich people rather than essential items for all people. Surely the perfect economy would strive to fulfill all the essential needs first and luxuries second and then only if the resources were available to support it. There is presently no continuously effective or politically possible control for the rate and the direction of growth in the economy. A profound reorganization of the economy must take place—a green economy with more investment in resource efficiency and less in labour efficiency. This will reduce the need and the desirability for increased consumption and economic growth.

Our economic system is failing to control resource use, pollution, the pressures in the environment caused by ongoing population expansion, and the unprecedented dangers of global warming caused by burning fossil fuels. The economy provides perverse incentives that ignore these external costs and perpetuates an inefficient use of resources. Our economy must instead motivate the development of technology and the building of infrastructure that will reduce resource consumption in the long run.

How do we design an economy that doesn't have to grow but where prosperity, defined as the happiness and wellbeing of people, increases instead? Technological advancement, improvements in design, scientific research, and associated development should continue. Ingenuity is required to maintain wealth as resources decline. It is also required to solve increasingly complex problems of pollution, global warming, and maintaining food and water supply with ongoing population growth. We must learn to deliver infrastructure, housing, food, essential tools and appliances, and services more efficiently so that more people in the world can rise out of poverty to a reasonable standard of living.

In this chapter, I have described how available resources limit the advance of civilizations and population growth. Civilizations have collapsed unexpectedly when the population exceeds the capacity of the environment. The advance of European civilization, the industrial revolution, and exponential population growth was possible first with the discovery of North America, and second with the invention of ways to harness fossil fuels. Although it may seem like there is no end to economic growth because of techno-logical adaptation, there is an upper limit to available resources.

The remaining chapters of Part One demonstrate that the increase in consumption that has occurred in the past forty years has resulted in little growth in prosperity, that economic growth is unnecessary for prosperity, and that we can structure the economy to be healthy without growth. The following chapter explores the limitations of growth. There is an assumption in our economy that the more we consume, the more prosperous we are. However, the positional aspects of excess consumption and continual novelty increase our prosperity inefficiently. A lot of our consumption is wasteful and does not increase our prosperity in proportion to the resources consumed. With the right production, including better technology and smarter design, we could consume less yet receive more benefit.

TWO THE LIMITATIONS OF GROWTH

The man whose whole life is spent in performing a few simple operations, of which the effects are perhaps always the same, or very nearly the same, has no occasion to exert his understanding or to exercise his invention in finding out expedients for removing difficulties, which never occur. He naturally loses, therefore, the habit of such exertion, and generally becomes as stupid and ignorant as it is possible for a human creature to become.[20]

—Adam Smith

Once upon a time, there was a fishing village where fishermen caught fish that they sold to the local villagers. The villagers provided services such as boat building, food preparation, laundry, and medical care for themselves and for the fishermen. It was a closed and steady state

---

20   Adam Smith, *The Wealth of Nations*, (Harmondsworth: Penguin Books Ltd., 1776, 1982), 734-735.

economy. The fish were always harvested sustainably and the community functioned like this for as long as anyone could remember. There was no industry or technological improvement. People were fairly poor by our standards, but comfortable and relatively secure and happy.

One day a great wizard called Smith, who looked a bit like Robert Carlyle, came to the village. He said he had powerful magic to make them all rich beyond their dreams.

"You must specialize your talents, pool your savings, and invest in new fishing technology," he said. "You need bigger boats, nets, and electronics that will double the productivity of the fishing fleet and only require half the fishermen."

The villagers complied and the cost of fish came down; the villagers gained a richer diet that cost less. Those that pooled their savings earned a substantial return on their investment because of the larger volume of fish sold and the lower labour costs. Half the fishermen were now unemployed, but they became entrepreneurs and developed other products and services in which the investors, who had even more spare cash, could invest. New technologies were developed that reduced the need for manual labour and provided many possibilities for exciting leisure activities.

The economy grew and grew. They had more and more stuff, every convenience that could be imagined. The things they owned accumulated to such a degree it filled up their houses. No problem, they would build bigger houses. When these filled up as well, they built storage lockers behind the houses. Their possessions piled up to such a degree they became a burden and a curse. Air and water in their tiny village became polluted, causing sickness and ill health.

The villagers cried to the wizard, "How do we stop this madness of economic growth?"

The wizard smiled and said, "All magic comes at a price. There is no cure for economic growth."

Growth is a kind of deus ex machina, the god in the machine of the economy that conveniently, but irrationally, solves the problem of inequality and unemployment. As long as the overall economy continues to grow, the poorest will be better off, even if the rich continue to get richer. The unemployed will eventually get jobs, and we will ultimately solve the problems created by industrial production with new technology.

However, once this growth dynamic is established, any slowing of economic growth will cause unemployment and increasing social costs, while tax revenues decline. Because of the environmental costs, growth of the economy is unsustainable in the long run, but a lack of growth of the capitalist economy is unstable. This dilemma puts the public at the centre of a false debate. On one hand, we know that the environment is suffering from our actions, but on the other, we worry that any action will cause us to lose our jobs and the standard of living to which we have become accustomed.

One obvious benefit of economic growth is to raise an economy out of a condition of perpetual poverty. According to American economist Jeffrey Sachs, a leader in sustainable development, countries can generally escape from poverty traps and the need for foreign aid when their per capita income reaches about $4,000 per person measured at purchasing power parity (PPP), or roughly $1,000 (US dollars) at market prices.[21] Another benefit is

---

21   Jeffrey D. Sachs, *Common Wealth: Economics for a Crowded Planet*, (London: The Penguin Group, 2008), 246. PPP is a common exchange rate where the value of each international currency is in equilibrium with its purchasing power. Poorer countries tend to have lower wages and pay less for the goods and services they consume. Therefore, PPP is higher than international market prices in less developed economies. Unless otherwise indicated, all other ($) amounts will be in United States Dollars.

the ability to support democratic institutions. A study by Adam Przeworski and Fermando Limongi found that democracies in countries with per capita incomes of less than $1,500 survived just eight years. Countries with incomes between $1,500 and $3,000 survived ten years, but those with a per capita income of $6,000 survived indefinitely.[22] With this rough gauge, looking at the developing world and the obvious advantages of a democratic society, a goal of achieving a per capita income of $6,000 or a little more is very desirable.

Pollution increases with industrialization at about $2,000 per capita, but after about $8,000, people become rich enough for things like catalytic converters on their cars, and switch to unleaded gasoline and many other pollution-reducing technologies. According to the investment bank UBS, $13,000 is the per capita income at which consumption increases dramatically.[23]

In the year 1900, GDP per capita in the United States was $4,310. From 1900 to 1950, GDP per capita rose to $9,561. In 1973, GDP per capita rose even more to $16,689. Life got even better with modern conveniences such as refrigerators, vacuum cleaners, colour televisions, stereo high-fidelity music, and relatively trouble-free automobiles. Most of the improvements associated with modern life occurred in this period and democracy became more secure. Going from 1973 to 2000, per capita income almost doubled again, but the differences to the quality of life are less obvious.[24]

22   Adam Przeworski and Fermando Limongi, "Modernization: Theories and Facts," *World Politics* 49.2 (1997), 155-183.
23   Dambisa F. Moyo, *Winner take All: China's Race for Resources and what it means for the World*, (New York: Basic Books, 2012), 68.
24   http:/www.eh.net "HS-8 The World Economy 1-2001."

We have a great deal more, but less of value. Almost all increases in quality are the result of technological improvements: televisions have bigger and flatter screens; cars are safer; computers have become more powerful and smaller. On the other hand, we have more television shows, but fewer worth watching; bigger houses, but made of less durable materials. We have more digital music but of lower fidelity than previous technologies, more information but less that is accurate, more social networking but less human contact.

Our true wealth is a measure of the earth's resources. This means that the people of Paleolithic times were phenomenally wealthy, like Bill Gates a hundred times over. But this wealth was all in the bank, saved like the wealth of the thrifty millionaire who amasses his fortune without the slightest luxury, passing it on to successive generations. We the people of the modern world spend like the instant lottery winner until nothing is left, thinking that spending is what makes us wealthy. That we are poorer than previous generations is obvious. The early hunters and gatherers had the whole earth to divide among a few million people. We have an earth to split among seven billion. There is more polluted air, less pure water, more spent soil, and fewer intact forests. Increased happiness due to increased wealth does not characterize modern life; instead, we see more stress and ultimately less quality of life due to increased capital cost.

Even if things are not that bad, we must consider another factor: a relatively small proportion of the earth's population, approximately one billion out of seven, enjoy most of the benefits and are responsible for most of the harm. In the ocean of economic development that has occurred in the past 250 years, a tsunami of wealth has gone to 1 percent of the world's population. The output of the world economy is approximately $51 trillion. This provides an average per capita income of over $7,000 per year for every person on the planet. But this average is highly unequal, with 2.7 billion people living on less than $700 each year, while those in the rich part of the world, on average, consume goods and services worth over $40,000, and the top 1 percent, if they wished, over $400,000. Because populations will grow to nine or ten billion people, and the wealth of developing countries will tend to converge with rich countries, the size of the world economy will at least triple in the next fifty years.[25] If we carry on with business as usual, our already high impact could become three times as great as now.

Extremes of wealth and poverty are the worst-case scenario for solving the problem of overpopulation, unsustainable resource use, and high levels of pollution and greenhouse gases. The financially insecure, now including the middle class, will not care, or care less, about solving the problems of the environment. They will be more concerned with their own immediate survival. On the other hand, luxurious air-conditioned houses in gated communities with private security forces cushion the ultra-rich from the effects of pollution and global warming. In the future, there will be fewer resources to distribute to increasing numbers of people, all of whom will aspire to a better lifestyle. We cannot continue maximizing production without consideration of what we are producing and what the environmental cost is.

Economic growth for the past forty years has added many costs with only incremental benefits. The drive towards high labour efficiency has forced us to work more intensively. Community and social relations have suffered. We are materially only slightly richer, but spiritually poorer than ever.

---

25   Jeffrey D Sachs, *The Age of Sustainable Development*, (New York: Columbia University Press, 2015), 194-199.

UNCERTAIN GAINS

There have been some obvious improvements to our lives in the last century. We can place these into three categories. First, there are the improvements due to technology. This includes airplanes, automobiles, radios, televisions, computers, and cell phones. These changes in technology resulted in dramatic changes to our culture and made our lives more comfortable, enjoyable, and rewarding. But by 1929, twenty-three million Americans already had auto-mobiles; eighty-five percent of Americans had electricity and therefore could buy washing machines, toasters, refrigerators, and radios. Television was invented in 1923. By 1939, there were 20,000 TV sets around London, England. Full commercialization occurred in the 1940s and 50s. In 1946, the United States (US) army developed the first general purpose electronic computer. Computers were in common use by the 1980s. Long-playing records, or LPs, invented in 1948, still provide superior sound quality to digital formats. Most of the technologies making sig-nificant changes to our lives were already well established forty years ago.

Secondly, there have been ongoing incremental improvements that result from persistent economic growth and marketing pres-sures. Television screens have been getting bigger, and the latest cell phones include cameras and music players. Marketing pres-sures continuously induce us to upgrade to the new model. The cost of doing this is huge, but the benefit is increasingly marginal.

Thirdly, we have more, but often with a sacrifice of quality. We have bigger houses, bigger cars, more televisions, and more com-puters. Items that were formerly a luxury have become a necessity. Having more provides little additional benefit. A bigger house is harder to clean and maintain. More possessions increase prosper-ity up to a point, but then just add to clutter.

Life expectancy

Is it better to be alive now than at the turn of the twentieth century? Life expectancy at birth has increased significantly in the last century, but this does not have that much to do with economic growth. If you were born in 1900, your life expectancy would be forty-nine years, as opposed to sixty-eight if you were born in 1950. You would have to accept a probable loss of nineteen years to your life, which is not a good trade. But if you were ten years old in 1900, your life expectancy would jump to sixty-five as opposed to seventy-one in 1950. Life expectancy at birth has increased primarily because of the reduction in infant mortality at birth, the use of antibiotics, and the control of infectious diseases. At fifty years old, life expectancy was seventy-one in 1900, seventy-four in 1950, and eighty in 2000. Increases in life expectancy mostly affect the young. An article in *The Economist* suggests that, "the biggest increase in life expectancy pre-dated the introduction of national healthcare systems." Most of the improvements came from nutrition, sanitation, hygiene and housing, rather than medical care.[26]

As an economy grows to about $10,000 per capita of GDP, other factors more heavily influence life expectancy and infant mortality.[27] Some countries—such as Cuba, Japan, and Argentina—have been able to maintain and even enhance national health despite severe economic downturns. Others—such as the ex-Soviet states—have not, mainly due to the elimination

---

26   "The Health of Nations: A survey of health-care finance," *The Economist*, July 17, 2004.

27   Tim Jackson, *Prosperity without Growth: Economics for a Finite Planet*, (London: Earthscan, 2009), 56-61.

of state-financed healthcare. This indicates that social support is much more important than the size of GDP for better health outcomes. America spends the most money on healthcare of any industrialized nation, but this does not translate into gains in life expectancy over other nations that spend less. Evidently, high economic growth and technical innovation have not increased our life expectancy, but rather low-technology interventions and more socialized medical care.

More choice

In a sense, everything in the economy is based on a need. However, the extent to which these needs are satisfied is relative. Air, water, and food are primary needs, but other things such as healthcare, clothing, shelter, entertainment, fun, excitement, status, and exercise are also needs in that we cannot live a full and balanced life without them. We buy food because of a need to eat; healthcare is required to remain healthy; we buy a big house because of a need to be comfortable, an expensive car because of a need for status. We buy games because of a need for diversion and entertainment. Needs are not necessarily satisfied by the economy according to GDP per capita. We can satisfy some needs by spending more money, but not others. To display status, you have to have the best car, the biggest house, and the finest possessions. If the possessions of everyone else are improved to the same level, then the quality of the best also has to be improved. Similarly, if we all make do with less, the best can also be proportionately less. The purchase of luxury items and their price is subject to an escalation like a nuclear arms race. Economic growth in this area has no real benefit to society.

Maintaining full employment has required an increase in the range of products available to entice people with new technologies and to make subtle changes in products to make existing products seem obsolete. Economic growth is a matter of more choice of product, frequent superficial changes, and an entire industry devoted to advertising. The economy has grown, but what benefit have we received for this growth? Advertising pollutes newspapers, radio, television, and now the internet. More choice is not making our lives any better.

Happiness

One measure of how well an economy is performing is how happy citizens are. Recently, there have been surveys measuring happiness in different countries with various levels of economic development. The results are surprising. There is no simple, direct correlation between economic wealth and happiness.[28] People in some poor countries are quite happy, whereas the very rich do not seem that much happier than people with average incomes are. People do not become happier as they earn more money. Happiness is not a binary condition of being happy or not happy; rather, it is multidimensional because there are many factors that cause one to be happy. In *The Human Condition*, Hannah Arendt indicates that the quest for happiness as an end in itself is mainly by those that are forced to labour for their livelihood, what she calls the *animal laborans*. Those who receive satisfaction from their work or their action within a community do not expect to be

---

28   Mark Anielski, *The Economics of Happiness: Building Genuine Wealth*, (Gabriola Island: New Society Publishers, 2007).

made happy: "For only the *animal laborans*, and neither the crafts-man nor the man of action, has ever demanded to be 'happy' or thought that mortal men could be happy." Arendt further warns that as spare time is only spent on consumption, and as these appetites become more sophisticated and more concentrated on superfluities, there is a grave danger that "eventually no object of the world will be safe from consumption and annihilation through consumption."[29]

As wealth per capita increases, so too does happiness, but only up to a point. Two conditions define overall happiness in economic terms: one is having enough, of having basic needs fulfilled; the other is having the security that this fulfillment will persist. A high GDP per capita does not guarantee financial secu-rity. Such security is as likely to exist in poorer countries as our own. We can achieve security with relatively little financial wealth if the economy meets certain conditions. Perpetual growth of the economy is more likely to create financial insecurity and states of constant stress. We do not need more to be happy; we only need enough.

Suppliers of goods and services within the free market system have an interest in expanding needs, not just fulfilling them. In other words, they strive to create unhappiness. The result is an unstable economy that must always grow to achieve an acceptable dynamic equilibrium. Any happiness created is fleeting. As one is left behind, the feeling of not having enough relative to everyone else becomes overwhelming. One is motivated to spend remain-ing resources to have as much as most other people.

---

29   Hannah Arendt, *The Human Condition*, (Chicago, London: The Uni-versity of Chicago Press, 1958), 133-134.

More leisure activities that are more stimulating and don't take as much effort

The economy has grown to produce more diversions and entertainment. This growth has come in various forms including massive and expensive stadiums for professional sports, and a huge infrastructure of telecommunications to transmit sports events and movies made with special effects to be more stimulating than real life. People spend millions on games that simulate reality and provide intense excitement. Perhaps this extra excitement is a good reason for ongoing economic growth. There is benefit to some growth in this area, but:

- These diversions are expensive in terms of resource consumption. Because most of these diversions are passive, they soon become boring. There is a constant need to create new movies, new games, and new technology.

- Many of these diversions are addictive. There is indeed a link between artificial happiness and addiction. An alcoholic is happy while drinking, a gambler while gambling. This happiness is not a meaningful state of bliss; it is a rather a perpetual state of seeking and briefly attaining a sort of happiness without ever being able to stop, lest one sinks into despair.

- These diversions in general do not involve much effort. They do not develop the body or the mind.

Despite the huge amounts of resources devoted to these diversions, games that are more traditional and physical sports have not become obsolete. People need challenges. Their bodies need exercise. Their minds need obstacles to grow. This can be done in a low-tech way. The game of soccer requires just a ball, and it remains the most accessible and popular game on the planet. Chess, still one of the most mentally challenging games, requires a very low investment in hardware, with no need for software. The amount of technology required creating products for diversion and entertainment is relative. More money spent on a game does not necessarily make it more fun. Many old, low-tech games continue to entertain. Hundreds of games can be played with a deck of cards. Live singing, dancing, and theatre still compete with movies and high definition television. Growing the economy to provide more high-tech entertainment could be worthwhile if it increased prosperity. There is no guarantee that this will happen, especially if people have to work harder to buy technologies for leisure and then have less free time to use them.

Much of technology ostensibly improving the quality of our lives is just compensation—television, radio, recorded music, telephones, and the internet re-establish continuous social contact, the norm in previous societies where people lived and worked together. Leisure activities such as downhill skiing, videogames, and movies compensate for the boredom inherent in industrial culture because of isolation, repetitive work tasks, and the lack of exhilarating and stimulating physical activity in our everyday lives.

CERTAIN LOSSES

The degradation of the environment and the extinctions that have occurred during the last century are sources of great sadness to many people. On top of this, pollutants and many thousands of chemicals added to our food and water have unpredictable effects on our health. If, at the start of the last century, we took a map of the world with shades of grey representing levels of pollution, we would see black spots emerge in several areas—mainly in Europe where the industrial revolution began. Moving through the last century, we would see several blackened spots in North America as well, including Los Angeles and New York City. However, for most of this period, much of the surface of the earth would be a pristine white. Now, while many of the black spots have become a moderate to dark grey, there are even larger black spots in other parts of the world that continue to produce the products we use, and the entire earth's surface is a disturbing off-white.

Although health and mortality have improved in richer countries, minor ailments and stresses have increased. There are also self-inflicted problems such as not getting enough exercise, eating too much, smoking, and recreational drug use. While many life-threatening illnesses have been prevented, various other incapacitating conditions that are not life-threatening have increased, reducing the well-being of everyone. The bi-products of industrialization may be the partial cause of various diseases and conditions including allergies, chemical sensitivities, chronic fatigue, and migraine headaches.[30] More of us breathe poorer quality air in our cities and in our homes. Even those who live in the country have to put up with indoor air pollution from household furnishings, sometimes worse than the most polluted cities. These effects perhaps do not substantially reduce the length of our lives, but they do reduce the quality.

------

30   See Rick Smith and Bruce Lourie, *Slow Death by Rubber Duck: How the Toxic Chemistry of Everyday Life Affects our Health*, (Toronto: Alfred A. Knopf, 2009) and Theo Colborn, Dianne Dumanoski, and John Peterson Myers, *Our Stolen Future: Are We Threatening Our Fertility, Intelligence, and Survival?—A Scientific Detective Story*, (New York: Plume, 1996).

Industry has introduced many chemicals to our indoor environments. These chemicals, sometimes providing marginal benefits, are often untested and unregulated. Due to the large number of interacting factors, proving specific health effects is exceptionally difficult. Using mortality rates to determine the cost of pollution is misleading and greatly underestimates its impact. An illustrative example is noise pollution. Noise pollution kills no one, but increases stress, disrupts sleep, and makes life less pleasant. Similarly, various chemicals have negative effects on our quality of life. What we do know is that many conditions that significantly affect quality of life are on the rise. Autism, learning disorders, attention deficit disorders, and depression have all increased in recent years. Prevalence of all allergies and other sensitivities have increased exponentially for the past fifty years.[31] Food allergies among children, unheard of even thirty years ago, have increased 50 percent from 1997 to 2011.[32]

Various factors such as excessive hygiene and decreased ventilation may have contributed to this increase, but the most likely explanation for most of the increase is that modern conveniences, more prevalent in higher income countries, have introduced new chemicals from synthetic materials, flame-retardants, and preservatives to indoor environments. These are now more significant because of more time spent indoors with less ventilation. Phthalates used to soften plastic, found in cosmetics and personal

31   Prof. Ruby Pawankar, MD, PhD, Prof. Giorgio Walter Canonica, MD, Prof. Stephen T. Holgate, BSc, MD, DSc, FMed Sci and Prof. Richard F. Lockey, MD. *White Book on Allergy*, (World Allergy Organization: 2011-2012) "Executive Summary"

32   Jackson K et al. *Trends in Allergic Conditions among Children: United States, 1997-2011*, National Center for Health Statistics Data Brief. 2013. Retrieved from www.cdc.gov/nchs/data/databriefs/db10.htm.

care products, floors and upholstery, exist in high concentrations in the dust of our houses. These have been shown to be a major cause of asthma and allergies.[33] Whereas volatile organic compounds (VOCs), also a serious cause of health problems, quickly gas out of most indoor materials, phthalates persist in the indoor environment for long periods.

With a lifetime risk of mortality slightly more than one in a hundred, the riskiest thing most of us ever do is anything to do with motor vehicles. The risk of dying in a fire is far less, at 1,442 to one, but the certain harm from flame-retardants, while small, affects us 24 hours a day and seven days per week.[34] The benefits of flame-retardants are greatly over-estimated. Flame-retardants may prevent some fires from starting, but result in far more hazardous chemicals being released once the fire starts. Female firefighters have six times the national average rates of breast cancer.[35] Drops in fire related deaths have more to do with better building codes, sprinkler systems, fire alarms, and self-extinguishing cigarettes. Without flame-retardants, we may experience a slight increase in the risk of death by fire, easily mitigated with a few precautions, but offset by better health for everyone.

---

33   Bruce Lourie and Rick Smith, *Toxin Toxout: Getting Harmful Chemicals out of our Bodies and our World*, (Toronto: Alfred A. Knopf, 2013), Chapter 5. 40,000 children tracked in 5-year increments since 2000. The study found no relation between moisture related exposures and allergies, but the more phthalates were found in household dust, the higher the rates of allergies.

34   www.iii.org/fact-statistic/mortality-risk.

35   A 2012 Chicago Tribune investigative series called *Playing With Fire* documented how fire-retardant chemicals fail to provide meaningful protection from furniture fires.

Halogenated flame-retardants (those containing chlorine or bromine) have been shown to cause reproductive, thyroid, endocrine, developmental, and neurological disorders.[36] Hard plastics used in televisions and computer cases can have 10 to 20 percent flame-retardants by weight. Polyurethane foam found in soft furnishings and underlay of carpet can have up to 30 percent. As these materials age, the toxic compounds are gradually released. High levels of these compounds are also found in household dust. Some manufacturers including Herman Miller (office furniture) and Interface (carpet tiles and fabrics) are starting to eliminate halogenated flame-retardants from their products. But since these substances bioaccumulate in the environment and comprise such a large proportion of our interior environments, they will be a persistent problem for many years to come.

Pesticides are the cause of general developmental problems, cognitive deficits including attention deficit disorder, low birth weight and smaller brains, an increased risk of asthma in children, and reduced sperm counts in adult males.[37] Hormone disrupting chemicals such as BPAs used in plastics and parabens used as a preservative for countless consumer products are mistaken for estrogen in our bodies and are responsible for genital malformations, neurobehavioral changes, increased allergies, pregnancy loss, metabolic disorders, reproductive disorders, and behavioural changes in children.[38]

---

36   Bruce Lourie and Rick Smith, *Toxin Toxout: Getting Harmful Chemicals out of our Bodies and our World*, (Toronto: Alfred A. Knopf, 2013), Chapter 5.

37   Ibid, Table 5 in Chapter 2.

38   Ibid: Table 3 in Chapter 1.

Chemical fragrances are added to virtually every household product for no reason. Fabric softeners made of natural ingredients were developed in the 1900s to soften fabrics made harsh with the dying process. Over the years, fabric softeners have become more effective with ingredients that are more toxic, but are also less necessary with modern fabrics.

Why is all this important? A lot of economic growth is the result of value added production of chemicals that add enhancements of negligible benefit, but add up to considerable harm. Not only is much of this production unnecessary, we would greatly benefit from there being less. Minor benefits are magnified with clever marketing, while environmental and health costs are ignored. Corporations are established based on this business proposition and lobby fiercely to prevent regulation.

Climate change

There seems to be a strong and durable consensus of scientists that global warming is taking place and is a serious problem. According to the Intergovernmental Panel on Climate Change (IPCC), total carbon dioxide must be kept under one trillion tonnes (metric tons) to keep global warming below two degrees Celsius by the end of the century. If we continue on our present course, total temperature rise could increase between three and ten degrees. This range indicates considerable uncertainty in the computer-generated climate models used for prediction. But, whereas the low end may be manageable, anything over about four degrees could be catastrophic. Average temperature has already increased 0.9 degrees since the start of the industrial revolution. Oceans are absorbing most of this heat, which is causing reduced summer sea-ice cover in the Arctic Ocean. Oceans have already risen twenty centimetres since 1880 because of the expansion of warmer water. Another metre or more is possible by 2100. Rising temperatures increase the atmospheric capacity to hold water. Because of this, winter storms are more intense and occur more frequently.

As of this writing, the hottest year on record is 2015. One thousand people in India and Pakistan died during heat waves. Another 47,000 were hospitalized in Japan.[39] In 2015, California experienced a prolonged and severe drought. My own province of British Columbia has had devastating forest fires. Overall, 2.4 million hectares of American forests were destroyed.[40] The Arctic is warming twice as fast as the rest of the world and may release vast amounts of methane gas, one of the possible tipping points that could lead to catastrophic effects such as the melting of the Greenland ice sheet.[41]

---

39   "Climate change: The hottest year on record: 2015," *The Economist*, January 21, 2016.

40   Warming since 1901 has caused a significant trend toward drought in California. This has made forest fires much more likely. See "Contribution of anthropogenic warming to California drought during 2012–2014," A. Park Williams, Richard Seager, John T. Abatzoglou, Benjamin I. Cook, Jason E. Smerdon, and Edward R. Cook, *AGU Geophysical Research Letters*, 2015.

41   For more information see William Nordhaus, *The Climate Casino: Risk, Uncertainty, and Economics for a Warming World*, (New Haven & London: Yale University Press, 2013); Naomi Klein, *This Changes Everything: Capitalism vs. The Climate*, (Toronto: Alfred A. Knopf, 2014); Jeff Rubin, *Why Your World is about to get a Whole lot Smaller: Oil and the End of Globalization*, (New York: Random House, 2009).

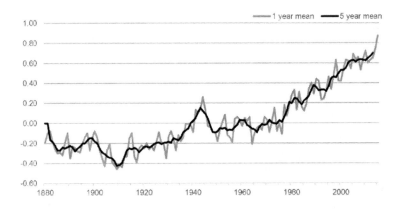

Figure 2: *Global surface temperature, deviation from 20ᵗʰ century average, °C. Source: NASA's Goddard Institute for Space Studies.*

The loss of leisure time

Industrialization and new household technologies should reduce the amount of work we have to do. With increased production, we should have more free time, as predicted by twentieth century futurists. The loss of free time is one of the mysteries of the modern age. Production requires less time; we sleep less since the invention of the light bulb. Before the industrial revolution, people may have worked harder physically, but they had time to spare.

At the start of the industrial revolution, there was little incentive to work in factories. Samuel Johnson observed that peasants could make a pair of traditional Scottish brogues (shoes) at home in one hour, but required three days of labour to earn enough to buy commercially made ones. Those that did work had to work long hours in factories, sometimes seventy to eighty hours per week. Since then work hours have decreased to a more manageable level of forty or so hours. However, it is an enduring myth that we have more leisure time because of our industrialized economy. The medieval workday was rarely more than eight hours and the pace was considerably slower than today. Much work in agriculture was seasonal, sometimes requiring long hours of work per day but only for brief periods of the year. It was unusual for servants to work a whole day. In addition, up to a third of the year consisted of public holidays and days off from work.[42]

In their book *Cradle to Cradle*, William McDonough and Michael Braungart speak of how nature more effectively incorporates waste, whereas industry tries to eliminate waste, but ends up with unusable parts or pollution.[43] The same thing happens with the modern use of time. Time spent to prepare for an activity or to get from one activity to another is either a kind of blank unproductive time or a downright finger-tapping unpleasant time fragment. In the past, a drive or a train ride from one place to another was a relaxing, comforting, and introspective journey through a soothing countryside. Now it has become a series of short unpleasant jaunts through a maze of traffic lights, or time spent at bus stops and waiting rooms at airports. Increasing transaction times such as these are partly responsible for the growing poverty of time.

In traditional economies, the labour required to produce the needed goods and services involved physical effort, so a separate period for exercise was unnecessary. People that must labour hard to get things done, and mostly walk from place to place, need not exercise as a separate activity. Similarly, life was more integrated into

---

42   Juliet B. Schor, *The Overworked American: The Unexpected Decline of Leisure*, (New York: Basic Books, 1992).

43   William McDonough and Michael Braungart, *Cradle to Cradle: Remaking the Way We Make Things*, (New York: North Point Press, 2002).

continuous labour intermingled with social activity and ending with significantly more hours of sleep. In the modern age, work, leisure, exercise, and socializing have become separate and mutually exclusive activities. Work is without physical effort and is more socially isolating, creating a need for separate time blocks for exercise, social activity, and relaxing. In pre-industrial society, all time was used, if not for production, then for communication and social contact. Industrial society has eliminated this natural efficiency. The modern attempt to use time more efficiently and multi-tasking, that exhilarating but exhausting technique of doing several things at once, has introduced many small intervals of time useless for human consumption. Such intervals are too short for introspection, relaxation, or socialization. They suspend consciousness and promote irritability and depression. Logic would dictate that with increasing innovation and mechanization, we could all have less to do. Capitalism, however, dictates that most people must receive wages from a constant amount of work to buy essential commodities. The consumption of luxuries is the only way to guarantee jobs and therefore an acceptable standard of living.

Compared to the 1970s, we are working harder.[44] We have to do more in the same amount of time, more transactions per unit of time. On top of that, despite the tremendous growth in the service industry, we have to do more ourselves than we used to. Milk used to be delivered door to door. A strong young lad would

---

44   Juliet B. Schor, *The Overworked American: The Unexpected Decline of Leisure*, (New York: Basic Books, 1992). See also John P. Robinson, Geoffrey Godbey, *Time for Life: The Surprising Ways Americans Use Their Time*, (University Park, PA: The Pennsylvania State University Press, 1997, 1999). Detailed time diaries indicate that average work time is decreasing, but this fails to account for the rise in unemployment and underemployment in recent years. Some people are working much less while those that do have jobs tend to work longer hours.

pack your groceries and carry them to your car. Now you even have to scan the prices of your own groceries before packing them yourself. Those in business have to type their own letters, which was previously done by secretaries. Many new technologies seem to be about getting you to do something that someone else formerly did for you, like the self-serve gas terminals with automatic credit card swipes. There is a reduction of paid labour, but unpaid household labour increases.

The distortion and imbalance of the way we spend our time, the disappearance of social ritual, the increased transaction time, and decreased time for leisure explain the alienation of capitalist industrial society. Some leisure activities have increased, not because workloads have decreased, but because of the prevalent commercialization of leisure activities. In the unrelenting drive to make the luxuries of the past into essential items of the present, even leisure activities such as skiing, cycling, and snowboarding are becoming essential counterpoints to our hectic yet sedentary lives.

Even much of our present consumption of material goods is directed towards conserving a precious leisure time resource. We often see social rituals and even semi-social rituals associated with higher artistic events—such as going to the theatre—as time consuming. DVD players and wide screen televisions, although considered materially enriching, can be more cynically viewed as a way to save the time formerly required to go out to a live performance in the community.

Food shortage

Despite spectacular gains in wealth, good quality food remains scarce even in rich countries. The Food and Agriculture

Organization of the United Nations (FAO) has estimated one billion more tonnes of cereal equivalents will be required by 2030. At the same time, water scarcity and other effects of global warming will make this more difficult. Food wasted is equal to about 85 percent of food eaten in the United States. Rodents eat about one fifth of the world's grain harvest. Of what is left, 40 percent (70 percent in developed countries) is used inefficiently to produce meat. Pets in rich countries eat more meat than people in poorer countries.[45] Agriculture and industrialization have destroyed about a third of the forests that once covered 45 percent of the earth's surface. The rate of tropical forest destruction is currently 86,000 hectares a day (an area larger than New York City).[46] As of 2003, 29 percent of fish stocks have collapsed.[47]

Wealth is a measure of food security. Although western nations have a surplus of food to the point that a significant proportion of the population is overweight, the world as a whole does not. Also, obesity is not caused by the availability of too much food, but rather by the increased availability of cheap, industrialized, and poor quality food. Compared to 1950, top quality food is far better now. It is possible to get fresh food year round. Fresh fish, much of it sold as sushi in local restaurants, is available anytime for a price. However, the median quality of diet has declined. It is primarily the replacement of adequate nutritional food sources such as canned and frozen vegetables with cheaper high calorie

45   Clive Ponting, *A New Green History of the World: The Environment and the Collapse of Great Civilizations*, (New York: The Penguin Group, 1991, 2007), 246-247.
46   Ibid 252.
47   Jeffrey D. Sachs, *Common Wealth: Economics for a Crowded Planet*, (London: The Penguin Group, 2008), 141.

refined carbohydrates causing obesity and other health problems. The reduced availability of high quality food is the most important explanation of why a four-fold increase in wealth does not provide financial security. Without obtaining a certain level of wealth, the food quality you have access to will also be poor. Obesity and poor health will be the result. Poor quality food is the main reason you do not want to be stuck with a minimum wage job for long. Wealth per capita in the world economy has been going up. But, suitably nutritious food available per capita has been going down with population growth. Wealth determines access to good food.[48]

Lower quality products

Furniture is now most likely made of particleboard with a thin veneer of real wood or just a convincing facsimile. Materials in houses are similarly downgraded to simulated materials and comfortable substitutions such as wall-to-wall carpeting. Clothing is more likely to be made of synthetic materials with thinner fabrics that wear out more quickly.

Industry has responded to higher prices and the probability of reduced sales and profits by cutting the quality of the goods and services produced. Industrialization is unrelenting as a force that improves living standards by allowing us to produce more with

---

48   Jones NRV, Conklin AI, Suhrcke M, Monsivais P (2014) "The Growing Price Gap between More and Less Healthy Foods: Analysis of a Novel Longitudinal UK Dataset," *PLoS ONE* 9(10): e109343. doi:10.1371/journal.pone.0109343. Research indicates that healthy food and beverages are consistently more expensive than unhealthy ones and the gap is increasing over time.

less effort and to produce new and better solutions. However, technology is also used to produce goods of much lower quality, which through effective marketing are perceived as of equivalent value. Most products we consume are of considerably lower quality than fifty years ago. Usually this is done in a way that the consumer is less likely to notice. Cheaper materials are substituted for ones that are more expensive and reduced to the minimum functional requirements. New technologies are developed to provide the same functions in a cheaper way. Reduction in quality is most apparent in food, clothing, housing, and furniture. It is mainly in electronic products that improvements in the technology have compensated for the material reductions in quality.

Cultural degradation

The Index of Social Health is published annually by Fordham University's Graduate Center in Tarrytown, New York. The index, based on sixteen indicators including infant mortality, child abuse, poverty, suicides, drug use, dropout rates, average salaries, and health insurance coverage, shows a steady decline from 73.8 (out of 100) in 1970 to 40.6 in 1993, and increased slightly to 55.0 in 2006.[49] In contrast, GDP includes all expenditures, whether they contribute to well-being or not. It ignores crucial economic functions outside monetary exchange including unpaid housework, childcare, and volunteer work. It does not account for the natural resources used up. It ignores distribution of income and the amount of poverty in an economy. Spending on weapons, war, and crime is included, while the expenditures on education, healthcare,

---

49   http://iisp.vassar.edu/ish.html.

and social services do not include the intangible returns on investment of increased physical well-being, cultural advancement, and
the improved quality of the environment. This has often resulted
in a shortage of goods and services that matter and an overproduction of that which dilutes and degrades our culture.

Inequality

Defenders of our current economic system say that despite
rising inequality, the increase in productivity has created more
for all. Adam Smith proclaimed that the poorest people of his
day lived better than African kings did. The lot of the poor has
improved. As John Kenneth Galbraith once said, when the horses
get extra food, some of the grain makes it through the horse's
stomach for the sparrows. Even though disparity in wealth is
getting worse, the amount of poverty in the world is decreasing
and people are all gradually getting richer—so theoretically all
boats are rising.

If we look at the data for the last few years, not all boats seem
to be rising. An article in *The Economist* in 2006 reported that
workers' share of the cake in rich countries was the smallest in at
least three decades. In many countries, wages were flat or falling.
While labour productivity has risen 15 percent, real wages have
fallen by 4 percent since 2001.[50] America's top 1 percent of wage
earners now receive 16 percent of all income, compared with 8
percent in 1980. In another article in 2009, *The Economist* wrote
that from 1947 to 1979, the top 0.1percent of American earners

---

50   "The New Titans: A Survey of the World Economy," *The Economist*,
        September 16, 2006.

received about twenty times as much as the bottom 90 percent. By 2006, they were earning seventy-seven times as much.[51] In a special report published in 2012, *The Economist* indicated that the share of national income going to the richest 1 percent has doubled since 1980, and for the richest 0.01 percent, has qua-drupled from just over 1 percent to over 5 percent. This is an even bigger slice of the pie than received 100 years ago during what is referred to as America's first Gilded Age. Similar disparities of wealth have occurred all over the world.[52]

If costs are rising at a rate faster than benefits, the "all boats rising" argument has a problem. While true that as the economy grows benefits for all increase but costs are increasing faster. If a poor family lives in a large house because there is no alternative smaller one, has two cars because there is no other way for two wage earners to get to work, then all boats are not rising; rather, the boats we require to survive are becoming bigger.

Economic growth is unfortunately the glue that binds our economy together. Growth as a positive force, for the past forty years, has been a much-promoted fiction that has convinced most of us we are getting richer because we have been consuming so much more. In reality, the product, though delivered in higher quantities, is more diluted, like adding more water to the punch bowl to keep the party going. We are just consuming lower quality products and the quality of our lives diminishes. Poorer quality materials in houses have reduced indoor air quality to

---

51   Figures from Economic Policy Institute reported in "More or less equal," *The Economist*, April 2, 2009.

52   "Special Report: The World Economy: For Richer, For Poorer," *The Economist*, October 13, 2012.

the detriment of health of the occupants. Products that used to last five or ten years now last one or two, thus using up scarce resources even faster and generating more pollution. Many products have become so cheap it is more expedient to throw them away rather than to repair them.

Our feelings of financial security are not dependent upon overall wealth created, but on whether the economy is growing at a point in time. Despite incredible economic growth over the past century, we have not eliminated poverty; instead, we have increased inequality. Undeniably, the earth is in worse shape than ever before. Less production would not necessarily reduce our happiness and well-being. In fact, producing less may result in less stress and a healthier, more satisfying environment.

Many things have improved because of technology, but the present economy is mainly about increasing the quantity of production, often at the sacrifice of quality. The interesting thing about doing the reverse is that there is a justified increase in price, or economic growth, without corresponding environmental impact. The possibility of economic growth by increasing quality is the topic of the next chapter.

THREE **THE GROWTH OF QUALITY**

*I have learned to seek my happiness by limiting my
desires, rather than in attempting to satisfy them.*

—John Stuart Mill

Economic growth feels good. It is a positive force in civilization. Economic stagnation is the opposite. Benjamin Friedman,
a leading American political economist writes that economic
growth is not just good for improving living standards, "it shapes
the social, political, and ultimately the moral character of a
people." Greater opportunity, tolerance of diversity, social mobility, fairness, and democracy are all enhanced.[53]

As consumption becomes more pointless, Friedman's moral
dimension is brought into question. Economic growth has

---

53   Benjamin M. Friedman, *The Moral Consequences of Economic Growth*
(New York: Alfred A. Knopf, 2005), 4.

become the prime directive of our economy. All energies are directed to this one ambition—to produce more and more to improve living standards. During the past forty years, growth has still provided some of these positive aspects to our economy but, as I have argued, it comes with diminishing returns. There are other directives to consider. We know, for example, that war, although horrific and to be avoided if possible, gives life a purpose by making one want to work hard for the common good. There is no reason why the type of organization and effort that occurs with war could not be used to tackle other problems such as poverty or climate change.

Just before World War II, governments developed the measure of Gross Domestic Product (GDP) to determine economic output, essentially as a measure of the ability to produce bombs, planes, and guns for the war effort. This remained useful after the war to gauge the capacity of countries to rebuild and develop their manufacturing ability. It has also been useful for measuring the growth of developing countries. GDP is a measure of production capacity. It was never intended as a measure of welfare, but it is frequently given as evidence of such.

Economic growth occurs more in less developed economies. As an economy matures, growth rates slow down. Jeffrey Sachs, a leading expert on economic development and the fight against poverty, has suggested a simple rule of thumb to calculate the expected rate of growth per capita of a given country based on its level of development: starting with a mature economy such as the United States with a per capita GDP of $50,000 measured in purchasing power parity (PPP)[54] and a rate of growth of 1

---

54   See note 21.

percent, it is possible to predict the rate of growth of an economy half the size by adding 1.4 percent. Thus, an economy with a GDP of $25,000 will grow 2.4 percent per year; one with $12,500 will grow 3.8 percent per year, and so on. Typical growth rates for different sized economies are shown in the following table:

Table 1: *Economic growth rates relative to development in Purchasing Power Parity (PPP).*[55]

	Size of Economy	GDP	Growth
Growth Rates relative to development	Least developed	$1,613	8%
	Low income	$3,125	6.6%
	Lower middle income	$6,250	5.2%
	Upper middle income	$12,500	3.8%
	Lower high income	$25,000	2.4%
	United States	$50,000	1%

This implies that growth tends to slow as an economy matures but also, perhaps, that economic growth will stop for a completely mature economy. Canadian economist Peter Victor has created a computer model of the Canadian economy to test various growth scenarios from 2005 to 2035. In the business as usual scenario, GDP per capita doubles, unemployment goes up slightly and then comes down, government debt falls, and greenhouse gas emissions increase. Poverty, however, continues to rise. The main problem with the business as usual model is that resources continue to be used unsustainably and greenhouse gas emissions continue increasing to dangerous levels.

55   Jeffrey D Sachs, *The Age of Sustainable Development,* (New York: Columbia University Press, 2015), 194-199.

On the other hand, a drastic reduction of economic growth—its elimination over a ten-year period—leads to results that are even more disastrous. Unemployment and poverty skyrocket. Greenhouse gas emissions improve, but at the cost of economic collapse.

The third scenario, where economic growth is slowed over a longer period, such that the economy is allowed to stabilize, shows that unemployment drops, leisure time increases, and poverty is eliminated while greenhouse gas emissions decrease. A computer model is not reality, but it is interesting that the economy, in theory at least, could improve with less economic growth. Even de-growth—a transition to a more sustainable society with lower ecological inputs—could be possible.[56]

Population growth is slowing; people are getting older and having fewer children. The world in the future will require less housing, less infrastructure, and fewer child-related products. High economic growth of the past few years is largely due to the "catch up" of emerging economies. As all world economies become more mature, global growth will slow. We are running out of resources and the ability of the environment to absorb pollution. This will necessarily lead to more regulation and more taxation of external costs. Consumption is reaching a saturation point. The desire of the general population to limit consumption for the sake of the environment is increasing. It is also possible that although environmental impact is increasing along with economic growth, it is increasing at a lower rate.

------

56   Robert Dietz, Dan O'Neill, *Enough is Enough: Building a Sustainable Economy in a World of Finite Resources*, (Abingdon, Oxon: Routledge, 2013), 52-59.

DECOUPLING GROWTH FROM ENVIRONMENTAL IMPACT

Clive Ponting compares the transitions from one level of civilization to another to a "ratchet."[57] This means that certain developments in society do not allow the return to previous conditions. Societies did not instantly adopt agriculture as a better way of life. Rather, they were forced by circumstance over hundreds of years to intensify hunting and gathering techniques that ultimately led to an agricultural economy. Once agriculture became established, populations rose and a return to hunting and gathering became impossible. Similarly, rising populations have forced most people to abandon an agricultural way of life and adopt one based on industrial production. Each level change operates like a ratchet, preventing a return to an earlier level. This ratchet mechanism now continues with economic growth, technological advance, and rising populations. The world economy grows and what were previously optional luxuries for the rich have become essential goods and services for everyone.

Environmental impact tends to increase along with economic growth. The primary reason for this is the ongoing dependence on fossil fuel use in the world economy. While gains have been made in the rich industrialized countries with cleaner fuels, pollution controls, and more regulation, these gains have been negated by burning coal, fewer pollution controls, and almost no regulation in developing countries that now do most production. Impacts associated with extracting minerals have been rising due to "low

57   Clive Ponting, *A New Green History of the World: The Environment and the Collapse of Great Civilizations*, (New York: The Penguin Group, 1991, 2007), 37, 55.

hanging fruit" approaches in the past. Resources in general are getting harder to access. Ore grades are declining, requiring much more material to be processed and causing more disruption to natural ecosystems. More fossil fuel derived fertilizers and environmentally hazardous chemicals are used for food production now than ever before. Substituting synthetic materials for natural ones frequently involves the release of far more chemicals with unknown effects on the environment.

However, moving forward, the potential for impact decoupling does exist. We can replace fossil fuel energy production with non-polluting solar sources within a couple of decades. The availability of clean energy makes more decoupling possible. If the full and true cost of resource extraction is accounted for, then many other low impact sources of resources will come on line. Total CO_2 per person, for the United States, including imports, has declined slightly from twenty-three tonnes in 1973 to twenty-two tonnes in 2009.[58] Water use per person peaked at 7,500 litres per day in 1975. Since then it has declined to 5,300 largely due to efficiencies gained in agriculture. Sources of a few pollutants that we have decided to regulate have also dropped substantially in developed countries, although total world pollution continues to rise even on a per capita basis. CO_2 per person has increased by 10 to 15 percent, energy use by 50 percent, but GDP per capita has increased 80 percent. Making a tonne of steel in China uses twice the energy and releases twice the CO_2 as making the steel in the United States, South Korea, Japan, or Germany, showing that further decoupling is possible. The rate of deforestation is

---

58   This does not include other greenhouse gases such as methane and nitrous oxide.

also slowing: From 1990 to 2000, the amount of forests lost was 2 percent; from 2000 to 2010, the loss was only 1 percent.[59]

The rise in GDP was roughly equivalent to the rate of rise in resource consumption up until about 1950. GDP then increased at a much faster rate, even as resource prices declined. The authors of a report from United Nations Environment Programme (UNEP) conclude that the decoupling of the economy from resource use is starting to take place.[60] The biggest factor in this apparent decoupling seems to be population density. During the twentieth century, populations in all countries became much more concentrated in cities. Populations have increased, and the rate of resource use has increased, but at a lower rate than the increase in size of the economy.

Resource consumption rates of dense populations is almost half the rate of less dense and less urbanized areas for a given level of GDP per capita. Canada and the US, for example, consume resources at roughly double the rate of Europe. Low-density industrial countries have a metabolic rate (tonnes of resource use per capita per year) approaching twenty tonnes, whereas high-density industrial countries have a rate of only thirteen tonnes. Low-density countries in the rest of the world have a rate similar to Europe, while high-density developing countries have a rate of only about five tonnes.

59   Ibid, 276-280 for history of forest use and K. MacDicken et al., "Global Forest Resources Assessment 2015" *FAO*, 2016, for statistics.

60   UNEP (2011) "Decoupling natural resource use and environmental impacts from economic growth, A Report of the Working Group on Decoupling to the International Resource Panel." Fischer-Kowalski, M., Swilling, M., von Weizsäcker, E.U., Ren, Y., Moriguchi, Y., Crane, W., Krausmann, F., Eisenmenger, N., Giljum, S., Hennicke, P., Romero Lankao, P., Siriban Manalang, A., Sewerin, S.

Some of the divergence in the rates of resource consumption and economic development is explained by the increased financial cost of urbanization. Most notably, land prices escalate substantially. The cost of doing business rises, as does taxation required for services. From 1900 to 2005, world GDP per capita has increased from about $1,500 to $7,000—a roughly four-fold increase. During the same time, resource use has increased by only a factor of two. The average use of resources in 1900 was four and a half tonnes per capita per year. By 2005, this had increased to about nine tonnes.

Although resource consumption continues to increase (but at a lower rate than economic growth) the possibility of reducing consumption while the rate of financial value continues to increase is possible. One way of achieving this is by changing the way we measure economic growth.

Hedonic factors of growth

We pay more for smartphones, but they also do more. Computers provide us with extraordinary benefits as they have become more powerful and are available at lower prices. These subjective benefits of technology have not been generally included in GDP, but in recent years, economists have started to include these so-called hedonic factors in the measure of economic growth. This confuses GDP as an objective measure of output with a more subjective measure of welfare.[61] And technology has offered much more dramatic improvements in the past: from candle to lightbulb; horse and carriage to motorcar; radio to television. However,

---

61   Diane Coyle, *GDP: A Brief but Affectionate History*, (Princeton and Oxford: Princeton University Press, 2014), 88.

it does make sense for the economy to concentrate more on providing the hedonic factors made possible with better technology and less on gross increases in consumption. Whereas the resources consumed to produce tangible products are limited, the ability of technology to produce ongoing improvements to our lives is not.

Cultural, psychological, and spiritual growth are not constrained by physical limits, but how could these intangible benefits be linked to a dematerialized increase in GDP? In some respect, something like this has happened with the urbanization process. Moving to a city from a small town results in several increased costs. Much of what was free or of low cost in the small town, costs money in the big city. Rents for smaller apartments are higher. Higher fees are often required for gym memberships, clubs, and associations. There are also higher costs for entertainment, food, and daycare. To offset these costs, people receive intangible benefits including more stimulation, and access to cultural events and sports facilities.

Increasing the quality of housing could have a similar effect. If houses were built with better quality materials, with better technology to increase air quality and offer a more pleasing environment, the long-term costs could be reduced because the houses would last longer. The economy would be dematerialized to a degree. Less resource consumption over time, combined with the intangible benefit of a more comfortable home environment, would offset the higher economic cost. In general, economic growth has increased prosperity by increasing the quantity of production. The alternative to this is to increase quality. The economy will continue to grow, but only in a non-material sense of intangible benefits. We will enjoy higher quality products and pay more as overall consumption shrinks.

MEASURING QUALITY

When we look at GDP, we cannot be sure if it indicates an indulgent consumption of resources, a cost dealing with emerging environmental problems, or a responsible development or purchase of infrastructure that will reduce overall consumption in the long run. GDP per capita is a crude measure of economic progress. It is adequate to compare the condition of China today and ten years ago, or compare North America between 1900 and 1973, when GDP went from roughly $4,000 per capita to just under $20,000. However, as countries reach a certain level of economic and industrial development, GDP becomes increasingly irrelevant as a measure of prosperity.

The measure of economic growth, since its inception, has been concerned with the productive capacity or quantity of production of services. For the past forty years, consumption of goods and services has increased along with increased greenhouse gas emissions and increased environmental impact overall. But for 90 percent of the population, increased consumption has been matched with poorer quality, little increase in income and increases in levels of debt. The economy has grown because of inflation of rewards for the top 10 percent and not because of this increased production. This means that reducing consumption and increasing the quality of what we produce could drive future economic growth if quality is reflected by price.

Other measures of prosperity proposed do not have the cool objectivity of the Gross Domestic Product. A single number— the GDP—describes the size of the economy, and another—the yearly increase of GDP—the apparent health. The size of economic output defines the strength of the economy and a growing economy has lower unemployment. It is no wonder that governments wish to maximize it. We now use GDP as a measure of prosperity, the theory being that the more we consume, the more prosperous we are. Economic output is a positive measure, indicating the strength of an economy. Consumption, on the other hand, describes the indulgence of society, and does not necessarily increase prosperity. Instead of tracking and encouraging the growth of GDP, we need to measure and increase economic efficiency. Instead of Gross Domestic Product, there should be a measure of Gross Domestic Consumption that would include all the external costs related to the depreciation of the environment. We should aim to minimize it and use other indicators to measure quality of life. A true measure of GDC that provided the yearly consumption of resources, together with a more objective measure of prosperity, would offer a better measure of economic efficiency.

A true measure of GDC should accurately measure resource use on a yearly basis. If resources are used to construct infrastructure that will last a hundred years, then only 1 percent of that consumption should be included each year. Much of the double-digit rise of GDP in developing countries like China and India is for the construction of infrastructure, including transportation networks and whole cities. Their present consumption may be more sustainable in the long run than we think. In North America, in contrast, infrastructure is crumbling and consumption of products is increasing unsustainably.

Two resources are not in short supply: labour and money. Yet austerity programs limit public services, our infrastructure is crumbling, and we unnecessarily ration healthcare. Unemployed workers that could reduce these deficiencies sit idle because of under-taxation. Wealth concentration makes the rationing of resources with markets ineffective. The rich can increase their consumption of scarce resources to obscene levels. Meanwhile, labour-based goods and services that should be plentiful, including healthcare, education, and police protection, are unacceptably scarce for the poor. There would be plenty of resources for housing, transportation, and infrastructure for climate mitigation if money was spent wisely for large-scale projects.

Economic growth should occur in the short term to develop infrastructure and products that last longer, but the intention will be to use resources more efficiently in the long term. Our material wealth may decline in the years to come, but it could do so in such a way that less will actually be more. We can build smaller houses filled with fewer possessions, but these houses will be more comfortable to live in and products could be more satisfying to use.

We should not attempt to end economic recessions with more consumerism. Instead of corporate stimulation of the economy to produce more things to buy, we need to ration scarce resources and encourage community-based stimulation of the economy to create what is deficient: low cost housing, enough food, better education, and healthcare.

An alternative way to measure the economy would be relevant for an economy of decreasing quantity and increasing quality of production. In such an economy, GDC would be an objective measure of environmental impact, and it would go down instead of up. GDP would continue to indicate economic worth. To account for increased quality of production, there would be a steady increase in prices, or inflation. This inflation must be carefully monitored by governments. Prosperity would increase along with inflation if inflation was accompanied with better quality goods and services, increased median wages, less inequality, and less poverty. Controlling the economy with the money supply and maintaining a low level of inflation is what central banks routinely do now. Productivity gains or labour efficiency is used to determine the difference between economic growth and inflation. Instead, a measure of resource efficiency and quality gains would determine the difference between growth and inflation.

A fiscal stimulus of the economy to develop new technologies that will provide increased prosperity with reduced impact, combined with policies that reduce superficial consumption, may cause the economy to stop growing or even shrink in size in a material sense, but will still feel a lot like economic growth because of the dynamism inherent in the economy. This is in contrast to the past forty years when people were stimulated to consume for no great benefit and without corresponding increases in wages; the economic growth that occurred, with high levels of debt and underemployment, felt more like stagnation.

CREATIVE DESTRUCTION AND REDUCTION

Countries with higher poverty rates and more inequality tend to have less efficient economies, as it takes much more economic growth to get people out of poverty. Most of the gains for economic growth flow to the rich and have a much smaller effect on the poor. We can reduce poverty more efficiently by transferring funds from the richest members of society. This has a negligible effect on the prosperity of the rich but a large effect on the prosperity of the poor, and overall consumption levels do not have to change.

Globalization and the liberalization of trade in the last century have been effective in moving many people out of poverty. However, massively higher consumption in the rich world has achieved only a relatively small increase in consumption in the poor world. Research by Andrew Simms and David Woodward, of New Economics Foundation (NEF), has determined that in order to achieve $1 of poverty reduction, $166 of extra global production and consumption is required—with associated environmental impacts that hurt the poorest most.[62] Their prescription is to move decisively away from the inefficiency of relying on global growth for poverty reduction.

Normally, economic efficiency refers to the ability of an economic system to produce the most with the smallest input. This definition ignores the benefits of such production. If the economy produces more than necessary, the economy is not efficient. The efficiency we need is the greatest benefit for the most people while using the fewest resources—more for less. Our economic system motivates everyone to produce as much as possible and then figure out what to do with the excess later. Instead, the economy should be based on limiting consumption when resources are limited and focusing growth where required, rationing if necessary. This is what rational people would expect an economic system to do.

Joseph Alois Schumpeter was an Austrian economist pessimistic about the long-term prospects of capitalism, but he provided important insights into how the economy works. In Schumpeter's view, economic growth proceeds from a theoretical stationary point of no growth. In this environment, entrepreneurs create innovations that attract investment. New products are developed and with it new markets for consumption. New businesses are created. Others are destroyed. This process of "creative destruction" is not smooth and continuous, but proceeds with disruptions called recessions. Periods of economic growth together with recessions comprise a business cycle. The reason this occurs is that early entrepreneurs, who Schumpeter called the pioneers, at first create truly significant innovations that prove

----

62   David Woodward and Andrew Simms, *Growth Isn't Working: The Unbalanced Distribution of Benefits and Costs from Economic Growth*, (London: New Economics Foundation, 2006), 17.

very successful. This encourages other entrepreneurs and investors to get into the market to do similar things, with further innovation, and more incremental benefits. More investors are drawn to the market expecting easy money. The market becomes increasingly heated; the benefit of innovation becomes more questionable. Economic growth, increasingly, attains a less socially useful, more frenzied, and even desperate characteristic. Eventually, Schumpeter believed that the economy would become stationary with "nothing left for entrepreneurs to do.... Socialism of a very sober type would almost automatically come into being. Human energy would turn away from business. Other than economic pursuits would attract the brains and provide the adventure."[63] Entrepreneurship and creative destruction are going to provide the most benefit to society as inefficient technologies are replaced. But this will not necessarily result in overall growth in consumption. As the economy matures and mainly fulfills people's needs, economic growth becomes unnecessary and a measure of cost that should be minimized rather than maximized. New industries that replace old industries, that pollute less and use resources more efficiently, will continue to be developed. The economy switches gear from one that produces more and more, to one that produces better and better products. Businesses compete based on the quality of the goods produced as well as the technology. Even if newer, more appealing products using newer technology replace old products that still work well, emerging second hand markets develop to find other users. Only the businesses that make the best products will thrive.

------

63   Joseph Alois Schumpeter, *Capitalism, Socialism, and Democracy*, (George Allen & Unwin, 1976), 131.

As ongoing economic growth becomes less viable in the world economy because of peak oil extraction, other resource shortages, population stabilization, and aging demographics, local economies will have to be reformulated to expand production that more completely utilizes local resources. As the national economy contracts, economic growth at a local level will use labour and resources more sustainably. This form of growth will increase real wealth, but the size of the overall economy may shrink.

At present, governments are preoccupied with economic growth because of the misconception that it is the only way to create wealth and solve the problem of underemployment. In the future, the focus of all levels of government must be on ensuring appropriate levels of employment instead of economic growth, ensuring fair distribution of essential goods and services, and placing limits on excessive optional consumption.

By insisting that everyone earn a living from productive work funded by capital investment, we are consuming unnecessary resources because much of this production is frivolous, and we are wasting much human effort that could potentially be put towards other more useful activities. Economic growth requires and results in a growth of capital goods. Increased capitalization results in increased unemployment, which in turn requires more economic growth. Developments in technology and increased capitalization in the economy have resulted in a slow rise of unemployment, underemployment, and socially useless employment. This implies that the nature of employment has to change.

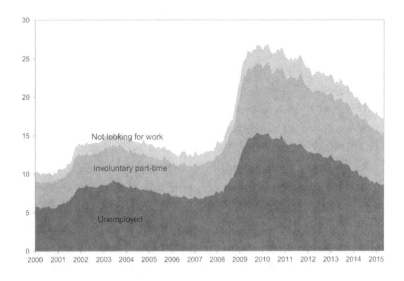

Figure 3: *Number underemployed in US (millions). Source: EPI analysis of Bureau of Labor Statistics' Current Population Survey public data series.*

Everyone should have a job to do that is useful to the community and that can provide a livelihood. The present economy depends on consumption and growth. One supports the other and as such, constitutes an engine of economic expansion. Growth fulfills needs, creates further needs, and ideally solves problems of unemployment and poverty. The economy, however, cannot continue growing in this fashion forever.

A community can produce everything needed within it. This guarantees full employment, but is less productive than an economy that involves more specialization and trade. Trade and industrial development can increase productive output if labour shortages develop or if by doing so more goods are produced with lower resource consumption. In general, this is not the case. Free trade and more intensive capitalization results in more goods produced in less time, but often with an increase in resources consumed. The local economy should be protected from competition to the degree that full employment is maintained.

The most significant feature of our economy is the division between labour and capital. As the economy moves towards a mode of industrial production, it changes from an economy in which capital is at the service of labour to an economy in which labour is at the service of capital. This switch from a labour-based economy to a capital-based economy is primarily responsible for the huge increase in productivity we have experienced in the last few centuries. In Part Two, I explore the differences and special relationships of these two economies.

It is clear that our economy produces a lot that has made improvements to our lives. We have computers, high definition televisions, smartphones, and numerous other electronic devices. While many of these advancements are a benefit, they represent a small and superficial component of our prosperity while creating many negative side effects including clutter, over-choice, and pollution. In Part One, I argued that in terms of prosperity, we are not that much better off than we were forty years ago. This is a prime indicator of the failure of our economic system as it now exists. Wealth in terms of the things that really matter—financial security, the quality of our food, the quality of our households, and the quality of our environment—have either not improved or have declined significantly.

On the other hand, simply stopping economic growth will not automatically stop global warming or environmental destruction as some environmentalists hope. It will simply lead to economic stagnation and a lack of development of new technologies we need. Economic growth may also continue, harmlessly, as costs increase with more urbanization and better quality products. Our focus should be on making our economy more efficient by consuming fewer scarce resources. As this occurs, the size of the economy may eventually reduce on its own.

Technology removes the need for skilled labour in the economy, but labour will be required more and more to process and protect available environmental resources. We will need technological advance to deal with the problems of living in a crowded and resource-depleted world. Whereas a great deal of skill and knowledge is required to participate in the capital-based economy, this knowledge capital will become irrelevant for a growing proportion of the population because of advancing computerization and the automation of services.[64] Wages will become lower and unemployment will increase. Resource conservation, however, will require labour of a different sort—a range of services requiring basic skills. In the resource-based economy to follow, our present measure of economic growth as a growth in quantity will stop being a positive force. The degree to which our economy can preserve resources will determine prosperity rather than the growth of capital. What I hope to show is that the required transition from an economy that requires specialized human capital to participate, resulting in high unemployment, to an economy with a more distributed employment of ordinary labour is not only possible, but also desirable.

Technological advancement should be in the direction of using resources, rather than labour, more efficiently. Technology, now directed towards economic growth and increasing profits of corporations, maximizes consumption. More effort is spent

---

64   Richard Susskind and Daniel Susskind argue that all professions will ultimately be replaced with technology. *The Future of the Professions: How Technology will Transform the Work of Human Experts*, (Oxford: Oxford University Press, 2015).

marketing products than developing them. Furthermore, economic growth is no longer increasing overall prosperity in rich countries. Production efficiency has increased so much that unemployment and financial insecurity are more problematic than any real deficiency of manufactured goods. Poverty and the risk of poverty at some stage of life is now more of a threat than ever, despite the rising abundance of everything.

Schumpeter coined the useful phrase "creative destruction" to describe how existing established businesses were destroyed by the creation of new technologies and new business models, like the work of a sculptor who destroys part of the stone to create. In the same vein, I propose to call the reduced consumption we must confront a "creative reduction." This recalls the work of the architect Ludwig Mies van der Rohe who famously declared "less is more." Technological efficiency will cause both creative destruction and reduction and this may cause unemployment to increase. I argue in Part Two that this is not a long-term problem.

The next big economy based more on labour than capital will be an extrapolation of the present leisure economy. This economy will include not only what is commonly referred to as the leisure industry, but also arts, crafts, and low volume production–those activities that require more labour, and are personally more satisfying. As long as there is wealth to support it, such labour can expand without limit.

... there's the respect
That makes calamity of so long life.
For who would bear the whips and scorns of time,
Th'oppressor's wrong, the proud man's contumely,
The pangs of dispriz'd love, the law's delay,
The insolence of office, and the spurns
That patient merit of th'unworthy takes,
When he himself might his quietus make
With a bare bodkin? Who would fardels bear,
To grunt and sweat under a weary life,...

—William Shakespeare, Hamlet

PART TWO UNEMPLOYMENT

... there's the problem
With the environmental movement.
For who would bear the recycling and conservation,
The reusable shopping bag, the carbon tax,
The pangs of a despised Gaia theory, Kyoto's protocol,
The insolence of eco-friendly products
That the climate change denier takes,
When he himself might his SUV drive
With air conditioning? Who will bear the burden,
To grunt and sweat with no more fossil fuels,...

FOUR LABOUR, WORK, AND ACTION

If labour is abundant, then why is it expensive? After all, money is an abstraction that measures scarcity. So paying for labour with money such that the money earned can buy more labour services, should enable a free and circular economy. Therefore, it is odd that labour is so expensive relative to the goods produced and the capital and resources used to produce them. To answer this puzzle, we must delve into the relationship between labour and capital notoriously expounded by Karl Marx.

The relationship between labour and capital is that in pre-historic times, and even much later, after the agricultural revolution, labour was the basis for survival. Karl Polanyi, in *The Great Transformation*, noted "the absence of the principle of least effort; and, especially, the absence of any separate and distinct institution based on economic motives" in pre-industrial societies. Techniques of reciprocity and redistribution ensured order in production and distribution rather than capital-based market exchanges of labour skills.[65] Resources were available, but limited by how much one was willing to work. In general, no one had to pay for labour. All of this changed with the industrial revolution. Capital increasingly became the basis of survival.

Capital includes factories and machinery, but also the store of human knowledge, skills, and special talents. The value of capital has become the clearest store of value in our economy. Labour is only valuable if it increases the store of capital. Household labour and the raising of children have no value in monetary terms and professions such as serving coffee and waiting tables have relatively little value. A rare talent such as being able to sing well has a high value because many people are willing to sacrifice their hard-earned capital—in the form of money—for a chance to listen to it.

Since capital (money) is what is required to buy the essentials of life, and labour (a job) is the only way for most people to obtain capital, labour tends to be expensive, regardless of whether it creates capital or not. Although labour that creates no capital has no value, it requires capital earned by economic growth to supply the conditions of livelihood when someone is employed. This is why it is worthwhile for corporations to find ways to minimize labour.[66]

In her book *The Human Condition*, Hannah Arendt proposes three fundamental human activities: labour, work, and action.

65   Karl Polanyi, *The Great Transformation: The Political and Economic Origins of Our Time*, (Boston: Beacon Press, 1944, 1957, 2001), 49.

66   See also Michael Perelman, *The Invention of Capitalism: Classical Political Economy and the Secret History of Primitive Accumulation*, (Durham and London: Duke University Press, 2000).

Labour corresponds to "the biological processes of the human body, whose spontaneous growth, metabolism, and eventual decay are bound to the vital necessities." The human condition of labour, according to Arendt, is life itself. Work provides a world of human artifacts "distinctly different from all natural surroundings." Action creates political bodies and thereby "creates the condition for remembrance, that is, for history."[67]

In economic terms, work is productive activity. Something is created; projects are completed. Work is what builds our capital stock and increases our standard of living. Although work is potentially infinite in scope, it is always limited by our resources. Work earns a livelihood and lack of work in our society is termed unemployment.

Labour is what we do to maintain ourselves. It is the constant chores, the housekeeping duties, and all the repetitive toil required to maintain our environment. Action, in Arendt's terms, is what is done in the political arena to make the decisions that maintain our civilization and move it forward. This is not only the burden of leadership, but also the burden of democracy. Action corresponds to those activities that define relationships among men and women. It therefore includes the affairs of political action—the countless meetings, discussions, and newspaper columns that determine how people relate to each other and contribute to government. It also encompasses the constant social interactions that allow social relationships to grow and the rituals surrounding major life events such as marriage and death.

In our modern world, "labour" is personal hygiene or household chores; in economic terms, it is encompassed by the household economy or by what could be called the labour economy. The

---

67   Hannah Arendt, *The Human Condition*, (Chicago, London: The University of Chicago Press, 1958), 7-9.

incentive for doing labour is the most natural one: the basic need to fulfill the requirements of life and well-being. What is essential for life is that which is produced by one's labour. It is by definition non-permanent and done repeatedly, like washing the dishes and cooking meals. Although seemingly limitless, it is technically finite. The household work that is never done can in fact be complete at any point in time. However, needs can be expanded to suit the availability of labour and the availability of labour can easily and arbitrarily be reduced by the increase of rest, for example, or social ritual—an increase in "action." There is no such thing as unemployment within a labour economy that functions primarily based on what is essential to life.

Work, on the other hand, provides artifacts and products that have a certain degree of permanence. The incentive to do work is unnatural—it requires the motivated discipline of the self, the hierarchical and powerful chain of command of the state, or the abstract incentives of the market. What is optional to life and therefore to society is infinite in scope. There is no end to what projects can be started, from building the pyramids, landing a man on the moon, or finding a cure for cancer. This work, as opposed to labour, often produces artifacts that are longer lasting. What is essential and what is optional—that which requires labour and that which requires work—defines our economy.

In our society, it is the drive to do optional projects that directs innovations and provides the impetus to expand the production of artifacts. The activities of optional work are primarily, though not exclusively, directed by the market-based economy. The market also absorbs what was once essential labour of the household and turns it into an optional service that only a few can afford. In general, work creates capital in our economy. Capital in the form of money also allows this economy to function. For these reasons, we could call it a capital-based economy.

The economy of traditional societies was labour-based to a high degree. There was a direct relationship between people's labour and their production. In antiquity, the part of the economy that was capital-based, like the building of the pyramids or the development and maintenance of the Roman Empire, was generally quite separate from the more labour-based agricultural societies underlying it.

However, for as long as humanity has lived distinct from other animals, it has depended on capital for survival. During Paleolithic times, without the specialized skills and technologies needed to build essential tools (human capital), humanity would have been restricted to a few small habitats, the population kept in check by limited natural resources and survival dependent only upon instincts. Numerous skills were needed, such as the ability to make fire and the ability to domesticate animals and plants. Later, agriculture demanded even more reliance on capital. Land, machinery, and techniques of farming were required to live off the soil.

It was capital in the form of knowledge—all of the invention that sparked the industrial revolution—and the nearly inexhaustible energy sources derived from fossil fuels (natural capital) that made ongoing population expansion with increased consumption possible. Without our advanced farming methods, our science, and technological innovations, our huge and growing populations would ultimately starve. We now need capital the way previous ages required land. There is a relatively clear division between what labour and capital produces. There are two separate economies, each with separate needs. Isolated from social requirements, capital only requires growth. The labour economy, on the other hand, is intimately bound to social needs of community. It is true that capital augments labour and increases its efficiency, just as digging with a shovel is more productive than digging with one's hands. Labour also augments capital by performing functions that would be difficult to mechanize. Investors, or capitalists, require capital in the form of money to achieve growth. The labour economy requires sufficient resources created by capital. Capital increases the amount of resources available by increasing productive efficiency and by making previously inaccessible resources accessible.

Industrialization prompted an economy where labour was at the service of capital instead of what had existed before, which was a labour-based economy where capital was at the service of labour. This subtle yet profound change is primarily what caused the stunning increase of productivity brought on by the industrial revolution. The industrial revolution itself started with a dramatic increase in capital made available with the discovery of North America. Capital, in the form of gold and silver from the New World, funded the development of new technologies by providing a huge concentration of wealth made available to the new industrial capitalists. New production processes incorporated labour and natural resources previously untapped. Capital created more capital. Capitalists separated production from the needs of community and it gradually became an end in itself. The production of goods brought wealth to investors and producers. Whereas before people would work only reluctantly for the fulfillment of essential needs, the new capital-based economy demanded ongoing work regardless of need. As the requirement for wage labour became universal, the only way for the largest proportion of society to attain the minimal amounts of money for subsistence was to do work to produce those products and services that ordinarily would not be required. Because of these incentives, the sheer intensity of innovations, new technologies, and ever-higher aspirations of culture have accelerated to an unprecedented degree. People have no choice but to work for the advancement of civilization. As their work is essential for their survival, this optional work becomes the essential labour for the household. Civilization progresses.

Diseases that once killed are cured. The speed of transportation becomes supersonic. The local solar system becomes part of our domain. Computers augment the already awesome powers of the human brain. This continual advancement of technology, though fundamentally optional, has become essential in an economy so strongly biased in favour of capital.

Up to a point, there is nothing wrong with the great incentive to produce more in our economy. New technologies, the large budget movies with spectacular special effects, and the development of fast computers are of great benefit in many ways. The problem seems to be a significant asymmetry between certain areas of the economy and others. For example, there seems to be no limit to how much money is available for blockbuster movies, video games and the whole leisure industry, yet money for healthcare, education, and crime prevention is scarce. Consumers willingly pay for entertainment but prefer to pay no taxes. The capital-based economy, controlled by private markets, over-produces what is optional and over-rations what is essential.

As we use more capital via more technology to extract more resources from the environment, the economy appears to be unlimited. We have used up resources accumulated over millions of years and added pollution that may take millions more for the ecosystem to absorb. In short, what our intensive capital-based economy has done for a mere few hundred years is to provide unparalleled comfort and the survival of an unprecedented number of people, while the previous epoch of human development and survival lasted many hundreds of thousands of years.

It has been a goal of civilization since its inception to provide or to protect existing resources to maintain or establish a labour economy. Generally, this occurs with the existence of elite members that own land and capital. Until the modern age, labour, which did not necessarily require special skills or talents, determined survival for most people. Only lack of resources could limit survival. It was the job of the elite, whether intentional or not, to collect and orchestrate capital to make resources plentiful enough for the many to survive. With diminishing resources, the elite could assure survival for themselves by accumulating enough capital. This capital would then be used to buy remaining resources, at whatever cost, to sustain the lives of the elite in ongoing comfort, to build fortifications, and to pay armies for protection. The poor had few alternatives but to compete for jobs to service the rich in order to survive. Whenever the elite concentrated capital purely for their own ongoing comfort, and ignored the plight of the common peasants that did the real work of production, their riches merely delayed the collapse of their civilization.

In general, labour and capital have coexisted. It was only during the Paleolithic era, before civilization began, that a pure labour-based economy existed with a minimum of capital required. It was not until the agricultural revolution that a capital-based economy, isolated and independent from a labour-based economy that supported it, came into existence. And not until the modern industrial period can we consider the possibility of an economy that does not include a viable labour-based component at all; that we can consider the possibility of a pure capital-based economy where machines and a small subset of the population are responsible for all production, with the rest barely surviving or perpetually engaged in consumption through investment and transfers.

The labour economy tries to conserve existing resources. Labour is minimized, but at the same time, existing labour is utilized to share the burden of production. The time required for production is also rationed according to other needs including sleep, social obligations, and other requirements of the household and community. On the other hand, the capital-based economy strives for innovation. It is an effective economy as long as resources are plentiful and labour is scarce. The capital-based economy left to its inherent tendencies does not try to conserve resources or to utilize all labour. It cares nothing about the needs of the house-hold or the community. Work demands complete dedication to the employer and to a career. As the labour economy is subverted by the capital-based economy, life becomes consumed by work. Working hard is not rewarded with more rest or time for social interaction, but with money, which is used for more consumption. Whereas labour is unlimited, work is limited by capital.

We have traded human effort for more capital. Less effort is required to accomplish production in our economy. More skills are also required to work in the capital-based economy. We have to build more schools and universities and spend more time and money preparing for the workforce. In other words, it requires more human-capital to establish a career. Because eco-nomic activity is concentrated in urban centres, property values get higher near the centres of cities. It requires more capital to establish living accommodations. It also may require two incomes to raise a family, and two incomes may require two automobiles. We pay dearly in capital terms for a few years of extended lifes-pan. The elderly have to live in special homes. Medical interven-tions require high cost medical equipment. More hospitals and extended care facilities have to be built. The concentration of economic activity in urban centres and more cars on the road create more congestion. Finally, the increase in leisure activities has created a need for more capital to buy airplanes, snowmobiles, audiovisual equipment, and computer games.

We depend on the crutch of technology to maintain our health and well-being in the face of far fewer resources per person. We can no longer do without technology or the corresponding capital investment that makes it happen. This is why seeing technology that has become essential to keep us alive, like central heating in a wintry climate, as a benefit and a source of our wealth, rather than a cost, is questionable.

This is not to say that life is not good in the developed nations, but merely to challenge the prevailing view that our quality of life is the best it has ever been. There are periods in the past when people had more resources at their disposal. They rarely innovated because they had no real need to. Their lives were good enough as they were. We, on the other hand, have to innovate as a means of our survival.

A typical North American family of the 1950s had sufficient land and time to provide their food if required. Now, while the houses are bigger, they are of lower quality, and they sit on smaller plots of land not useful for producing anything. At the same time, the capital requirements for staying alive in the modern industrialized world have greatly expanded.

A refrigerator would have been considered an incredible luxury in 1900; by 1930, a luxury costing a small fortune; by 1950, a standard item that most people could afford; by 1980, when the fridge broke down, there was no longer any choice—it had to be repaired or replaced. Luxuries eventually become essentials and we have to pay for them. People in 1900 had no refrigerators, but they had cold rooms, marble slabs, and convenient shops close by. We do not, so we must work hard enough to buy this and other former luxuries. Access to an automobile contributes to wealth, but on the other hand, if I am not able to live and work without an automobile, then that automobile is a cost, not a benefit. A few years ago having a computer was a luxury. Now having one for every member of the family is becoming a required cost of living for school, home, and work. Similarly, printers, fax machines, digital cameras, and software are required to varying degrees and they become obsolete quickly because of the rising tide of technological advance. Capital requirements for staying alive are continuously increasing. At the same time, labour requirements are decreasing.

The capital economy minimizes labour and uses it as efficiently and productively as possible. The labour economy absorbs labour, making it easier and less time consuming for everyone to get jobs done. The capital economy thrives on social capital but does not have the time resources to create it. The labour economy, by expanding labour and reducing time required for production, provides ideal conditions for the building of social capital. This suggests that a labour-based economy and a capital-based economy are complementary.

We need to restore the balance between labour and capital that existed for many thousands of years before the industrial revolution. We need to create capital to advance civilization, but only at the rate we can afford. We need labour to build strong communities and to ensure sustainable production of what we need to survive.[68]

The next chapter describes how a more labour-based economy could reduce unemployment.

---

68   Sources consulted for this chapter: Thomas Homer-Dixon, *The Upside of Down: Catastrophe, Creativity, and the Renewal of Civilization*, (Toronto: Alfred A. Knopf, 2006); Tim Jackson, *Prosperity without Growth: Economics for a Finite Planet*, (London: Earthscan, 2009); Jane Jacobs, *Dark Age Ahead*, (Toronto: Random House, 2004); Jay, Peter, *Road to Riches: or the Wealth of Man*, (London: Weidenfeld & Nicolson, 2000); David S. Landes, *The Wealth and Poverty of Nations: Why some are so Rich and some are so Poor*, (New York: W. W. Norton & Company, 1999, 1998).

FIVE **THE NEED FOR A LABOUR-BASED ECONOMY**

For much of civilized history, people gained their liveli-hood primarily with the sweat of their brows. Less than a hundred years ago in the US, agriculture employed almost half of all workers, with only the barest minimum of experi-ence necessary. Other occupations such as barbers, shop-keepers, carpenters, and butchers required only a brief apprenticeship and provided the certainty of employment. Doctors, lawyers, and other professionals required more training, but there was sufficient demand to absorb most that had the required aptitudes and were willing to spend the time in education and training. Throughout the agri-cultural revolution and well into the industrial revolution, until fairly recently, it was still possible for most people to rely on their ordinary abilities as an ultimate safety net for survival. Small garden plots, food preserves, cooking, baking, and sewing allowed families to survive with basic needs fulfilled.

Fast forward to the present day. Many professions demand more than ordinary talent. With newer technologies, fewer, more talented professionals can do the work of many less talented ones. To live in our modern economy, we must have skills attained with long years of education, requiring a higher than average level of intelligence or a rare talent. Supreme beauty can pave the way to becoming a supermodel or a movie star, high intelligence to becoming a scientist, speed and agility to becoming a star athlete. Coming up with inventions such as Velcro, or having talents at stock market speculation, may be other roads to financial success.

During the Great Depression, there was 25 percent unemployment. There was no employment insurance or welfare. Yet people survived because, for many, especially those who lived on farms, self-provisioning was still possible. After the depression, governments in many parts of the world nationalized many industries including healthcare, transportation, and coal production. In the 1980s, doctrines of right wing economics reversed policies of nationalization and reduced taxes for the rich. Since that time, the command economy has been shrinking and the opportunities for self-provisioning have been diminished by increases in population density and economic factors, resulting in a more commercial and capital-based society than the world has ever seen.

Here lies the defining line between a strong labour-based economy in which labour and ordinary talent ensure a comfortable livelihood, and a capital-based economy, which is highly competitive, requires extraordinary talents, large amounts of capital, and in which livelihood is less certain.

There is nothing wrong with a capital-based economic system as long as the base currency of survival for all the population is basic unskilled labour. What distinguishes the modern era from previous periods of history is that the viability of the labour economy is threatened. As soon as there is a race within society to gain the most capital and people see capital as the only means of survival, it is no longer an economy that works for the benefit of all. It is an economy that can guarantee wealth and survival for only a few.

Capital has dramatically reduced labour requirements for our essential production, but it paradoxically takes just as much time for people to gain their livelihood. We now have to devote more time to satisfying our living requirements than ever before. It takes two wage earners to provide an adequate standard of living for a family. This is because capital requirements, driven by optional consumption, have risen dramatically. In other words, our economic system trades extra capital in the form of more resources and energy consumed to reduce human effort, but simultaneously demands more consumption to reduce unemployment.

The problem of unemployment and therefore of poverty can be solved by dividing the economy between labour and capital. This allows the labour economy to expand and contract as required to ensure that there will always be full employment, and that everyone has a reasonable standard of living within the resources available. More teachers can teach fewer pupils, and doctors can have fewer patients. On the other hand, if the market or society makes demands for optional projects like building a road, developing a new technology, or fighting a war, then what is regarded as essential can be restricted to needs that are more basic. Adjusting the money supply of both currencies can effectively regulate the two economies. What is necessary for a labour-based economy to be viable is the provision of sufficient common capital: guaranteed accommodation, public transportation systems, public land, parks, and public streets for walking and cycling. A labour economy could do most of the maintenance required for the common capital. Discarded items would provide much of the capital required to live. In other words, as now, capital transfers would prevent extreme poverty but in such a way that the functioning of the market economy would not be negatively affected. The labour-based economy would function in much the same way as a peasant economy. It would not be a luxurious existence but it could be a comfortable existence, free from poverty and with plenty of time for household and community activities.

As a society, we can decide how much labour we need or want for providing such things as education, healthcare, and growing food. There are only so many hours of labour available, so a currency that represents that labour is self-regulating. This means that anyone who supplies at least the minimum number of hours of labour should receive at least the minimum benefits of society. Unemployment is impossible because there are always things to do. Meanwhile, the capital currency in the other capital-based economy continues to do what it is supposed to do, which is to ration capital. Both the labour economy and the capitalist economy involve economic freedom, as each participant can act according to his or her own self-interest and this is more or less in harmony with the ambitions of society. Labour is limited to twenty-four hours a day and it can easily be artificially regulated by social agreement to sixteen, twelve, eight, or even four hours per day, depending upon how much needs to get done. This suggests a need for a separate economy that does not represent a scarce resource, but one that is both limited and abundant: labour. Because it is limited, it is easy to control the money supply and inflation is impossible.

The benefits of having a viable labour economy are guaranteed full employment and a natural urge to conserve scarce natural resources. The capital-based economy, at present, functions because of unlimited natural resources. If growth is essential, then the preservation of the environment is a secondary requirement. With the addition of a viable labour economy, it is possible to require the capital-based economy to sacrifice growth and ration scarce resources. If the labour economy provides people with a non-extravagant but nonetheless fair and adequate means of making a living, this prevents producers in the capital-based economy from hiring workers for below subsistence wages.

One of the unnoticed trends of the past forty years is the steady increase of what could be termed a labour economy. The labour economy is what is done outside of paid work. There are three categories: unpaid household labour, unpaid labour in the real economy, and work that is viable only because it is funded by the welfare state or by charitable donations.

Household labour has been reduced since the turn of the century by labour saving devices such as automatic washing machines and vacuum cleaners. Easily obtainable food has made having a private garden for growing vegetables unnecessary. But since the 1970s, a countertrend has increased the demands on the household, including new tasks such as recycling, pumping gas, and packing groceries. Child rearing has become more demanding as children undertake a wide range of organized activities. It is now more common for a parent to have to take their child to school and pick them up. For a variety of reasons, children are now also more likely to require attention for conditions such as autism and other special needs. The high cost of housing has led many to renovate, both to save money by buying an old fixer upper and to increase the value for resale.

People doing work for no reward (the second category) is a new phenomenon no one could have predicted. While people have always contributed time for volunteer work or internships, people are now also spending countless hours writing blogs, articles for

Wikipedia, reviewing books for Amazon, and even writing books for uncertain profit. People are doing this work for rewards other than money, such as recognition from their peers or just the satisfaction that comes from doing something that interests them and doing it well. A great deal of software is now open source, written by programmers in their spare time and made available for anyone to use or improve. The advantage to the economy is immense. The combined efforts of many people working for free in this way provide much benefit to society and this suggests an alternative to market based solutions based on monetary rewards and restrictive patents.

Social media and the internet have been instrumental in this trend, but the welfare state has also played a role. Despite high rates of underemployment and low wages, programs of social support including unemployment insurance, guaranteed healthcare, and welfare programs have helped to make this shadow economy viable. People prefer to be useful. Laziness is rare, and it could be that the cruel incentives of the market economy are not always necessary and may be counter-productive.

The third category is the paid labour that the welfare state makes possible. As two income earners are now required instead of one, childcare and care for aging relatives has become more of a burden for the household economy. Wages for most jobs are not sufficient to pay market rates for these services and so only become viable with subsidization by the welfare state.

COMPLEMENTARY CURRENCIES

Bernard Lietaer, as an economist with the National Bank of Belgium, was instrumental in implementing a convergence mechanism for the creation of a single European currency. For the past twenty-five years, he studied complementary currencies (CC) and considers their presence in the world economy essential.

These currencies have become increasingly common since the 1960s. Some well-known examples include the Local Exchange Trading System (LETS) developed in Vancouver and the Ithaca (HOURS) system used in New York City since 1991. Today, over 2500 different Local Exchange systems operate throughout the world.

Since 1995, Japan not only has the highest number of CC systems—over six hundred in 2003—it also has the biggest diversity in type. Many grass root systems developed from models such as LETS and HOURS tend to be smaller and locally based. Complementary currencies are merely agreements within a community to use a locally devised currency in addition to conventional money as a means of payment.[69]

Japan suffered a prolonged economic recession triggered by the real estate crash of 1990. It may be the earliest example of a global phenomenon showing growth of capital assets not supported by corresponding wage growth and consumption, followed necessarily by increasing unemployment. Japan's unemployment rate increased from near zero percent in 1990 to 3.4 percent in 1996 and 5.4 percent in 2006, despite aging demographics. The Japanese first tried conventional solutions, including reducing interest rates to as low as zero, investment tax breaks, and public investments in infrastructure. All have failed. The Japanese are highly motivated to find alternative solutions to their economic crisis. Kato-Sama, a Japanese

---

69   Bitcoin is another alternative currency, but this is an open source alternative to conventional money. It may have some advantages, but it is not complementary in the same way as these time-based currencies are.

bureaucrat, developed a regional development strategy that included a new concept of regional currencies that he called "eco-money." He also created an Eco Money Network to analyze the needs of the community, design a CC to fulfill those needs, support its introduction, and analyze the results. These currencies are experimental and run for only one and one half to three years. They focus on services only and their scale varies from small communities to whole cities. The largest ones, such as the LOVE (Local Value Exchange) are managed with smart card technology to integrate several different activities including welfare, education, disaster prevention, environmental protection, enterprises providing natural food for children, and at home care for the sick and elderly.

Generally, these currencies are time-based and therefore could form the monetary basis of a labour economy. This sector could include all unskilled labour and those not otherwise employed. Money is available for anyone who needs to work. Resources include unused land borrowed for growing local organic food, pre-owned products, and recycled building materials. People can build houses with recycled materials and produce food on unused land like vacant lots, between buildings, on rooftops, and in parks. Old people, the sick, and the mentally ill can be given care. Theatrical groups and bands playing used instruments can entertain. Governments must ensure that there are always sufficient common resources for this economy to operate.

Complementary currency in Bali

The Banjar is a social unit that has been operating in Bali since 914 AD. It operates in rural and urban communities and in a defined geographical area consisting of between 750 and 1,200 members, with the largest ones in urban centres. Community based projects are organized and funded using two separate currencies. One, called the Rupiah, is the national currency, and the other is time-based. Communities hold regular meetings about once a month to determine allocation of time and money for projects. The unit of time-based currency, called the Nayahan Banjar, roughly translates to "work for the common good of the Banjar." The Nayahan is a block of time of about three hours that can take place in the morning, afternoon, or evening. Smaller communities do not bother keeping track of the time, but in larger communities everyone's contribution is recorded in a book called the Klian Banjar. According to Bernard Lietaer, the Banjar has given the Balinese culture extraordinary resilience in the face of a massive influx of tourists.

Each Banjar starts seven to ten projects every month and expects each family to contribute time and Rupiahs. In poorer communities Rupiahs are more constraining, but in richer communities time, the Nayahan Banjar, is scarcer. For the Balinese, "Time is a form of money," and more important for the strength of the community.[70]

Dual currency systems are a pragmatic solution to the division of essential staple items from non-essential luxury items. Experiments with complementary currencies should continue. They expand local production and consumption at the expense of imported goods and services. As such, they can have the effect of

---

70   S. DeMeulenaere, Bernard Lietaer, *Sustaining Cultural Vitality in a Globalizing World: The Balinese Example,* International Journal of Social Economics, Vol. 30 No. 9, 2003.

reducing overall economic activity, just as tariffs and subsidies do. However, stimulation of a local economy is more likely to stimulate production that would not otherwise have occurred. If I do work on my own house because I cannot afford to hire someone to do it, I am doing work that otherwise would not be done. Even though the work is done less efficiently than if a professional was hired, my labour is producing something in addition to what is normally produced in the main economy. Local currencies extend the productive capacity of the household by bartering services and utilizing labour that cannot or has not been utilized by the market economy. As such, it is an antidote to recession. Lower economic growth with increased employment is a legitimate response to excess production or a limitation of resources. The activation of a local currency encourages the mobilization of local labour that is underused because of a slowing economy. A thoughtfully established system of local currency at the municipal level would allow governments to regulate economic growth at the national level. If an economy is over productive, the money supply can be restricted. As labour is freed up because of rising unemployment, municipal based local currencies can expand to encourage less labour efficient, but more resource efficient local production.

This is no different in principle from what naturally happens when jobs are scarce. The household economy expands. People grow gardens and keep chickens in their back yards. Local municipal based economies would be less productive than national economies based on free trade between countries, but more productive than isolated household economies.

Industrialization has made labour more productive, but largely at the cost of depleting scarce resources. The capital-based economy, like the incandescent light bulb that consumes a large amount of energy relative to the amount of useful light, uses excessive resources to ensure that even the poorest have the barest minimum for survival. There is unnecessary production of products, often with many unnecessary features, just to make them appealing at the point of sale. Products are produced with poor quality to lower costs and increase sales, rather than with higher quality to make them last longer. The private industrial sector tends to develop expensive technology to solve small problems for an immediate market, rather than larger problems for an uncertain return.

Work is required to earn a living, and lack of work is termed unemployment. As industrialization advances, fewer workers are required. Economists maintain that there should be no long-term unemployment problem. Displaced workers from agriculture, for example, found work in factories. When factory production moved overseas, the service industry expanded. A growing economy should provide jobs for all who seek them. The evidence for this, however, is largely inductive. There is no reason in theory why the number of workers required for a given level of production should match the number of people who require jobs. In fact, we can now imagine an economy where machines do all the work. Without a base in labour, and unless we can afford for the economy to expand continually, unemployment will increase.

The next chapter looks at what happens to labour with extreme capitalization.

SIX EXTREME CAPITALIZATION

Machine breaking or Luddism as it came to be known, began in the seventeenth century and continued until about 1830. However, this was more a reaction against unemployment or wage reductions in general rather than to technical progress. There was no special hostility to the machine when it did not disadvantage the worker. Eric J. Hobsbawm notes in "The Machine Breakers" that there are "several examples of the straightforward opposition to machines which threaten to create unemployment or to downgrade labour even today." The worker "... was concerned, not with technical progress in the abstract, but with the practical twin problems of preventing unemployment and maintaining the customary standard of life, which included non-monetary factors such as freedom and dignity, as well as wages. It was thus not to the machine as such that he objected, but to any threat to these—above all to the whole change in social relations of production which threatened him." [71]

Imagine a society in the distant future, in which advanced technology has eliminated the need for any work, including all production, services, decision-making, and distribution. People would work or spend time at home where they would sleep, prepare meals, and satisfy other needs including relaxation, exercise, social contact, and sexual fulfillment with artificial media such as television, video games, and internet—all of which are commercialized.

The resulting economy would have 100 percent unemployment. There would be no demand for production or services without the intermediary actions of government and the enlargement of the welfare state. In such an economy, 100 percent socialization of the economy would be required. If 100 percent unemployment is possible because of technological innovation, then by extension, technological innovation is plausibly the cause of present underemployment.

In a capital-based economy, there is a tendency to find the best qualified, the most talented, and the hardest working to do most of the work, leaving the rest of the population less productive. This creates a condition that is perhaps the most overtaxing of the environment: those overworked do not have the time or the energy to invest in conservation. They are more likely to use their increased income for increased consumption of luxury products and labour saving devices. The rest will not have the financial resources or motivation for conservation. Such a stark division

---

71   Eric J. Hobsbawm, "The Machine Breakers," *Past & Present*, No. 1 (February 1952), 57-70.

does not produce leaders of communities or opportunities for cooperation that utilizes the talents and abilities of everyone.

As resources diminish and population increases, opportunities for providing material needs to those who can afford them become reduced. Healthy incentives change to unhealthy desperation. People desperately try to find meaningful and long lasting jobs, companies search for new products to market, and whole industries try to find more resources to exploit. This is a central problem of the capital-based economy—that ongoing growth is essential, even though we arguably have a superabundance of almost everything. This desperation within superabundance is the central paradox of a capital-based economy.

It is possible to find someone desperate enough to perform any service. Some of the sex trade and the illegal drug industry are obvious examples, but increasingly, manufacturers are also desperate enough to manufacture anything. Corporations use any tactic, and advertisers use sophisticated propaganda to persuade people to buy products they do not need or even want. Advertisers now pitch to young children even for adult products.[72] This desperation points to an obvious flaw in the economic system and a growing shortage of employment opportunities despite (or because of) rising abundance. Therefore, we should not be surprised that the degree of socialization of the economy is trending upwards despite neoliberal sensibilities at the helm. I discuss this further in Chapter Seven.

---

72   See Juliet B. Schor, *Born to Buy*, (New York, London, Toronto, Sydney: Scribner, 2004) and Shari Graydon, *Made You Look: How Advertising Works and Why You Should Know*, (Toronto, New York, Vancouver: Annick Press, 2003).

Outsourcing, but mainly automation, has caused a loss of jobs in our economy. Telecommunication technology has allowed the outsourcing of knowledge-based tasks to India. Competition from developing countries has encouraged companies to reduce labour costs. This has caused a downward pressure on wages and a continuous state of underemployment.

As technology improves, the rate of automation can only increase. Driverless vehicles will eliminate the need for long distance truck drivers as well as taxis drivers. Automated checkouts, online shopping, and more home delivery will reduce the need for staff at the retail level. Advances in manufacturing will further reduce employment requirements. Some forecasters are even predicting a singularity at which machine intelligence learns to develop technology far beyond the ability of humans to comprehend and the pace of technological change becomes so great that progression is no longer observable.[73] If machines truly gain such intelligence and technological abilities, they could easily solve economic problems along with global warming and other environmental issues. However, they may become so advanced that they would consider us large parasites or at best, maybe pets.[74] There may come a point where we may wish to limit progress.

Capital is clearly required to improve quality of life, to counteract diminishing resources, to satisfy the requirements of rising populations, and to develop new knowledge and technologies. This will ultimately reduce our impact on the environment. But continuous economic growth for the sake of full employment and

---

73   Ray Kurzweil, *The Singularity Is Near: When Humans Transcend Biology*, (New York: Penguin Group, 2005).

74   In a BBC interview on December 2, 2014, Stephen Hawking warned that artificial intelligence could lead to the end of the human race.

stability is a recipe for catastrophe. Such growth is like a cancer, with no endpoint and no maturity, ultimately overwhelming all resources.

Different cultures in all periods of history have had difficulty dealing with the unemployed. Most economists have discounted the possibility of automation destroying jobs. They even have a name for this misplaced view—the Luddite fallacy.

Technology and automation do take away jobs, but until now economic growth has created other jobs that provide more goods and services than were there before. Despite the apparent ability of the economy to create jobs and keep people employed, there is no guarantee that the number of jobs created will equal those that are lost. The tendency to reduce overall employment and cause hardship because of it is not a new thing.

Technology has been displacing human labour for thousands of years. This labour displacement has not generally created unemployment but rather a redeployment of skills and efforts into other areas that society ultimately found useful. A segment of the population gains an increase in spare time and considers alternate ways to direct efforts. These efforts change or even evolve civilization in unpredictable ways. When humans developed techniques for hunting large mammals, people had more time for painting on cave walls, religious rites to celebrate birth, marriage, and death, and the further development of culture. The beginning of agriculture led to the development of the city-state and the building of empires. More recently, the industrialization of agriculture has led to the growth of manufacturing and now technology threatens to remove the need for productive work entirely. Whenever an economy becomes more efficient and therefore more productive, the excess capacity is directed toward other ends such as religion and military expansion.

Labour displacement is a complex process of cultural change, sometimes enormously disruptive and often the cause of war and economic turmoil. Civilization has offered many solutions to the sudden emergence of a relative state of unemployment or labour surplus. These solutions were evident in the last century and were the main cause of ideological conflict and the near constant state of war that occurred.

In a hunting and gathering economy, labour is required for survival either directly for food production or indirectly for the domestic concerns of food preparation, child rearing, clothing, and shelter. For the hunter and gatherer, the prime directive is simply staying alive. With agriculture, the support functions of the economy expand and the prime directive shifts to the control and expansion of territory. All efforts in the economy and the competition among nations are directed towards the expansion of empire and the defence of borders.

The industrial economy required restructuring such that labour was directed, not primarily for producing food but for creating various goods and services. Consumption of optional goods and services and the required marketing efforts is the driver of this economy. Almost all labour is detached from the real needs of society, such as food production and essential goods and services. This means that most people can only survive in a parallel economy of manufacturing by selling their labour, which is employed for optional needs, and using the money earned to buy the essentials for survival.

At one time, a whole family only had to invest about forty hours of labour per week to receive the capital required to sustain their lives. They could use the remainder of the time for household duties, community service, recreation, and social activity. As capital growth demanded more labour, not only did GDP grow, but also with it the size of the capital-based economy at the expense of the labour economy, which previously sustained the household and the community.

Industrial production has progressed to such a degree that there is no longer any real limitation of what and how much is produced. We are emerging from an economy in which it made sense to produce as much as possible to one in which a limitation of production for the sake of environmental sustainability is necessary. We must now begin to impose limitations on production, including the resources used and the pollution generated. It is now a matter of how much we can afford to produce. This is possible without undue hardship only if we accept human labour as an alternative to capital-based production, and full employment with a fair living wage as essential.

Where human effort is involved, resources are used more conservatively. For this reason, labour-based technologies tend to be more efficient in resource terms. An automobile, for example, may have an engine with the power of three hundred horses. However, only one horse is required for transportation and even the power of a single human can provide much useful transport, especially when coupled with the technology of the bicycle. But neither a bicycle nor a horse can propel us at one hundred kilometres per hour.

Labour saving technology has become a cultural obsession. We go to great lengths to minimize human effort. However, such reductions in human effort require more technology, energy, and resources. The dramatic increase in the needs of capital to run Western civilization has depleted resources, increased pollution, and caused global warming. At the same time, the reduction in human effort has not resulted (contrary to expectations) in a reduction in time spent working. We have to work faster and more intensively, with increased levels of stress. People need exercise to remain fit. Replacing labour with capital-intensive labour saving devices has made us overweight and unhealthy.

There is a lot of work that does not have to be done. It is often not a shortage but an excess of products, and the need to produce more and more, that is making our lives more unpleasant and more alienating. When we make purchases, we often have so much choice that we cannot find what we really want. On the other hand, reducing production would be a benefit from many different perspectives, from reducing pollution and global warming to conservation of scarce resources. Since we already have so much more than we need, it would seem reasonable to assume that having less would not have a great effect on our wellbeing. If we could reduce the capital that we need and at the same time increase what could be achieved with only labour, it would seem that this would be of benefit to our society.

By increasing labour without increasing resource depleting production, we could repair cars instead of replacing them, walk more instead of driving, improve health with more labour intensive preventative healthcare, and build better and more durable products by spending more time on design.[75]

This is not to suggest that we should dig holes with our hands, but perhaps in some cases we should recognise human labour as a form of alternative energy. We can do this by making a firm division between an economy in which the full utilization of labour is essential, and another type in which labour for capitalized production is optional. Households and communities can always use labour and this is generally not destructive to the environment. Even if actual productive work is not required, the economy can

---

75   Shameless promotion: see form3.com.

still provide incentives for less intensive resource use. About ten years ago, Mexico replaced cash handouts with conditional cash transfers (CCTs). They gave money to the poor if their children stayed in school, had regular checkups, and if pregnant mothers took nutritional supplements. This program was so successful that New York City as well as Britain and other European countries have considered similar steps.[76] These transfers provide the resources and the incentives for the poor to do what is essential in their lives in the long term. This can also form part of the basis for a household-centred labour economy by providing funding for some household labour. This labour is not productive, but it reduces long-term costs to society and comes closer to how a typical middle class household once operated. At one time, the wages for employment of one family member were adequate for the needs of the whole household. Thus, the household as a whole could afford the labour required for the long-term interests of the family. This ended when two wage earners were required to earn only enough for the short-term needs of survival in a growing impoverished class of people in otherwise rich developed countries.

Capitalism creates a condition of material abundance for some, but rising population ultimately succumbs to resource scarcity. Just as insufficient land existed in feudal times, insufficient capital now exists for many to survive in the lifestyle defined as normal. With an abundance of products not directly related to real survival, capital cannot increase sufficiently for all to obtain the essentials of life. More capital investment is required for smaller returns, and the spoils of capital investment are spread ever more

---

76   "When bribery pays," *The Economist*, March 15, 2008.

thinly. People have to work harder for capital but more and more capital is required for basic survival.

We cannot stop logging, because people would lose their jobs. Nor can we stop unsustainable agricultural practices or shut down industries that pollute too much or produce nothing of real value. The capital-based economy produces an artificial world with pressing internal problems. This is blocking rational action, causing us to do things that make little sense. If we were acting rationally, given what we know about global warming, pollution, overpopulation, shortage of water, the shortage of fertile land, and the increasing cost of resource extraction, would it be reasonable to continue living the way we do? The stakes are high. Yet we carry on insisting on our wasteful and extravagant lifestyle. I am not referring only to those who are unaware of the seriousness of our plight or those who deny that there is enough evidence to be certain. I am talking about those, like me, who recognize the problem but must choose other more pressing and personally important priorities: food for their families, a roof over their heads, and a job that pays the mortgage.

As it stands, our economic system, based so totally on capital, seems ill equipped to deal with recently exposed problems. Pollution, including the greenhouse gases that cause global warming, the collapse of ecosystems, and species extinction are all, in the end, economic problems that threaten the long-term viability of civilization as we know it. The solutions that these problems would seem to suggest often contradict the smooth functioning of the economy. Continuous growth of the economy, required for low unemployment, is generally not compatible with lower levels of exploitation and destruction in the environment. Although luxury and quality of life may improve, a capital-based economy, taken to its ultimate extreme, is much less stable. Civilizations can be vulnerable to collapse because ongoing growth in consumption becomes essential for survival, even though resources are scarce.

The loss of jobs caused by the agricultural revolution was compensated for by the growth of manufacturing. When manufacturing jobs were lost due to automation and outsourcing to other countries, the service industry expanded. Nonetheless, underemployment is a persistent feature of an advanced industrial economy. Service industry jobs are often lower paid. And what happens when service industry jobs are also automated? Hypothetically, machines could do all work, including all service industry jobs. If the current trend towards full capitalization of the economy continues, we could imagine a world where there is no work to do, with 100 percent unemployment. Logically, this is possible.

Millions of workers from China, India, and the former Soviet Union compete for jobs previously supplied by a handful of rich developed countries. With seven billion people in the world, there is a glut of labour in the world market. Most people in the world, until recently, could support themselves with agriculture. Overpopulation has made this impossible for most and more have to compete for jobs in the industrial sector. The result is unemployment, low wages, illegal employment in the drug and sex industries, and outright slavery.

Wages are too low, especially in developing countries, to absorb the huge increases in production. Instead, aggressive marketing has persuaded consumers in rich countries to take on more debt. Since debt can only grow so high, the economy at some point has to stall. The present state of the economy, similar to many other depressions that have preceded it, is characterized by wealth concentrated in a small section of the population, a high amount of debt or negative wealth in the remaining population, and a huge stockpile of luxury products, some of which will never be consumed.

Growth is required to solve the problem of unemployment in an industrial, capital-based economy. Such was not the case in a traditional labour-based economy. The argument put forward is that as industrialization has developed, the ever-present labour economy that has coexisted until recently has gradually shrivelled. The labour economy is an old-fashioned economy based on the idea that everyone shares according to the effort that is provided. Labour-based communities tend to be poor, so capital based economies are required to produce wealth, to expand civilization, and to solve problems in the world. This suggests a complementary relationship and an antidote to unsustainable growth.

Automation can take away jobs. The answer for the Luddites was to stop progress by destroying the machines that were taking away jobs. The machines are now an established part of our economy, but now a modern version of the Luddites believes that the only way to preserve jobs is with increasing material consumption. Every Christmas there is a newspaper editorial encouraging people to buy more presents for the good of the economy.

In any economy, there is no guarantee that there will be full employment. This seems borne out by the statistics. But because labour, as opposed to work, is always a requirement for receiving the benefits of society, it makes sense to consider the idea of a labour economy distinct from a capital-based one. In the capital-based economy, there can be unemployment but the labour economy can always expand and contract as required.

This is where the distinction between work, labour, and action becomes important. While machines could do all the work and most labour as well, there could remain a requirement for types of labour, like those tasks that maintain the body and the mind, or cultural pursuits. This is not productive work, but in a fully capitalized economy, productive work is not required. Action—as in the awareness of political affairs and the need to participate in decision-making—could also be a need of such a society.

This chapter was introduced with a thought experiment about what would happen if the economy were 100 percent capitalized. We concluded that there could be 100 percent unemployment in such an economy. The corollary is that capitalization increases underemployment. The only way that economic growth can reduce unemployment is through labour displacement. As jobs are eliminated by technology other uses and applications for labour must be found.

THE NEXT BIG ECONOMY

Until fairly recently, the economy was fundamentally agricultural for the vast majority of the population in North America. The agricultural focus began to change in the late nineteenth century. Falling prices for agricultural products due to too much land under cultivation and improvements in productivity due to technology led to over-production. The Long Depression from 1873 to 1879 was the result of this stagnation. Later, food shortages in Europe absorbed this excess production and a brief expansion of the economy occurred in 1890, beginning the Progressive Era. World War I also provided some impetus for economic growth, but by the 1920s, severe problems returned. The so-called Roaring Twenties did not have a healthy economy but instead created a huge bubble ready to burst. There was huge investment in new technology such as the motorcar and attempts at private stimulus of the economy with easy terms on credit. However, the underlying dependence of the economy on an agricultural base led to the economic crisis and stagnation of the 1930s. Despite huge speculative growth of the industrial sector, and with that the stock market, the wage of the average family hardly grew at all during the 1920s. Efforts to keep up with the growth of the economy led to increases in debt and the eventual failure of about a third of the banking industry by 1932. We can characterize this period from about 1890 to about 1940 as the gradual demise of the agriculturally based economy in the United States.

What emerged with World War II was a new prime directive. Manufacturing became the new focus of the economy and technology the basis of the power of nations. Economic growth became the focus instead of expansion of territory. The steady growth of manufacturing and technology through much of the twentieth century and especially at the end of the Cold War made it possible for the United States to become a leading power in the world. The economy grew to raise incomes, to increase household consumption, to reduce unemployment, and to make the country militarily strong. All activities, including food production and services, became the support function for the manufacturing industry.

After 1970, productivity in manufacturing and outsourcing increased to the point of economic stagnation. The economy still grew but, as in the last stages of the agricultural economy, it became harder for the majority of the population to make a living. What will emerge, hopefully without a world war, will be a new base for the economy. The production of food and all the goods and services required for staying alive will become easy for the economy to provide and relatively few people will be required to create them. What will form the basis of this new economy?

When new technology is developed, it has a profound effect on the economy. Robert J. Gordon, an economic historian at Northwestern University, points out that recent new technology does not have impact on our lives comparable to early industrialization.[77] When television was invented, no one had any product like it. A new market was created that increased the size of the economy. Labour saving appliances, airplanes, highways, telephones, central heating and air conditioners all provided new benefits and contributed to a new economy with high economic growth in the 1950s, 60s, and 70s. Now consider the smartphone, a revolutionary new product, which has created a new market, but also, has diminished the need for a pocket calculator, a flashlight, a home telephone, yellow pages, maps, mail, newspapers, books, television, and games. Disruptive technologies provide benefits not available before and, therefore, new markets. Emergent technologies, like the smartphone, do the opposite: they provide an alternative to existing technology. Whatever benefits the smartphone and other new digital technologies provide, they do not necessarily cause the economy to grow or provide more jobs. Of course, there are sales of smartphones and associated services, but there is also a pronounced reduction in the sale of products and services replaced.

There is one aspect of the current economy that is more resistant to both outsourcing and automation: work that is associated with leisure, arts, and crafts.

---

77   See Robert J. Gordon, *The Rise and Fall of American Growth: The U.S. Standard of Living Since the Civil War*, (Princeton and Oxford: Princeton University Press, 2016).

The new leisure-based economy

The natural successor of the industrial economy of manufacturing is a new leisure-based economy. Manufacturing and the service industry will automate more and employ fewer people. This is an exact parallel to what happened to the agricultural economy with increased industrialization. The leisure economy, including travel, tourism, dining out, theatre, movies, music, performing arts, professional sports, physical recreation, television, books, magazines and internet based entertainment, even now is a substantial portion of GDP. Employment in this area is the most automation proof. Although technology, in principle, could replace all work, it is less likely to be used to replace leisure industry jobs. The reason is simple: while few people complain that retail jobs, work on an assembly line, or long distance trucking are disappearing, people enjoy working in leisure-oriented industries. In professional sports, the use of performance enhancing drugs is both illegal and disapproved of by spectators. The possibility of android athletes replacing human ones, for this reason, is remote. Similarly, audiences will appreciate real actors, real musicians and real artists more than digitally produced alternatives. There are computer programs that can paint as well as Picasso and compose music like Mozart, but few want to buy this output. Human creativity will not only have an edge over the artificial equivalent for some time, there will also be a persistent preference.

Although unemployment and underemployment will remain a significant problem for some time, the Luddite scenario of complete automation is not likely to happen because society will react. Even now, there is enormous political pressure to solve the problem of unemployment. In addition, those who are unemployed will continue to be highly educated and resourceful. They will gravitate towards more craft-based and artistic endeavours. The trend for more automation will be met with a counter trend towards low volume production. At the same time, consumers will shy away from the machine aesthetic towards more individual expression.

Since 1972, the Real Ale movement in Britain has challenged mass production of beer. More recently, in North America thousands of craft brewers have taken over about 20 percent of the market and the share is rising rapidly. Craft style production, embracing emerging technologies of low volume manufacturing, may now be a more practical solution to underemployment than economic growth. This transition can be streamlined if the welfare state rather than the market economy supplies most of the essentials of life including food, shelter, and medical care.

Universities will move away from their role of producing highly trained technicians and engineers for industry and back to their traditional role of teaching the humanities and higher sciences. Research and development into new areas will remain a highly important aspect of the economy despite the level of automation.

The highly capitalized and passive entertainment industry is more a part of the old industrial economy than the new leisure economy. Tourism depends mainly on travel by air. Movies, sports, and recreation depend on expensive equipment. However, efforts to reduce environmental impact will have far less effect on this industry than on manufacturing and retail. The environmental footprint of the leisure industry can easily be reduced with increased employment opportunities. Theatre, music, recreation, sports, gardening, arts, and crafts all present low capital and high labour possibilities.

Although there are professional athletes, actors, and artists that earn huge amounts of money, there are substantially more that will work for free. Though work in the leisure economy will be less susceptible to automation, much of it will also be underpaid or unpaid. Leisure and work will be highly integrated in the new leisure economy, much the same as labour was often unpaid and integrated into the activities of the household in the agricultural economy. More arts and craft oriented production will become both a part of leisure and a part of livelihood in the new associated household economy.

In the new emerging leisure economy, the state will have a greater role in basic production. The state may come to own the means of production, while the private sector continues to innovate and find new ways to profit from innovation. A small entrepreneurial fringe will also provide many of the goods and services required in a more personalized way, and will arguably be an extension of the leisure economy. Perhaps only 20 to 40 percent of the workforce will be required to provide food, housing, and all the services that are essential to people's lives. And perhaps 60 to 80 percent of this will be distributed universally, in a similar way to how publically funded healthcare is distributed now. In this scenario, work will not be obsolete but will be redefined in terms of arts, crafts, theatre, sports, and personal development including fitness and education. Volunteering and humanitarian aid could evolve into new occupations. This is analogous to how work evolved to replace agricultural output. Goods and services that were previously produced within the household were instead manufactured and monetized, forming the basis of new employment, not only in manufacturing but also in retail and marketing. The leisure industry will also evolve into a new way of making things and new ways of solving problems. People will work in meaningful and fulfilling jobs, attempting to solve problems not for profit but for personal satisfaction.

Leisure accounts for much that makes us human. Festivals, celebrations, cultural pursuits, political organization, and protest are all activities that can absorb labour and form a more meaningful basis for livelihood than the sterile world of manufacturing. The leisure economy has much in common with the agricultural economy, in that labour and the affairs of the household can be integrated. The leisure economy also has the potential to take on those projects that industry does not find profitable, such as ending poverty, providing housing for the poor, and attacking disease and malnutrition. In the end, the very idea of leisure as a counterpoint to work will disappear in favour of labour as a fundamental human condition.

In Part Three, I discuss the role of government and markets in allocation of goods and services. What really happened to cause the crash of 2008? Yes, there was a bubble, but there was also a sort of global panic about the lack of good residential housing stock, close to waterfronts, high quality urban amenities, and pleasant natural surroundings. Rumours of peak oil and dramatic increases in food prices from 2004 to 2007 also contributed. This panic helped to bid up prices. The market may have overshot, but scarcity of resources may have been at the root of the crisis. The market economy has created an abundance of things like smartphones and online movies, that at the end of the day do not matter that much, while the things that really matter like energy, food, and water are becoming scarce.

Our civilization may already be in the early stages of collapse. Although our problems and appropriate actions have been obvious for some time, the elite have tended to focus more on concentrating wealth than solving problems. It is a curious feature of collapsing civilizations that the wealthy seek aggressive means to extract even more wealth from the already impoverished. Jared Diamond describes how kings and nobles in the collapsing Maya civilization failed to recognize and solve obvious problems caused by overpopulation, deforestation, and climate change. Their attention was focused instead on warfare, building monuments, and disproportionately enriching themselves by extracting food from the peasants. Diamond compares how "Maya kings sought to outdo each other with more impressive temples" with the "extravagant conspicuous consumption by modern American CEOs."[78] This response, like that of the Rapanui chiefs discussed in Chapter One, who competed for the largest statues, seems a common response of the elite to ensure that as resources decline, sufficient wealth will ensure current living standards, even though the eventual collapse will occur more quickly. This is what makes the current predicament difficult to solve.

An economy based on selfish individualism undeniably has several advantages, including stunning advancements in technology. It also has many disadvantages that are now becoming more significant, including gross inequality of wealth. Such an economy is more likely to inspire social unrest and an attitude of trying to guarantee personal survival rather than create a solution to world problems. The environmental movement is mainly composed of the middle and upper classes, for they are the only ones that can afford to pay more for fuel-efficient cars, organic food, and ethically produced goods.

More wealth means more power. Present conditions in the United States aptly demonstrate how people with wealth are able to strongly influence and even control government to the point that a large proportion of the population no longer bothers to vote in general elections. A country with a high concentration of wealth can become similar to a dictatorship. Although it is possible for a democratically elected government to enact controls and regulations such as restrictions on political contributions, in practice this becomes less likely to happen the more that wealth

---

78   Jared Diamond, *Collapse: How Societies Choose to Fail or Succeed,* (New York: The Penguin Group, 2005), 157-177.

is concentrated in fewer hands. [79] Implicit control of democratically elected government by a small non-elected elite amounts to
a system similar to that created by fascist movements in Europe
before the Second World War.

The stresses accompanying the transition from a capital-based
industrial economy to a more labour-based leisure economy are
exactly parallel to the traumatic changes experienced with the
declining role of the agricultural economy. The public is becoming restless. Populist movements in many countries are gaining
ground. In the United States, public figures such as Donald
Trump, skillfully exploiting popular sentiments from all over the
political spectrum, have achieved a remarkable following.

We should be concerned about the future.

---

79   Robert B. Reich, *Saving Capitalism: For the Many, Not the Few* (New
York: Alfred A. Knopf, 2015). See Chapter 18 for a discussion about
the loss of countervailing power in American politics. Corporations
spent 56 times more than labour unions in lobbying. The richest 0.01
percent provided 10 percent of total campaign contributions in 1980,
soaring to 40 percent in 2012. Only 58.2 percent of eligible voters par-
ticipated in the 2012 election, and only 33.2 percent in the midterm
elections of 2014.

But that the dread of something after death,
The undiscover'd country, from whose bourn
No traveller returns, puzzles the will,
And makes us rather bear those ills we have,
Than fly to others that we know not of?
Thus conscience does make cowards of us all,...

—William Shakespeare, Hamlet

PART THREE DISTRIBUTION

But for the dread of environmental collapse,
The unconfirmed future of computer simulation
No time traveller attests, puzzles the will,
And makes us rather accept the way the world is
Than consider others that we know not of?
Past failures thus make cowards of us all,...

SEVEN CORPORATISM AND THE WELFARE STATE

The truth is that men are tired of liberty.

—Benito Mussolini

As technology has progressed, displacing jobs from productive occupations, labour has moved into more service-oriented endeavours. From the primary function of food production, labour moved first into the many institutions of the city-state, including governance and military occupation, later into manufacturing as the industrial revolution developed, and finally into knowledge-based services. These service-oriented professions, however, are the overhead of the economy and are supported by what is considered productive. So, while true that much of technological progress need never create mass unemployment, the welfare state must support newly created employment in one form or another. Those who are productive and own capital must support the others who provide service. In earlier times, this could be a balanced partnership with farmers producing food, bakers baking bread, and blacksmiths providing shoes for the horses. Some form of taxation always supported the city-state and later the nation-state.

A few predictions can be made for the coming century. We know that the world population is going to increase by almost a third. Two to three billion people will be added to our already large population of seven billion. It is also obvious that we will run short of many resources. Even now, many countries are short of water. The growing lack of surplus grain since 2007 and the threat of food scarcity in the coming years are alarming.[80] Population growth will be highest in poorer regions. Extreme poverty and hunger can only increase without intervention. Some of the poorest countries are failed states with ineffective governments and are breeding grounds for terrorist groups. Violence is common and pirates in nearby seas make transoceanic shipping dangerous. However, rich and developing countries will continue to cause most environmental impacts. The large populations of China and India, which are emerging from poverty with their impressive economic growth in recent decades, will face huge challenges with resource shortages. Conflicts over resources with neighbouring countries are likely, as a condition of desperation sets in. Major war somewhere down the line is almost inevitable if we do not make significant changes to the world economy now.

Diminishing resources and a lack of rich world markets for manufactured goods, in proportion to the growing list of poor

---

80   See Lester R. Brown, *Full Planet, Empty Plates: The New Geopolitics of Food Scarcity* (New York, London: Earth Policy Institute, 2012).

countries seeking to emulate Japan and China with export-led growth, may lead to a protectionist backlash. Less US hegemony may make the present period of globalization less viable.[81]

In the developed countries, economic malaise and public discontent will continue to prevail for some time. A shortage of world resources will restrict economic growth; technological advances and outsourcing to poorer countries will continue to restrict employment opportunities. Ongoing underemployment and increasing social unrest will be the likely future scenario. This part of the story is not inevitable, but is somewhat likely if history is our guide. The rise of fascism in Italy and Nazism in Germany after the First World War occurred alongside similar stressors.

THE FUTURE MAY BE THE PAST

Historically, technological change and greater productivity have resulted in increased militarization both to protect resources developed by the agricultural economy and for the expansion of empire. Beginning at the end of the nineteenth century, governments looked for peaceful means to reduce the stresses of industrialization and the unequal distribution that resulted. The First World War, the Great Depression, and the Second World War were periods of stress that ultimately motivated increased democratization and socialization of the economy. Governments wanting to appease citizens at risk from unpredictable changes of industrialization—labour displacement— brought in publicly funded insurance to offset job loss, poverty in old age, and ill health. Growing inequality promoted progressive taxation

81   Kevin O'Rourke, "Politics and trade: lessons from past globalisations," *Bruegel Essay and Lecture Series*, 31 January 2009.

and the development of institutions such as schools and universities that would provide greater equality of opportunity. Publicly funded education also met the needs of industry for better-trained workers. Public funding was found to be more efficient for providing comprehensive infrastructure for transportation and communication than the piecemeal efforts of private enterprise. The welfare state grew along with the economy from the late nineteenth century until 1973. Various governments have encouraged or resisted the growth of the welfare state, but the trend line is unmistakable. The welfare state has grown with increased industrialization, resulting, especially in Western Europe, in a predominantly socialist society controlled by a parliamentary democracy within a market economy.[82]

After the long conflicts of World War II and the ensuing Cold War, the welfare state became the favoured alternative to non-market socialism and fascism, for the modern industrial state. Without the adoption of the institutions of the welfare state, the hardships caused by labour displacement would be a great deal worse. Under the present circumstances, the welfare state, defined as having a free market component and a state-run planned component, is arguably the best economy possible.

No economy has ever been completely planned. Most socialist state-run communist countries such as the Soviet Union and China have always had a sizeable black market economy. In the Soviet Union, it constituted approximately 20 percent of the economy. In Maoist China, the ratio of market-oriented activities was even higher. In contrast, even in the most capitalist of countries, many parts of the economy are socialized and planned.

---

82   See Francis G. Castles, Stephan Leibfried, Jane Lewis, Herbert Obinger, and Christopher Pierson, Editors, *The Oxford Handbook of The Welfare State*, (Oxford, New York: Oxford University Press, 2010).

It is obvious that socialist and market-based systems can coexist comfortably, and the effort to suppress either one due to ideological requirements is doomed to failure. What led to the collapse of the Soviet Union and Chinese communism is not the relative composition of socialized and market-based aspects of their economy, but the overly bureaucratic and centralized control of the economy; the failed attempt to set all prices for goods and services without the benefit of formal markets.[83]

Pure market economies are also rare. They do a remarkable job of balancing incentives and rewards, and become a dynamic engine of economic growth and material progress, but they have difficulty in equitable distribution of goods and services produced as a sizeable fraction of the population eventually loses the competition for a share of the wealth. Luck is a major ingredient for success and those that manage to gain even a small amount of it then find it much easier to gain more than those that must use all their efforts for mere subsistence. Were it not for the adoption of the welfare state, the Luddite scenario of rising unemployment would have occurred a long time ago.

Prior to the Great Depression wealth became concentrated and wages were lowered. People found it more difficult to make ends meet. The response of government was to create easy credit terms to replace missing wages. When debt became too high, the economy collapsed and unemployment exploded, becoming as high as 25 percent. Mass unemployment during the Great Depression led to the establishment of new institutions, including a growth in government, universal programs for healthcare, housing, and education, and safety nets for job loss, old age, and disability. This differed markedly

---

83   Francis Fukuyama, *The End of History and the Last Man*, (New York: Avon Books, Inc., 1992).

from the techniques of pure socialism in that the market economy remained intact, providing ongoing incentives for working and gaining wealth for wants as well as needs. New Deal policies proved inadequate at resolving the crisis, however. The huge military effort to defeat the Axis powers utilized spare capacity. For years after, the economy ran at full tilt to rebuild what had been destroyed by war. Wages increased to the point where people could afford to buy what the economy produced, resulting in considerable prosperity for most people.

World Wars I and II were fought to determine a new way to organize the economy. Socialism and fascism were the main contenders as alternatives to the inhumane version of capitalism that was then prevalent. During the Great Depression, capitalism failed to provide employment and an equitable division of wealth. It was the welfare state and the industrial build-up for the war effort that provided the impetus for the strong growth and full employment.

This enlargement of government allowed for a great expansion of employment that had not before existed, including many government services required for the distribution and administration of universal services. This insurance policy gave people the confidence to gain more education and consider alternate careers.

MODERN BASES OF POWER

There are three bases of power and influence in the modern industrial economy. The first is government, ideally elected and answering to the people. Second, there are free markets where producers and consumers interact and determine what is produced and for what price. Third, there are the non-democratic forces of private wealth and large corporations. Private wealth manipulates governments while corporations manipulate markets with propaganda. While the partnership of elected government and free markets created the welfare state, the power of the conservative elite and corporations has strived to dismantle it. Propaganda of the wealthy and powerful has forged a false link of corporate power with the freedom of markets and democratically elected governments with the oppression of non-market forces. In reality, free markets and freely elected governments provide the best chance of resisting the imposing power of corporations. It is corporate power that uses its wealth and influence to manipulate governments, just as the Fascists wanted to strip power from democratic institutions. The ideology of free markets with reduced government involvement has mainly served to concentrate wealth and power in non-elected institutions. What was already clear to Adam Smith, and even clearer by 1930 as the Great Depression started, is that markets do not run by themselves. Markets based on self-interest offer freedom only if they are controlled and regulated by free governments elected democratically.

Unfortunately, the belief that markets can run by themselves has taken a long time to die. This is not only because of the intellectually appealing idea that markets alone can organize a large industrial economy, but also because the holders of wealth and power can easily use their influence to manipulate markets and are loath to give this up for democratic process. A conservative ideology of free markets (meaning free from governments, but effectively manipulated by corporate power) attained a clear dominance towards the end of the last century. This has threatened the strength of democracy and the financial viability of the welfare state.

Although the movements of fascism and Nazism ended with World War II, and the movement towards state communism died with the fall of the Berlin Wall and the end of the Cold

War in 1990, socialism and fascism remain visible components of modern capitalist society. The ideals of socialism survive as the humanizing face of capitalism in the welfare state, as unemployment insurance, guaranteed employment, social assistance, and universal medical care. On the other hand, some of the ideals of fascism—collectivism, the rejection of history, glorification of technology, and the glorification of war—survive in the modern corporation and popular culture. Some charge that the predominantly corporate control of the United States, and increasingly the world, is fundamentally a fascist ideal.[84] I believe libertarianism, which aims to reduce government and give power instead to the individual and by extension to the corporation, leads to a fascist form of society. Libertarianism, of course, is a long way from fascism, but it rests on philosophical principles that are ultimately impractical and self-contradicting. It is a naïve philosophy prevalent in sparsely populated frontier societies, mainly in the United States and in a few pockets of other Anglo-Saxon countries. Libertarianism only works in relatively good economic times or by ignoring the poverty that results for those who do not thrive in the individualistic framework. It depends on the good character and self-reliance of participants, and abundant resources. Apply any pressure, such as diminishing resources, and bad things are sure to occur. And one of these bad things is fascism.

The tendency to reduce government control, ostensibly because markets are better and more efficient, has had the subversive effect of concentrating wealth and power. Markets are a part of the commons, and spontaneously occur whenever civilization has traded its surplus production. Shared resources (the commons)

---

84   Noam Chomsky, *Secrets, Lies, and Democracy*, (Odonian Press, 2002).

form the basis of community and have always required communal agreement and government for proper functioning. The larger the commons, the larger the government that is required. That markets could replace government in communities is a strange idea that has occurred only because small communities have disappeared. The welfare state is now the commons of the new industrial state. There is now no serious debate about whether we should have markets to control distribution. The debate has shifted to determining the right flavour of capitalism.[85]

For a while, free markets, and thus capitalism, were firmly planted in a humanist and rationalist base, but the ideas of fascism did not die. As fascism borrowed from the corporation, the corporation also borrowed the ideas of fascism. Fascism sought to eliminate the uncertainty of democracy by turning the government itself into a huge corporation. And just as the corporation can hire and fire, the fascist regime sought to eliminate and scapegoat whole sections of society. A chasm now exists in our society between the humanist ideals of socialism and the practical collectivist ideals of fascism. Also, the nationalistic and expansionist goals of fascism continue to promote the need for ongoing and ultimately destructive economic growth.

We can thus characterize US consumer culture by apparent and indulgent personal freedoms, but this freedom is manipulated by an ever-present media that influences actions far more effectively than traditional authoritarian structures ever could. What's more, this total control is in accordance with the needs

85   See David Rothkopf, *Power, Inc.: The Epic Rivalry Between Big Business and Government–and the Reckoning That Lies Ahead*, (New York: Farrar, Straus and Giroux, 2013).

of industrialization and the corporation and is often directly opposed to the needs of society and the environment.

The state no longer uses propaganda exclusively to brainwash the public into its nationalist framework. Propaganda is now decentralized, pushing people in many different directions at once, encouraging an increasingly fragmented culture, but with a surprisingly consistent directive. Propaganda exploits the limit to our understanding, our inability to grasp all of the knowledge in the world at the same time, our resort to heuristic determinations based on believing who we trust, and even worse, copying what others around us do, say, and believe.

If you were to ask people if they are influenced by the torrential amount of propaganda they are subjected to from the media and advertisements, most would deny that there is any influence whatsoever.

Because propaganda is ubiquitous in our culture it has become invisible, like the air that we breathe. Since the effect on all of us is uniform and we have no way to compare with people within our culture who are unaffected, it is difficult to measure.

Advertising explicitly promotes the product. Secondly, it implicitly promotes a type of product: cigarette advertising makes smoking look cool. Thirdly, advertising promotes a set of values, including instant gratification and that doing what makes you happy is the best option. These values are often not the same as the values of society. For the media, delayed gratification is counter-productive. Considering the consequences of present actions is similarly irrelevant. Advertising presents leisure as better than work and the democratically elected government, rather than the undemocratic corporation as the source of oppression.

Capitalism, unlimited production, and unrestrained economic freedom in the market place have led to a distortion of traditional values. Much of what constituted good character in ages past—such as persistence, hard work, and the value of delayed gratification—the ever-present media has subverted. Laziness is now a virtue and immediate gratification is just good mental health. Individual freedom of the greediest and most powerful now supersedes the freedom that all people used to have.

Nowhere is this manipulation of behaviour more apparent than in marketing to children. For kids, marketers convey the view that wealth and aspiration to wealth are cool. Material excess, having lots of money, career achievement, and a lifestyle to go with it are all highly valued in the marketing world's definition of what's hot and what's not. Juliet Schor in *Born to Buy* concludes, "Children have become conduits from the consumer marketplace into the household, the link between advertisers and the family purse.... Living modestly means living like a loser." Marketers have also created a sophisticated and powerful "'antiadultism' within the commercial world."[86] Nickelodeon, for example, promotes "... an antiauthoritarian us-versus-them sensibility that pervades the brand.... In the kid-centric hip world, adults are the bothersome, the nerdy, the embarrassing, and the repressive." Behaviour is promoted that is "annoying, antisocial, or mischievous."[87] As children grow and mature, they have a natural tendency to separate from their parents, to be contrary and oppositional for a while, ultimately finding their own character. Advertisers have exploited and capitalized on this tendency and exaggerated it to great detriment to our society. Whereas our parents wanted to save and not waste, we have learned to consume more and not waste the opportunities presented in the media for greater happiness. Our children, with the media's ever-present encouragement, have turned

86 Juliet B. Schor, *Born to Buy*, (New York, London, Toronto, Sydney: Scribner, 2004), 11, 48, 51.
87 Ibid 52-54.

consumption into a form of cultural expression. The media perverts even the urge to be ecologically friendly, taking a moral imperative to consume less and diverting it into a guilt free mandate to consume more "green" products in even more elaborate, but "greener" packaging. While you can find people in the United States who have rejected this work-and-spend lifestyle, few of these "downshifters" have children. The modern media as the instrument of the modern corporation, isolated from democratic influences, has hijacked our culture, stolen the hearts of our youth, and now threatens our future.

Fascism is associated with far right politics, but in reality, it is a populist union of various right and left ideals. In contrast with other totalitarian governments, fascism is born from a movement within an otherwise democratic society. It depends on popular support and ongoing recruitment for its power. Policies are crafted, not out of a consistent ideology, as in communism, but of a mixture of traditions and prejudices of the populace. It includes the corporations that have grown larger, more powerful, and more independent of the democratic influence of government but able to influence huge sections of the populace with powerful propaganda now called marketing. Corporations also grow in size and naturally resist the democratic control of governments. There is now more danger of surveillance, control, and oppression from the likes of Apple, Microsoft, Google, or Facebook than from any democratically elected government. Governments may be imperfectly controlled by representative democracy, but corporations are hardly controlled at all.

Fascism is primarily a philosophy of exclusion, responding to natural tribal propensities to join groups and to exclude those that refuse to join or are different. As such, it can become fiercely nationalistic or racist. Policies can range from the extreme left to the extreme right. Born out of democratic conditions, it may ultimately condemn representative democracy as lacking in decisiveness and requiring too much compromise. What is ultimately asked for and willingly given by those who join fascist movements is unquestioning acceptance to evolving ideals and charismatic authority. There is much in current popular culture and especially the child-centred, brand-motivated culture of creating the idea of cool, which suggests a fascist sensibility in the works.

Neil Postman suggested in 1985 that media such as television (or now the internet) is ideology because it imposes "a way of life, a set of relations among people and ideas, about which there has been no consensus, no discussion and no opposition."[88] Such technology has succeeded far more effectively than Adolf Hitler's *Mein Kampf* did in creating a new culture that excludes traditional values. "Huxley grasped, as Orwell did not, that it is not necessary to conceal anything from a public insensible to contradiction and narcoticized by technological diversions."[89]

The welfare state, in contrast, represents a philosophy of inclusion, accepting all races, all religions, and even all points of view as valid. It is internationalist rather than nationalist and seeks a global solution to problems such as poverty, global warming, and pollution. It is a democratic union of the right and the left—a series of compromises that allow socialist and statist institutions to coexist with free markets and competitive corporations. The ideals of the left and the right sit in an uneasy compromise, shifting one way and then the other according to the practical needs of the economy. It is the official, accepted form of government for most of the developed world, but it rests on a sea of conflicting and contrary popular sentiments, and entrenched political views that seek to dismantle what has been built over the past century.

88   Neil Postman, *Amusing Ourselves to Death: Public Discourse in the Age of Show Business*, (New York, London: The Penguin Group, 1985), 157.
89   Ibid, 111.

There is no reason for all industries to be privatized. Nationalized education, transportation, healthcare, postal service, and police protection are sustainable and in many ways create conditions more beneficial for society. Private healthcare in the United States is a disaster. Transportation networks devoted to the automobile have resulted in hopelessly clogged streets and ruined cities. Limited public radio and television has resulted in a consumer culture nearly devoid of social or environmental responsibility and devoted almost exclusively to diversion and play.[90]

The proposal here presented is that we maintain and extend the institutions of the welfare state, including universal distribution of essential goods and services. To control markets effectively and to solve the many and complex problems that emerge, governments will likely have to be larger, not smaller. The only alternatives of smaller governments and more power to individuals will increase the power of corporations and special interest groups, and make a return to fascism that much more likely. The welfare state is not a brief experiment that failed, but the extension of the city-state that is the very basis of civilization. Rather, the neoliberal experiment of completely free markets was brief, and failed miserably.

It is possible that the current economic malaise began in the early 1980s as neoliberal factions enacted free market policies and tried to reduce the size of the welfare state. In almost all cases, this resulted in less than adequate social outcomes including more poverty, more inequality, and underfunded healthcare, but did not reduce overall expenditure. This indicates, I believe, that ongoing technological change demanded increased social expenditures, not

90   Benjamin R. Barber, *Consumed: How Markets Corrupt Children, Infantilize Adults, and Swallow Citizens Whole,* (New York, London: W. W. Norton & Company, 2007).

less, for little evidence exists that the efforts to roll back benefits were in any way beneficial to society or to the economy. While some reform was necessary, the heavy-handed and ideologically motivated privatizations, tax rate reductions, and deregulations led to a bubble economy in the 1990s and a severe financial crisis after that. Movements of popular sentiment, libertarian values, and neo-conservativism continue even now against sensible liberal strategies to reduce unemployment by increasing expenditures on public works such as needed infrastructure repair, and to reduce inequality and government debt with needed tax reforms. These movements proclaim that government growth is responsible for sucking money out of the economy and for reducing the effectiveness of the private sector by increasing taxes.

In reality, the welfare state, including the enlargement of government and institutions such as universal pensions, employment insurance, and welfare programs offering a safety net for the growing threat of job loss and unemployment, is what was responsible for the growing prosperity from 1950 to about 1973. The recent restrictions on the growth of the welfare state have limited prosperity to a few and threaten to dismantle the whole edifice.

There is great suspicion and prejudice of big government, but a large welfare state is not just a necessary evil, it is more efficient for the operation of a large part of the economy that involves the rationing that will be required and the universal distribution of essential goods and services.

In the last century, industrialization, automation, and outsourcing drove down wages and increased unemployment. Economic growth and the growth of the service industries have replaced some of this job loss, but not all. Unemployment has grown, and wages for 80 percent of the population have not kept pace with what one would expect from the economic growth that has occurred. The welfare state has grown in reaction to these trends. First, the growth of government provides more jobs, replacing many lost in manufacturing. Secondly, government programs provide funding for research projects and universities, which have been responsible for the spontaneous development of new industries including computers, the internet, biotechnology, and many more that will come on line in the next century. Government subsidization has also made it possible for immature industries to develop, and for individuals to take more risks in the search for a career and additional education.[91]

AUSTERITY AND THE WELFARE STATE

The welfare state emerged in Europe because of the huge risk associated with the industrial economy, first in Germany between 1878 and 1881 as a form of publicly funded social insurance for the threat of unemployment, illness, and poverty in old age. It also counteracted the threat of communism that was then the popular alternative. The required mobility of the workforce made the extended family less viable and land, even a small garden plot, stopped being a safety net. The welfare state, gradually improving in response to crises, provided necessary support to use excess labour by supporting research and development for new industries and by funding education and training. After the Great Depression and World War II, the welfare state grew to preserve a state of democracy, the market economy, and political freedom rather than the threatening alternatives of fascism and communism. The cost of the welfare state grew with increasing

---

91   For more information on fascism see Kevin Passmore, *Fascism: A Very Short Introduction*, (Oxford, New York: Oxford University Press, 2002); Robert O. Paxton, *The Anatomy of Fascism*, (New York: Vintage Books, 2004); Brian E. Fogarty, *Fascism: Why Not Here*, (Washington: Potomac Books Inc., 2000).

industrialization. There was constant pressure, however, to keep tax rates low and to control increases in public funding. When the economy stalled, as it often did, there were calls on government to reduce spending at a time when there was more need for services than ever. Policies that result in a reduction of government services are referred to as austerity measures.

Calls for austerity may seem appropriate, but history has proven repeatedly that this is counter-productive. Mark Blythe writes in *Austerity: The History of a Dangerous Idea*: "Austerity is a form of voluntary deflation in which the economy adjusts through the reduction of wages, prices, and public spending to restore competitiveness, which is (supposedly) best achieved by cutting the state's budget, debts, and deficits." It is difficult to find a country in the last 100 years that has benefitted from austerity measures during recessions. Reduction in spending in the 1930s extended the Depression in the United States and other countries. The Asian economies grew, not with austerity, but with significant Keynesian type stimulus. South African countries endured economic hardship and crisis by following the rigours of the Washington Consensus. As exception to the rule, there is only Denmark in 1982-86 and Ireland in 1987-89. In both cases, a fall in interest rates counteracted the cuts in spending and provided a wealth effect for private interest.[92]

This conservative response of austerity turns an economic crisis into a moral problem. Governments and citizens have been spending too much, thereby causing the crisis. So now, they must reduce spending and reduce their debt levels. While it may seem morally expedient to pay down debts, it makes no sense to do this in an economic recession. What governments that engage in this practice are

---

92   Mark Blyth, *Austerity: The History of a Dangerous Idea*, (Oxford, New York: Oxford University Press, 2013), 3-4, 187.

saying is that because they have so much debt, they cannot afford to put people to work. People will have to stay unemployed until the state can afford to pay them. But working is what creates wealth, builds infrastructure, and gets the economy out of debt in the long run. Tough austerity measures in Europe since the economic crisis in 2008 have failed to bring these economies back to health. As countries cut their budgets, their debts became larger still. Greece's debt load went from 106 percent of GDP in 2007 to 170 percent in 2012, despite severe austerity cuts.

In 1925, a return to the gold standard in Britain required substantial cuts in the wages of workers. Prices fell and unemployment increased. The result of this austerity was devastating to the economy. Winston Churchill, who was the minister of finance at the time, later said the return to the gold standard was the worst decision of his career. Strong economic growth—the fastest in British history—did not return for six years when Britain finally dropped the gold standard.[93] At the beginning of the Great Depression, Germany tried a similar measure of austerity to cure the economy. Government expenditure was cut severely. Some argue that the resulting damage to the economy contributed to the rise of Adolf Hitler. In the United States, the introduction of austerity as a counter-measure to the excesses of the 1920s almost certainly made the Great Depression worse.

Since 2008, policy makers have engaged two futile strategies: austerity and stimulation of the economy with quantitative easing. If the cause at root is a growing cost of resource extraction, then austerity will not work because demand on those resources is simply shifted from public to private. Austerity programs applied

---

93   Florian Schui, Austerity: *The Great Failure*, (New Haven and London: Yale University Press, 2014), 75.

by government tend to fail because they affect those parts of the economy that are most essential to people's lives, such as healthcare, education, and pensions. Cutting back on these programs simply transfers the burden less efficiently to the private sector. Subject to limited private budgets, low cost medical interventions may be delayed, requiring care that is more expensive later on. People get less education and training than is optimum for the economy. The poor endure hardship while the incomes of the governing elite are maintained or even inflated. Austerity transfers the costs of consumption from public to private, from investment that would more efficiently reduce fixed costs, to the debt-ridden restrictions of private finance. Adding money to the economy also does not work because debt levels are already too high for more consumption. Besides, overconsumption is part of the problem.

Austerity measures imposed by governments, restricting previously agreed goods and services without a corresponding sacrifice of the elite, could be contrasted with a general strategy of rationing that places reasonable restrictions on consumption, but also seeks ways to compensate with alternative technologies. Reducing consumption is an appropriate response to declining resources. Restricting funds to governments for providing needed services is not. The most obvious solution is a fiscal stimulus of the economy along with higher rates of taxation of wealthy citizens. Infrastructure is badly needed for public transportation, for low carbon energy production, and for housing.

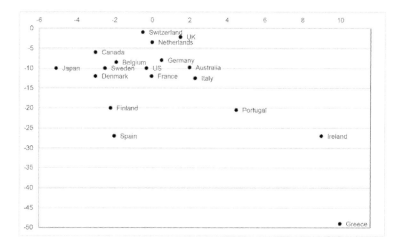

Figure 4: *An analysis by Paul Krugman in an opinion piece published in the New York Times called The Expansionary Austerity Zombie, indicates the effect of fiscal tightening on various countries since 2008.[94] In the graph above, the horizontal axis (using data from the IMF) indicates the degree of fiscal tightening as a percentage of GDP; the vertical axis shows the deviation from expected economic growth before the crisis (data from World Economic Outlook). The trend clearly shows that more austerity is associated with worse performance.*

Ironically, the United States was saved from a new Great Depression in 2009 by an automatic fiscal stimulus of its welfare system. Institutions established by existing New Deal policies replaced missing growth with automatic fiscal adjustments. Private incomes of about 10 percent of GDP were lost in the crisis. Quantitative easing, adding roughly 2 percent to GDP, was far too small to make up this difference. Low interest rates did not help as few loans were made. The most helpful response

---

94   Paul Krugman, "The Expansionary Austerity Zombie," *New York Times Opinion Pages*, November 20, 2015.

by far was an increase of federal government spending of more than 6 percent of GDP including higher health and security payments, more funding to Medicare, increases to social security, and payments to support unemployment.[95] As of 2015, the economy is growing and unemployment rates are going down.[96] Unfortunately, ongoing low rates of taxation have encumbered the state with high levels of debt.

A larger government requires more people to operate it. This may be inefficient in terms of how much is produced overall, but those not employed would have to be supported in another way. For this reason, the inefficiency of government bureaucracy is often overstated. Overall, governments do not do that badly.

First, governments, by standardizing output and buying in bulk, gain from vast economies of scale. Secondly, they are much better suited for that part of the economy that must deliver universal services. This is an area where private companies operating in the marketplace are much less efficient. Privatized healthcare in the US requires a huge administration to determine premiums and access. Public transportation services do not work that well when privatized. Companies for profit are unwilling to service routes with low ridership and compete redundantly for popular routes, yet a comprehensive transportation system is required to entice people away from their cars. It is a fallacy that private

95   James K. Galbraith, *The End of Normal: The Great Crisis and the Future of Growth*, (New York, London, Toronto, Sydney, New Delhi: Simon & Schuster, 2015), 185.

96   https://research.stlouisfed.org/fred2/series/U6RATE. Total unemployed, plus marginally attached workers, plus total employed part time for economic reasons has been going down from 17 percent in 2009 to about 10 percent in 2015. As noted earlier, underemployment, including discouraged workers (see Figure 3) is still persistently high.

enterprise eliminates needless bureaucracy. Means testing, complex insurance schemes, and other administrative bureaucracy are eliminated if government supplies or at least regulates and administers a universal service.

Thirdly, efficiency of labour is hardly the point any more. When private companies take over activities previously done by government, money may be saved, but more often than not at the cost of quality. Adding more labour for many services improves quality. More teachers and more doctors improve education and healthcare. Government can provide more jobs, if it has the funding to do so.

Finally, governments can provide safety nets in terms of employment insurance, guaranteed income levels, and pensions. This provides encouragement for people to move out of conservative occupations and become entrepreneurs, moving and developing the economy in unexpected ways. It allows people to be useful in other ways by doing more volunteering, engaging in social media, writing articles for Wikipedia, or a blog. People can spend more time in education and develop themselves more in intellectual terms. A better-educated population becomes a stronger and more capable democracy.

Growth of the welfare state should substitute for growth of the economy. This makes more sense mathematically. Exponential growth of the economy cannot continue forever. It will eventually grow beyond the resource base that supports it. The size of the welfare state, on the other hand, cannot grow beyond 100 percent, but rather to the most appropriate proportion of the economy. A fast growing economy with abundant resources can have a small government. As an economy matures and wealth concentrates among a few individuals and corporations, it is reasonable to find ways for the welfare state to grow to support the remaining population.

The process of industrialization has a beginning and an end. At some point, industrialization will grow beyond available resources. When this happens, economic growth can no longer be relied on to make up for increased unemployment. The welfare state answers the labour displacements caused by industrialization and supports the shift to a labour or resource based economy when resource preservation becomes the primary concern. Some see the free market as an alternative to the welfare state. But although markets go hand in hand with an industrial economy, they can never replace the welfare state completely and effectively. As resources become more important than capital, markets fail to account for the external cost of resource depletion and environmental degradation.

Mixed economies do better than either pure planned economies or pure market economies. Countries that spend a higher proportion of GDP on welfare programs have lower rates of poverty and less inequality. The growth of the welfare state as a proportion of the size of the economy is an inevitable part of the advancement of technology. Industrialization, beginning as far back as the agricultural revolution, displaces labour, which is then available for other uses. Labour is utilized with large-scale developments and infrastructure projects such as transportation networks that would not be practical to do with a market economy. It makes resources available for scientific research, the building of universities, and recently, whole industries such as the genome project, the development of computers, and the internet. The welfare state distributes goods and services that are required by everyone, such as healthcare, police, and military, more efficiently than a market economy.

The conventional wisdom is that the welfare state was a political choice. Countries tended to choose more or less social support as a response to the Great Depression. However, there is no indication that modern capitalist economies could have survived without it. This is not to imply that bigger government is always better. Some governments may be improved by cutting waste and inefficient bureaucracy.

As a general trend, governments become more effective as they increase in size as a percentage of GDP. Countries such as Nigeria, Sierra Leone, and Afghanistan have small, ineffective governments, while countries such as Denmark and Netherlands with very effective governments draw a high percentage of GDP. The outliers with relatively effective governments with low revenue are Japan, Singapore, and the United States.

The United States, however, seems to have the worst of both worlds—a small welfare state that is nonetheless bloated and inefficient. The United States was formed at a political level as a land of opportunity and unprecedented political freedom. Socialization of the economy remains anathema to a large part of the population. What is interesting is the degree to which the US has adopted many of the institutions of the welfare state despite this opposition. It is one of the few developed countries without a system of universal healthcare, yet it spends about the same amount, less efficiently, on the government-sponsored healthcare it does have. The size of its entitlement programs—welfare, unemployment programs, and pensions—is also comparable to other industrial economies. Total government revenue is 30.9 percent of GDP, but spending is 41.5 percent. In contrast, Denmark has a revenue of 55.7 percent and spending of 57.6 percent. Political scientist and bestselling author Francis Fukuyama calls the American government "rule-bound, uninnovative, and incoherent." Interest groups influence politics way out of proportion with their place in society, distorting taxes and spending, and leading, according to Fukuyama, to a crisis of representation.[97]

Riskiness of entrepreneurial ventures has been offset by bankruptcy protection, most notably in the US, allowing start-up firms to take much more risk in individual ventures, creating much more innovation and growth overall. Individuals are somewhat protected from financial pitfalls of job loss and healthcare costs by the same mechanism. The welfare state also offers low-income assistance and employment insurance. However, such de-risking of the economy has declined over the past forty years so that the average US citizen, despite high economic growth per capita, is financially less secure now than ever before, and therefore less able to participate in the economy in an innovative and creative way, motivated instead to find more sure-fire ways to survive.

How do the economies of the United States and Europe compare? In the US, the size of the welfare state is large, but does not deliver services efficiently or collect a sufficient amount of taxes. Europe has stronger social programs and less pronounced poverty. Underemployment is high in both regions. The United States may be stronger in the area of technological innovation— the incubating ground for companies such as Microsoft, Apple, Google and many others—although this is far from clear.

The Nordic countries, because of their strong welfare systems, have endured the current economic downturn much more effectively than other countries in the Eurozone that have cut social programs. Denmark, Finland, Norway, and Sweden devote about 52 percent of GDP for government programs. Of all the free-market countries

---

97   Francis Fukuyama, *Political Order and Political Decay: From the Revolution to the Globalization of Democracy*, (New York: Farrar, Straus and Giroux, 2014), 470-471.

in the world, they maintain the most comprehensive welfare states. Jeffrey Sachs writes in *Common Wealth: Economics for a Crowded Planet*, "… they have achieved vibrant well-functioning democracies that assure a very high level of social well-being for all of the citizens."[98]

They have extensive universal programs for healthcare, child-care, and care for the elderly. GDP per capita is consistently high. The average poverty rate among them is only 5.6 percent compared to 17.1 percent for the United States. These countries also score highly in the World Economic Forum Technology Index and in the number of patents per capita. They invest heavily in research and development, and in higher education.[99]

Table 2: *Indicators of innovation activity. Sources: Worker reallocation from Bassanini and Garnero (2012), other statistics from OECD (2010).*

	Indicators	USA	Sweden	Denmark	Finland
Economic indicators of Scandinavian countries compared to the United States	Patents per million (USA, Eurozone and Asian)	48.7	88.3	60.5	63.9
	Business expenditure on R&D as a percentage of GDP	2.01	2.78	1.91	2.77
	Researchers per 1,000 employed	9.5	10.6	10.5	16.2
	Venture capital as a percentage of GDP	0.12	0.21	0.16	0.24

98   Jeffrey D. Sachs, *Common Wealth: Economics for a Crowded Planet*, (London: The Penguin Group, 2008), 262-266.

99   http://www.demos.org/blog/10/20/15/united-states-vs-denmark-17-charts.

In contrast, in the United States, inequality of wealth has increased and there is less social mobility. Tax policies have consistently favoured the rich, while universal programs have been cut.

CONCLUSION

Our mission is to minimize consumption. Many of these changes will be controversial, especially if considered in isolation. Anything suggestive of socialism or any movement away from free market principles will be rejected in some quarters. In the next few chapters I argue that the economy is composed of a set of tools. The market mechanism is just one of these tools and is undeniably useful. Another tool is universal distribution. By using the most appropriate tool for the job to be done we will achieve the most efficient economy possible. Market transactions are frequently imperfect and government interventions can clearly improve the situation. Markets and governments are not an either/ or proposition; they form a complementary partnership. Markets address particularity while governments address universality.

Universal distribution of essential goods and services provides a solid base to the economy. It removes the requirement of perpetual economic growth and wasteful consumption. Centrally planned economies can be efficient at universal distribution if something has to be rationed and distributed equally to everyone, generally for essential goods and services. Free market economies on the other hand are good at satisfying diverse needs and wants—whatever is optional. We can conclude that although a centrally planned economy is not a good idea, the universal distribution of a few essential commodities such as food, shelter, and healthcare can make an otherwise free market economy much more efficient.

In summary, I suggest that the economy should be a balance between public and private interests. The boundary line between the two in economic terms is determined primarily by what is considered optional and essential by society. The free market works best for what is optional, whereas what is essential can be distributed more efficiently in the public realm.

The prisoner's dilemma, the topic of the next chapter, provides a good description of why markets without government regulation sometimes fail.

EIGHT THE PRISONER'S DILEMMA

Two prisoners are caught and independently interrogated. They are thought to both be guilty, but it cannot be proven. Before they are caught, the two prisoners agree that neither will tell the truth about the other's involvement. The authorities, however, offer a deal difficult to refuse. If one prisoner betrays the other, he will go free while his partner in crime will spend ten years in jail. If both prisoners cooperate, true to their word, it is unlikely the authorities can hold them for longer than a few days due to lack of evidence. Each prisoner realizes that not betraying is a better course of action as long as each can count on the other's silence. However, if one prisoner accepts the deal, it will result in the worst possible outcome for the other. Each prisoner asks the captor, "What if I am also named by my partner?" The interrogator, wanting to be sure of a conviction, says, "Perhaps you will get two years—not as bad as ten." So goes the prisoner's dilemma, the classic game of self-interest versus cooperation. It is obvious that if the prisoners cannot trust each other, the best choice they can make is to betray. While there are three possible outcomes, each prisoner has two choices—to betray or to cooperate. Of the three possible outcomes, having both cooperate is the best. The outcome where one cooperates and the other betrays is clearly the worst for the one that cooperates. There is thus an obvious third safe course for the prisoners, and by extension for society, and that is to base all decisions on self-interest. Both parties must betray the other. In a society based on self-interest and no trust, each member makes exactly the wrong decision, because it guarantees an outcome that is acceptable, even if it is the second worst.

In 1832 William Forester Lloyd, a political scientist at Oxford University, gave a lecture providing a plausible explanation for the over-exploitation of common pastureland in England. But it was an article in *Science* magazine by Garrett Hardin in 1968 called *The Tragedy of the Commons* that made these ideas famous.[100] Lloyd realized that each herdsman would gain a significant advantage by adding another animal to his herd, while the negative consequences to the commons would be shared by all.

The tragedy of the commons is like the prisoner's dilemma. Each herdsman is forced by the circumstance of his independence to choose what he knows is not the optimum solution for the group as a whole. It also describes an economy with a private and a public realm. The private realm is the individual farmer and his cows. The public realm is the commons. There are several solutions to the tragedy of the commons. The most obvious is regulation of the commons through collective agreement and enforcement. A second solution is to privatize the common resource by giving each farmer his own plot of land. However, this can lead to the complementary tragedy of the anti-commons. Rather than a tragedy of over-exploitation, this suffers from underutilization. A few rich farmers come to own the commons, leaving the rest to have none.

---

100   Garrett Hardin, "The Tragedy of the Commons," *Science*, 162(1968):1243-1248.

Adam Smith was perhaps over-fascinated with the juxtaposition of selfishness and moral behaviour. He believed that people would do more good by acting in their own self-interest than if they tried to arrange things for the good of everyone. Imagine a dinner party of fourteen guests and a pie cut into twelve pieces. One solution is to divide the pie equally among the guests. This would be very awkward. Guests would each receive 6/7 of a piece of pie and a few guests would have to take many small 1/7 pieces. The operation would be messy and time consuming. What would happen if more guests arrived, or if someone brings another pie? According to Adam Smith, and common sense, the best solution would be to let everyone take a piece according to their own self-interest. Likely, there would be guests not interested in pie, or some may share a piece. But self-interest does not mean greed. It would be poor form for one guest to take three pieces of pie. An underlying morality is important for this system to work. In fact, for Smith's system of self-interest to work, there has to be a spirit of cooperation, not competition.

Individuals sometimes act irrationally, but in aggregate act rationally. This is the basis for what has been called the "wisdom of crowds."[101] However, the collective actions of individuals can also

---

101   James Surowiecki, *The Wisdom of Crowds*, (New York: Anchor Books, 2004). Of course, what Mr. Surowiecki is referring to is not the distinctly unwise action of the mob or the proverbial committee that tries to design a horse but ends up with a camel. He is referring to a group of individuals all acting independently, but pooling results and then selectively determining optimum solutions. In short, he is advocating a marketplace of ideas created by individuals. The theory goes that everyone's decisions compiled together reach a consensus that is more accurate than any one decision. The outliers in the negative directions cancel the outliers in the positive direction, and the mean has a strong tendency to be exactly the right answer.

be irrational, even though each individual action is rational. This is the case in the prisoner's dilemma. Each prisoner acts rationally, but their collective actions are irrational. A similar result occurs in the tragedy of the commons, the nuclear arms race, and race to the bottom situations.

The phrases "self-interest" and "laissez-faire" are sometimes used to describe how markets work. However, the sentiments behind the remarks are different. When Adam Smith wrote, "It is not from the benevolence of the butcher, the brewer, or the baker that we expect our dinner, but from their regard to their own interest," he assumed that such self-interest was based on behaviour that was moral and law abiding. He imagined underlying morality, laws, and customs in which most people, while acting for their own self-interest, also acted within certain constraints and assumed a certain amount of trust. This meant that there was also a spirit of cooperation within a society. What Adam Smith realized as he wrote the *Wealth of Nations*, notably after *The Theory of Moral Sentiments*, there is an optimum degree of self-interest for certain economic decisions. Thus, the solution to the economic problem is not an extreme one of self-interest without trust; it is a sweet spot between extremes, of a degree of self-interest within an environment of trust based on laws, customs, and morality. It refers to a search for the common good based on self-interested actions bounded by mutual agreements. Self-interest has led to free markets and democracy. The idea of the invisible hand and free markets under the rule of law and moral principles is much more compatible with the philosophies associated with democracy. Democracy not only implies individual rights, but also group rights—a balance between the rights of the individual and the rights of the community.

French merchants who were frustrated by government interference with their trade uttered "laissez-faire," literally meaning, "leave to do." Laissez-faire is more concerned with the right to own property and to manage one's own affairs. Laissez-faire implies a return to natural selection. It is a call for natural dominance, a right to rule, a call to war, a belief in superiority by natural selection and battle. Although the term laissez-faire has recently become associated with liberal economies, the classical economists Adam Smith, Thomas Malthus, and David Ricardo did not use the term. In this book, the term self-interest will be reserved for egalitarian freedom within constraints, while the term laissez-faire will be used for the view that government involvement should be eliminated or minimized.

Self-interest, if based on underlying trust and cooperation, results in the efficient operation of free markets that allocate our resources in the most efficient way possible and accounts for much of production in the world. Without trust and cooperation, however, self-interest creates a situation like the prisoner's dilemma. A lack of trust forces people to make choices that are not ideal because choosing the ideal solution for society could lead to the worst solution for themselves. Without trust established by social convention and social institutions, an economy based on free markets will degenerate to the type of interactions that are common in criminal societies. Unregulated self-interest or laissez-faire policies lead to extreme economic solutions, like the creation of wealth only for a minority of people.

Laissez-faire is for allowing natural development without considerations of rules or morality. It is for the preservation of a state of nature—an attitude of survival of the fittest. At the extreme, the difference between self-interest and laissez-faire is the difference between civilization and nature. This is important because nature, like our economy, is productive but not efficient. Nature takes thousands of years to create significant changes. Efficiency is not the point. There is no waste, no lost effort, and no objectives.

In comparison, civilization has arisen in a breathtakingly short order. Civilization has occurred not so much by the laissez-faire actions of tyrants, but by the curbing of their excesses, by setting limits and redirecting their behaviour.

An economy based on self-interest requires government to preserve group interests and to prevent collusion of interests towards a greedy self-interest. This maximizes the possibilities for success and minimizes the overall consequences of failure. Each consumer makes independent decisions that provide feedback for similarly self-interested producers to adjust their own levels of production independently. If these actions are properly directed, it will lead to efficient production. If not, it may lead to production that has no benefit to society and may even cause great harm. A combination of democratic government, regulated commons, and markets based on rules, regulations, and fundamental trust results in the most efficient allocation of resources and provides the most benefit to society. It is the rules and regulations, the choices expressed by democratically elected government that can discipline the system and make it more efficient.

SPECIALIZATION AND COMPARATIVE ADVANTAGE

Adam Smith refuted a commonly held belief that wealth consisted mainly of gold and silver, by explaining how the production of many goods and services created real wealth. Two things enhanced production: specialization and the division of labour. Through specialization, a person or a company would become more proficient at producing one product or even a part of a product. The world economy could produce more by freely trading specialized services than if all countries tried to produce everything they needed for themselves. Through the division of labour, production was divided into small operations that could be done most efficiently by one person. A country could trade their excess production with the excess production of another country. By each country concentrating on what it could produce the most efficiently, both countries would end up with more.

In 1817, David Ricardo showed that even if one country produced nothing more efficiently, both countries would still be better off if each concentrated on doing what it was best at—its comparative advantage—even if the other country could do everything better. The principle of comparative advantage demonstrated that free trade would make countries richer than if they protected their markets.

To understand comparative advantage, consider two men who have to load a pile of boxes from a warehouse to a truck. One man is very big and strong, though a little clumsy; the other is small and weak, but very careful. Now if the two men want to get the job done as quickly as possible, the smartest thing to do is for the big man to leave all the small boxes for the small man to carry while he concentrates on the large and heavy ones. The ability to carry the small boxes is the small man's comparative advantage. Parents often use this principle when they allow their six-year-old son or daughter to set the table, even though they could do the job more efficiently themselves.

But what if the two men are in competition with each other? The strong man has a large family to support, so he offers to carry not just the big boxes, but also the small boxes two at a time. He who has the absolute advantage has the upper hand. As the larger man dropped several of the boxes, breaking the delicate contents, the smaller man, who is much more careful, sees a market niche. He specializes in the small boxes with the delicate contents. This does not seem to be a comparative advantage, but rather a relative advantage: the small man is forced to find a part of the market where he has an advantage in relative terms. The principle of comparative advantage assumes a spirit of cooperation between the participants. Without this cooperation, the relationship is more like the one in the prisoner's dilemma. Instead of the optimum solution, where everyone cooperates to ensure that everyone has a job to do most suited to their abilities, they must accept the next best solution where each works competitively according to their absolute advantage, hoping that they can find a market niche. Utilizing the principle of comparative advantage does not automatically result in full employment or a balance of trade. To increase wealth for all, trade requires a spirit of cooperation, not competition.

Why should an economy based on cooperation be better than one based on competition? We evolved to live in cooperative societies, in communities of about a hundred people. Cooperation gave humans an evolutionary edge. It was possible to survive in harsh environments by pooling resources and helping one another. This only worked if the community could monitor those who took advantage of the system. When groups were small, it was possible for people to keep track of who was giving and who was receiving, ensuring more or less equal efforts. Communities admonished or even ostracized those who tried to cheat. As groups became larger, coercion from a ruling class was required to ensure people expended the right amount of effort for what they received by group efforts. As civilization advanced and populations grew, such coercion also grew and often became more violent, but for the most part in the predominantly agricultural societies that formed, people managed to organize themselves into small communities that were mainly self-sufficient and independent of the ruling class's intrusions. With industrialization, this all changed. The need for labour in factories disrupted communities. The population became a huge proletariat that had to be controlled either by even more brutal coercion, as in the former Soviet Union and Communist China, or by an evolved system based on competitive laissez-faire that blocked or replaced our natural tendencies to cooperate, as in the United States.

For free trade to increase the wealth of nations there has to be a spirit of cooperation so that everyone produces according to their comparative advantage. If free trade functions only on competition, it will degenerate to each party seeking to gain an absolute advantage or a niche that will give them a relative advantage. This means that agreements have to be made and governments must sometimes intervene to protect local industries and to maintain the principle of comparative advantage.

One of the consequences of comparative advantage is that a trading partner may be better off producing what is least efficient if all other trading partners are less efficient still. Let's say that country A is 100 percent efficient at industrial production and 95 percent efficient at resource extraction. Country B is only 90 percent efficient at industrial production and 70 percent efficient at resource extraction. Without trade between the two countries, country A will produce 195 units of production (100 plus 95) while Country B will produce 160 units (90 plus 70). Total production will be 195 plus 160 equalling 355 units. On the other hand, if country B concentrates on industrial production because that is its comparative advantage, it will produce 180 units of industrial production. Country A, concentrating on its comparative advantage in resource extraction, will produce two times 95 units or 190. Together with trade, the two countries will produce 370 units of production, showing that by utilizing the principle of comparative advantage and free trade, much more will be produced in the world economy.

However, when one trading partner specializes in some form of industrial production while the other specializes in supplying unskilled labour or raw materials, the production capacity of the latter, including years of training, building factories, and developing agricultural land, goes to waste. The possibility of the less efficient industry becoming more efficient through ongoing innovation is lost. It is likely that more resources are consumed than necessary and that the most essential products are not being produced according to specific local needs. Comparative advantage is a valid principle to increase production, but not if utilized as a static and self-perpetuating arrangement. Countries should not be 100 percent dependent on resource extraction for their economy because resources will eventually run out.

A country that specializes in producing automobiles, for example, can invest in huge production facilities to reduce costs such that no other country can compete. The world is supplied with abundant automobiles in the cheapest way possible. By extension, with other countries also specializing in other types of products, a great deal can be produced with little effort. Production is maximized; labour is minimized. This is useful up to a point as world production increases. However, as markets become saturated, production must shift to other types of products, to new versions with more bells and whistles, to new wants and artificially created needs. In terms of resource use, this is inefficient. Whereas this type of economy is set up to produce as much as possible, what we need now is an old-fashioned economy that produces as little as possible but enough to satisfy everyone's needs. If the principle of comparative advantage works for trade between countries, it must also apply for production within a country and for labour as well as capital. Specifically, we should sometimes recognize a comparative advantage of local production despite the absolute advantage of imported production, and similarly a comparative advantage of labour with respect to capital.

The wealth of any economy is dependent upon the degree of industrialization achieved. Many countries can now produce an automobile for local consumption, or buses and trains for mass transportation. Each country will be better off industrializing for their own local needs first, and trading only what they have in surplus for what they are deficient in, rather than specializing for international trade.

At present, the world can produce vast quantities of any type of product, and markets ensure that what is produced is distributed to those that have the need or desire and the money to buy. But this top-down distribution, although satisfying wants of a wealthy class, does not begin to satisfy all the needs of everyone else. Local production scaled for local conditions represents a consolidation of world production capacity. Local production more accurately satisfies local needs, utilizes local labour, and more efficiently manages local resources. Industrialization provides the benefit of increasing returns through economy of scale, specialization, and trade with other similarly structured trading partners. Instead of the present model where industrialization concentrates in a few centres in a winner-take-all fashion, industrialization should diversify and allow regional expression.

Trade should be greatest within local communities and pro-gressively less between communities, countries, and international trading blocks. International trade should occur, not to maximize the amount produced, but to move resources from where they are plentiful to areas where they are scarce and for those processes that are complex enough to warrant such economy of scale and specialization.

The most efficient way to make music is to choose the best bands in the world, the best singers, the best musicians, and the best composers for each type of music, then record the music using the best technology available and make millions of copies for the world to enjoy. There is no need for anyone else to produce any music. Thankfully, this is not what happens, at least not exclusively. Local artists still produce music for local consumption. Why does this happen? Primarily because the diversity of expression and the warmth of a live performance are more valuable.

In a similar vein, does it not make sense for local communities also to produce food, furniture, and other products? Perhaps free trade should be more of a trade of diversity than a trade in efficiencies. Inefficient industries will learn to be more efficient over time just as local musicians will gradually become more talented.

Parents support their children until they can compete in the adult world. Companies and entrepreneurs with newly patented technologies are granted monopolies for a period so that they can recoup their initial investment and become competitive with mature technology products. Similarly, all countries in the world that have become wealthy have initially protected local markets.

Extremes of capitalism suppress the natural tendency of groups of people to cooperate. This can remove the efficiency of common ownership and the ability to set long-term objectives that ensure sustainability of the environment. This adversely affects the long-term viability of the community.

If maximum economic growth and consumption is the standard, it may be that laissez-faire solutions are best. If differences between rich and poor do not matter, then of course concentrations of capital may result in higher growth. But if the standard of evaluation used is fairness of distribution, the ability to ensure that everyone in society has the essentials of life, then more state controlled economies may have advantages. Extremes of wealth and poverty can also damage the environment. When people are forced to make economic choices rather than environmental ones, they will choose according to their short-term survival needs rather than the longer-term needs of the environment. In North America, even the relatively well-off middle class are not willing to make many financial sacrifices for the environment because of their economic insecurity.

AGE OF EXTREMES

Freedom is the characteristic most often associated with our free market economy, as if this is a justification for anything. But no one is ever completely free. If someone is free to steal from me, then my freedom is restricted. If everyone is allowed to act selfishly, then the freedom to live without fear is gone. In 1992, in a book called *The End of History and the Last Man,* Francis Fukuyama made the claim that our system of liberal democracy and capitalist markets are a pinnacle of human history and that no further advance is possible. However, Fukuyama also recognized the importance of trust. In his later book called *Trust,* he writes that without trust there can be a deficit of social capital. This is the ability of people to work together for common purposes in groups and organizations, the ability of people to associate with each other. Individual interests must be subordinated to the needs of the larger group.

The basis for an economy that does not play out like a version of the prisoner's dilemma is trust. Large corporations exist because it is costly to contract out for services with people one does not know well or trust. Markets have a place, but trust is far better and more efficient. Whereas markets are relatively easy to set up, social relationships must slowly develop trust.

The practice of socialism in the Soviet Union had negative consequences for civil society. Competition from other types of association including small businesses, unions, churches, newspapers, and even the family was suppressed by the state. The Soviet Union of the 1930s exhibited a "missing middle" with a powerful state, atomized individuals and families, and no intermediate communities or organizations.[102] What occurred in the Soviet Union by oppression has also happened in the US by placing too much faith in impersonal market forces.

In the last few decades, Americans have been less inclined to join volunteer organizations, family life has deteriorated, and rates of divorce and single parent families have increased. Communities based on neighbourhoods, churches, and work places have disintegrated. There is significantly more litigation. Individual rights have increased at the expense of the rights of parents, educators, and communities. Fukuyama claims that the US has a large fund of previously accumulated social capital that still provides a "rich and dynamic associational life, while at the same time manifesting extremes of distrust and asocial individualism that tend to isolate and atomize its members."[103]

Systematic problems with the economic system have existed since the early conception of liberal capitalism. Adam Smith was well aware of these problems. He realized that the people with capital would have an immense advantage over labour. The owners of capital would drive down the cost of labour to increase profits. He also realized that suppliers of goods and services would collude to keep prices high. He knew that legislation was required to minimize this tendency. He also saw the need for state funded education to counteract the mind numbing effects of factory work. Despite the problems caused by the

102 Francis Fukuyama, *Trust: The Social Virtues and the Creation of Prosperity*, (London: The Penguin Group, 1995), 54-55.
103 Ibid, 51.

concentration of wealth, economic growth would improve everyone's lot. In Adam Smith's day, the economy, like many developing countries today, had a lot of room to grow. Eventually workers did organize and fight back. Governments introduced legislation to limit working hours, to prevent child labour, and to set a limit to how low wages could go.

It is my belief that laissez-faire philosophies have undermined the trust that used to exist, which allowed families and communities to pool resources, make hard choices, and do the right thing. Our economies were never intended for extreme self-interest and no trust. We have made choices—different in each country—that reflect the degree to which an economy is based on self-interest and cooperation. Eric Hobsbawm, writing in 1994, called the twentieth century the age of extremes. Experiments of extreme socialism and laissez-faire policies were tried. While extreme socialism failed miserably, the neoliberal extremes of the past forty years have also produced results that are bad for society, bad for the environment, and ultimately bad for the economy. While right and left ideologies still dominate politics, fewer people would insist on centrally planned non-market socialism or a libertarian free market entrepreneurial society based solely on private enterprise. Severe free market solutions that have been demanded by the International Monetary Fund (IMF) in South America, in Russia, and in South Africa, as well as the right wing policies of Britain under Margaret Thatcher or the United States under Ronald Reagan have had many negative consequences that are now becoming apparent. Conversely, socialist policies of some European countries and the state control of Asian economies seem to have some advantages.

Corporations are imperfectly controlled by morality. Corporate responsibility takes a back seat to the profit motive. On the other hand, regulations are very effective. Most corporations are meticulous in following regulations from FDA to ISO standards.[104] Those that do not are easily policed. Individuals react in an opposite way. They resist regulations and routinely disobey them. Policing is only partially effective. Over 90 percent of drivers go over the speed limit. However, almost all drivers obey the moral imperative of driving at a safe and reasonable speed most of the time. Morality is the most effective way of controlling individual behaviour. People are generally ethical and responsive to group interests. Corporations are inherently sociopathic, but inclined (or more easily forced) to follow rules.

Free markets and the rule of law allow the economy to run without trust. That is its strength. But if we have trust as well, and can also cooperate outside of the market, the economy will run a great deal better for all of our interests not just self-interests.

Personal freedom and free markets are what characterize our politics and our economy. But freedom is not just a matter of letting everyone do whatever they want, for this would contradict the rights and freedoms of everyone else. The rights of the community must balance the freedom of the individual. Similarly, markets cannot be free from the intervention of the state because laws are required to ensure their smooth functioning.

THE UNFORTUNATE LOGIC OF THE PRISONER'S DILEMMA

Civilization must adapt rapidly to changing conditions in the environment, but the actions of individuals dictate the progress of

---

104   Food and Drug Administration (FDA); International Organization for Standardization (ISO).

our civilization more than the needs and aspirations of groups. In this chapter I discussed how such interest bias is represented by a class of problems such as the prisoner's dilemma or the tragedy of the commons, where the individual is prompted to act in a certain way because an advantage is gained, but at a smaller cost, because shared with the group. The logic of the prisoner's dilemma is such that a player is forced to make a less than optimum decision because of an uncertainty of how other players will act. This logic is common in market transactions, especially those that occur without the benefit of trust or strong regulations and contracts. The prisoner's dilemma is a result of a particular two-player game, but the unfortunate logic is a part of many aspects of the market economy. For example, the financial innovation of credit cards brought convenience and rewards to the consumer, but have increased transaction costs. Fees of 1 to 3 percent are charged, not to the consumer, but to the seller. In prisoner's dilemma-like fashion, consumers are encouraged to use their credit cards, each achieving a personal benefit of bonus points or reward miles, but everyone, even those who do not use credit cards, pays more.

There is also the race to the bottom, where competitors are forced to continuously lower prices (and quality), or to pay lower wages in response to what they fear their competitors will do. We are often not making the right decisions collectively because of these interest biases in our decision making process. These interest biases have always been with us, but now, because of the sheer size of our population and the impending limits of our resources, loom large as barriers to essential collective action. The existence of this cost/benefit discrepancy between individuals and groups is the reason for the need for regulations and the accounting of external cost to the group as a whole not accounted for by individual cost.

We can also put the needs of the environment in terms of the prisoner's dilemma. If we all cooperate, we will choose actions that have a minimal effect on the environment. We will use the least amount of resources, walk and cycle more, or use public transit instead of the automobile. We will consume less and live within the means provided by the earth's resources. However, if some of us take this course of action while the remainder defect, the few who cooperate will experience the worst of all possible worlds. The environment will still decline; pollution will increase and resources will run out. Sacrifices in comfort and convenience in the present will be made without any long-term benefit. In this case, the best decision we can make is actually the worst one: continue to consume and exploit the environment to the degree that satisfies our own self-interest. The best we can hope for is a degree of cooperation with new laws and regulations, but it may be too little too late.

The solution to problems of global warming, excessive pollution, and deterioration of the environment is not complicated. We have to reduce our consumption, produce what we need in the most sustainable way possible, using mainly renewable resources, while at the same time reducing or eliminating pollution as much as possible. We have to cut back on what is optional to the degree that is determined to be necessary. The only problem with this sort of solution is that it is not likely to happen. Reducing production and therefore consumption even slightly would throw a wrench into our economy, and without the trust that we would all cooperatively make the same sacrifices, we would end up with a world far worse in social terms and only slightly better in environmental terms. So we are inclined to make the worst choice that results in a less than optimum outcome for the environment and the economy. Instead of consuming less, we produce and consume more while still trying in small ways to do a little less damage to the earth.

The debate over the economy in the past century has covered the extent that free markets of private transactions should determine the overall direction of the economy, and to what extent governments can eliminate planning and other interventions of the economy in favour of what has been called a laissez-faire approach. Since 1973, the world economy abandoned more disciplined liberal principles for an ideological imperative to free up markets and reduce the role of government. The IMF forced Russia and Poland to do a complete about-face from centrally planned communism to laissez-faire capitalism, even though a more moderate change to free market socialism seemed more logical. After all, the highly successful western economies of Sweden, Norway, and Denmark were nearby. South American countries, suffering from hyperinflation, were also forced to eliminate any social-minded tendencies, often with great oppression and violence.[105]

What is now clear, forty years hence, is that such extreme policies do not work. The economy does grow, but so does inequality. A system based purely on competition creates winners and losers, and many more of the latter. The economy needs to be a balanced mixture of central planning by democratically elected institutions and free market enterprise. Private ownership of all resources is not necessarily the best approach. Private ownership promotes responsibility, but the commons has many benefits of resource efficiency that private ownership cannot provide. Markets do not eliminate the need for central planning. No intelligence determines the overall direction of the market. It does not prevent exploitation of things that are scarce. The cost of oil does not reflect the fact that it may or may not be running out; it only

---

105   See Naomi Klein, *The Shock Doctrine: The Rise of Disaster Capitalism*, (Toronto: Alfred A. Knopf, 2007).

reflects the current cost of extraction, refinement, and transportation. The market sets a price relative to the amount of effort expended by the producer, the needs and desires of the consumer, and the amount of money available in the economy. It does not account for externalities or prevent the depletion of resources. The scarcity of land causes the price of land to go up; it does not prevent or discourage someone from buying a plot of land. Scarcity makes a product more desirable.

The market sets a price to provide the proper incentives for producers and at the same time keep the commodity affordable. As such, it does something that would be enormously complicated for a centrally planned economy. The market is an essential part of a modern industrial economy, but we must not credit it with intelligence it does not have.

The supposed freedom offered by modern capitalist free market consumer society is not freedom at all. We are all forced by the inherent logic of the prisoner's dilemma to act selfishly according to our interests and counter productively according to the needs of the environment and of society. This often causes markets to fail. What follows in Chapter Nine is a discussion of the pillars of our politics and our economy: freedom, free markets, and the right to property. The intention is not to argue against prevailing philosophies in favour of their opposite, but rather to suggest that solutions must lie between extremes—a consciously designed economy instead of either a haphazard, laissez-faire economy based on individual self-interest and without communal responsibility or a micromanaged state-controlled economy. I argue that to maximize freedom, the most valued attribute of our economic and political institutions, it is not sufficient to allow irresponsible individual freedom, involving often conflicting, chaotic, and anarchic actions. Freedom results from the free movements within the constraints determined by community and by government.

NINE MARKET FAILURES

It is not very unreasonable that the rich should contribute to the public expense, not only in proportion to their revenue, but something more than in that proportion.[106]

—Adam Smith

In his *Principia*, published in 1687, Sir Isaac Newton developed the first laws of physics. For every action there is an equal and opposite reaction. Force is equal to mass times acceleration. In 1776, with the publication of *The Wealth of Nations*, Adam Smith sought to put economics on as firm a footing. His fundamental idea was that self-interest of the individual was the most effective way to organize an economy. Markets of people making self-interested decisions would do more good than any individual or group of individuals trying to do the best for all.

---

106   Adam Smith, *The Wealth of Nations*, (Harmondsworth: Penguin Books Ltd., 1776, 1982), 840.

Like Newton, he based his conception of the economic universe on absolute principles. The market would set an accurate price based on the rational behaviour of self-interested buyers and sellers.

In 1905, Albert Einstein published his special theory of relativity, disputing Newton's claim of an absolute universe. With his general theory of relativity, published in 1916, he sought to unify special relativity with Newton's universal laws of gravitation. Later, in 1936, John Maynard Keynes published the general theory of economics, not only incorporating classical economics, but also developing a general theory that disputed the absolute nature of the economic universe.[107] He believed that markets, although based on rational expectations, did not necessarily achieve the optimum equilibrium. The economy did not automatically tend towards full employment. It achieved a relative balance of demand and supply, but any fraction of the work force employed could achieve this balance. Like Einstein, his revolutionary theories were not complete. Not only was there a relativity inherent in the price setting mechanism of the market, but also people's actions were not entirely rational. While physicists sought to explain the seemingly irrational aspects of the quantum universe, new economic theories show that the market is a chaotic system that is neither random nor predictable; it is based on irrational and rational behaviours and a point of equilibrium is never reached.[108]

---

107   John Maynard Keynes, *The General Theory of Employment, Interest and Money*, (London: Macmillan and Co., Limited, 1936).

108   For a description of complexity economics see Eric D. Beinhocker, *The Origin of Wealth: The Radical Remaking of Economics and What it Means for Business and Society*, (Boston: Harvard Business School Press, 2006, 2007); See also Justin Fox, *The Myth of the Rational Market: A History of Risk, Reward, and Delusion on Wall Street*, (New York, London, Toronto, Sydney: Harper Collins Publishers, 2009).

Markets are a powerful tool in our economy. In fact, so powerful that some would believe that no other planning or decision-making is necessary. Private interests acting in concert, according to the dictates of the market, can much more accurately allocate resources than any central bureaucratic body. That the market mechanism must be part of a modern industrial economy is no longer up for serious debate. The ongoing debate concerns the degree to which the market should be relied on to control production and the distribution of goods, and the amount of control over the economy that government and other democratically elected bodies should have.

During the 1920s, markets were given free rein. The global economy grew with the benefit of free trade among countries. Then the Great Depression crippled markets and caused a major reconsideration of the role of government in the economy. John Maynard Keynes explained why the economic depression was taking place and what governments would have to do to end it. His theory forms the basis of present day macro-economic theory. The basic idea was that governments should borrow money when times are bad to get the economy moving and people working. When times are good, they should repay debts and save surpluses. The most controversial conclusion was that governments should intervene in the economy and not leave markets to function by themselves. President Roosevelt partially enacted his policies in North America with the New Deal, but the mobilization required to fight the Second World War gave the clearest indication that Keynes was right. If it could work in wartime, then it should also be able to work in peacetime.

KEYNESIAN BACKLASH

Friederick Hayek never accepted the Keynesian doctrine. In 1947, he wrote *The Road to Serfdom* to discredit the interference of governments in the economy. The easy to read and accessible book was a popular success, but scorned by mainstream economists. In an interview, Hayek later lamented, "When Keynes died, Keynes and I were the best-known economists. Then two things happened. Keynes died and was raised to sainthood, and I discredited myself by publishing *The Road to Serfdom*. And that changed the situation completely. And for the following 30 years, it was only Keynes who counted, and I was gradually almost forgotten."[109] But in the latter half of the twentieth century, Hayek has gained more influence.

In 1947, Hayek, who believed that freedom was in serious danger, assembled thirty-six economists, historians, and journalists to formulate the principles of a new economy based on the principle of free markets unfettered by government regulation of any kind. Chicago University's School of Economics later hired Hayek. The young Milton Friedman, who also attended, became the spokesman of this new economics of unrestricted free trade, low taxes, and privatization of all industries. This body of thought later became known as the Chicago School. All of this was presented under the banner of freedom, which generally meant freedom from government influence of any kind.

In Britain, Margaret Thatcher, who happened to read *The Road to Serfdom*, set the stage for privatization and unregulated

---

109 From "Hayek and Hazlett on the Decline of Keynes," *Free To Choose Network clip*, Thomas Hazlett discusses the legacy of Keynes with Friedrich Hayek.

markets. Markets were to be left alone to run their course like a force of nature. Thatcher privatized publicly owned assets and resisted the demands of labour unions. In North America, Ronald Reagan deregulated major industries, broke the power of unions, and lowered taxes for the rich to eliminate any impediment to economic growth. He enacted policies for greater liberalization of trade and privatization of industries, even services traditionally owned by the state such as transportation networks and telecommunications. Regulations that had safeguarded the economy from the excesses of the 1920s were removed. The supply-side doctrine provided justification for lowering taxes for the rich— more money left in private hands would stimulate the economy and ultimately place more money in government coffers than the taxes lost. During Reagan's term of office, the deficit increased from \$72 billion to \$290 billion. Similar policies by George H. W. Bush increased the deficit still further to over \$600 billion. In fact, supply-side tax cuts to the wealthy did exactly what common sense would expect: they made the wealthy even wealthier and the public sector deep in debt.

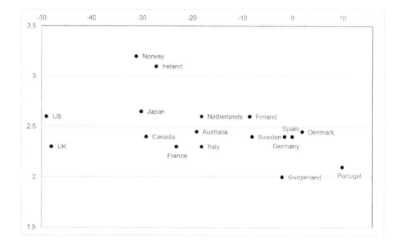

Figure 5: *Analysis by Piketty, Saez and Stantcheva indicates no correlation between lowering marginal tax rates (horizontal axis) and per capita economic growth (vertical axis). Source: top marginal tax rates and growth from 1960 to 2008, Piketty, Saez, Stantcheva.[110]*

For thirty years after the Second World War, Keynesian economics seemed to work well. Governments stimulated the economy during recessions to reduce unemployment. When inflation got too high, they cut down spending and paid down debts. After 1973, the economy faltered for various reasons. Because of the real growth in the economy since World War II, labour unions became organized and powerful. Wage demands continued to rise because of built-in expectations of rising standards of living. An

---

110   Thomas Piketty, Emmanuel Saez, Stefanie Stantcheva, "A Tale of Three Elasticities," *Paris School of Economics, UC Berkeley and NBER MIT*, November 2, 2011.

oil price shock encouraged higher prices still and reduced growth options in the economy, resulting in higher unemployment. This was enough to shift economic policy away from Keynesian theories favouring more government intervention towards more free market theories championed by the Chicago School of Economics. Those opposed to socialization of the economy seized on the opportunity to promote free market principles and to combat what they saw as a threat to freedom.

Privatization in Britain provided a temporary fiscal stimulus to the economy by lowering government debt. Deregulation in the United States allowed for more free competition and a lowering of prices. Most importantly, this philosophy of free markets led to free trade negotiations among countries. Globalization, encouraged with a liberalization of markets, led to an increase in economic growth in poorer countries such as India and China, who were thus able to raise their living standards. In richer countries, however, the benefits of globalization were less clear. More competition, outsourcing, and changes in technology meant that the rewards of economic growth were unequal. At the same time, governments reduced their tax revenues, first because of the mistaken belief that this would stimulate the economy, and secondly because corporations moved to countries with the lowest tax rates. More than ever, the world economy depended on the American consumer, who made substantial gains because of the cheapness of goods from China, and distributional efficiencies from large retailers such as Walmart, but overall was squeezed by increasing costs and stagnant wages.

China had a precarious comparative advantage in world trade: low wages. With the American consumer struggling and the lack of counterbalancing exports from North America, the value of the Chinese currency would naturally rise as it had done in Japan a decade earlier, and the advantage of low wages would be gone.

The Chinese used the excess in American dollars they received in trade to buy US treasury bonds, thereby artificially keeping their currency low. This allowed the US government to finance the growing debt caused by low tax revenue and to keep interest rates low. Low interest rates and the excess of money in the economy led to an inflation of assets, especially real estate. The combination of rising housing prices and low interest rates led to an apparent growth of household equity that in turn supported ongoing consumer spending. Meanwhile, the lack of regulation of financial services led to unprecedented leveraging of this fictitious equity with newly developed financial instruments. Financial institutions placed huge bets on the basis that the new economy of unrestrained globalized free trade would grow continuously and indefinitely.

High interest rates caused recession in 1975. In 1982, the economy plunged into the worst recession since 1930. From 1982 onward, with inflation checked, growth of the economy depended mainly on borrowed money. Consumption of goods increased, not because of higher wages, but because of the availability of much cheaper products manufactured in Asia. We should not characterize the period from 1973 to 2008 as one of economic growth, but one of extended stagnation involving huge transfers rather than growth of wealth. The nominal growth of the economy did not bring increased wealth. Real wages did not increase at all from 1973 to 1980, and then by only about 0.7 percent per year until 2000.[111] During this time, single income families became double income, work hours increased, and the pace of work, along with associated stress, increased. In other words, the economy "grew"

111   Paul Krugman, *The Conscience of a Liberal*, (New York, London: W.W. Norton & Company, 2007), 55.

by getting people to work harder while most of the wealth, if there was any created, was concentrated in fewer hands.

The average American citizen, forced to compete with labour in developing countries such as China and India, worked for lower wages and became starved for capital. Easy credit terms and inflating house prices supplied the missing capital for ongoing consumption. This growth in consumption did not solve deficiencies in people's lives, eliminate poverty, make healthcare more accessible, or reduce damage to the environment. Instead, it supplied greater luxury and private entertainment through new electronic products, and it increased inequality by extracting wealth from lower income people and adding it to those that were already wealthy.

It is likely that low wages in the US contributed to the current economic problem. Easy credit based on the equity of rising house prices supported consumption instead of higher wages that would be justified by economic growth. Legislated minimum wages have declined in real terms by the action of inflation. The balancing comparative advantage of labour in rich economies was the complementary opposite of the poor economies—information capital supported by an elite and smaller labour force relative to population size. Poor countries provided labour while rich economies provided knowledge capital, leaving a large portion of the rich world's population without a sufficient livelihood. The result was high unemployment and the growth of a lower paying service economy.

Instead of finding new uses for the labour displaced from manufacturing, the economy was stimulated to encourage consumption of more gadgets. People had to work harder to keep their jobs and make other people rich. The stimulus of more money in the economy inflated the stock market and the value of emerging high-tech companies. Wealth and GDP increased as dot-com related companies inflated in value. The year 2000 may have been the start of another great depression, just like the crash of 1929, caused by the same over investment of high-technology stock. Instead, money from Asia and oil rich countries flowed into the US and into the value of houses. From 2000 to 2006, the inflationary growth of housing assets almost wholly financed consumption and so-called economic growth. Eventually the whole thing came crashing down.

Most economic growth of developing countries has been dependent upon consumption that takes place in the United States, Europe, and other developed countries. Since wages have stagnated, growth of consumption in these countries has been able to occur by working longer hours, by adding a second wage earner per household (more working hours per household), and with an increase in debt. Paul Krugman writes in *The Return of Depression Economics* that many parts of the world economy have experienced severe recessions, including Japan in 1990, Mexico in 1995, Mexico, Thailand, Malaysia, Indonesia, and Korea in 1997, Argentina in 2002, and everywhere else in 2008. The cause of these recessions is insufficient demand to make use of the economy's capacity.[112]

THE GREAT DEPRESSION AND THE GREAT RECESSION

The current economic crisis represents a huge misallocation of resources that has occurred during the last few decades. During

---

112   Paul Krugman, *The Return of Depression Economics and the Crisis of 2008*, (New York, London: W.W. Norton & Company, 2009), 184.

the good times, houses were built too large, cars and trucks that used too much fuel were driven, and needed infrastructure that would have reduced our dependence on fossil fuels was delayed. When the crunch came, even more resources were wasted. Underemployment has grown to unacceptable levels, which is a tragic waste of human resources. Needed interventions to combat global warming are now on hold due to counterbalancing austerity measures to the extraordinary build-up of debt that has occurred.

We can place the blame on bankers, who greedily offered loans to those that were unlikely to be able to pay. Many commentators also blame the excess consumption of households financed by this easy credit. In other words, the lack of savings and profligate ways of the American consumer brought the economy down. One ends up with a series of circular arguments: the American consumer did not have to spend and banks did not have to lend. If we had behaved morally in economic terms, saving first and then spending or investing, the economic crisis could have been averted: the crisis occurred because we all forgot the useful habit of thrift, and bankers became reckless.

The correct analysis is more complicated and relates to the idea of external costs. Markets do not properly account for external costs, those costs independent of the judgements of buyers and sellers, that relate to shared costs as opposed to costs directly incurred by individuals. Within households, there emerged a new kind of external cost hidden behind a veil of complexity. The household budget became difficult to track for the average individual with limited time to devote to such matters. Accounting for all the costs of running a household, including savings required for funding university enrollment and later retirement, higher costs associated with dual wage earner employment, transportation costs, and higher taxes representing higher social costs associated with increased population density, became impossible. The amount of income required was often underestimated. Even when there was an obvious shortfall there was an expectation, that proved to be false, that wages for a particular career and wages in general would increase with economic growth that was widely assumed to be taking place. People made decisions to spend based on overly optimistic projections of future needs and future income. Real estate increased in value, simultaneously increasing long-term costs of home ownership while offering short-term equity for present consumption believed, at the time, to be justified by economic fundamentals. This inflation of equity legitimized current consumption by providing collateral for loans and lines of credit.

Homeowners cannot be blamed for the economic malaise. The homeowners who used the inflated value of their houses to borrow money at low interest rates for immediate consumption acted reasonably according to their short-term interests. Their actions also supported the economy and reduced unemployment. Given the financial environment, one could not expect otherwise. Bankers, also acting in their self-interest, exploited financial desperation and the lack of regulation in order to increase profits.

Costs escalated everywhere, creating a non-uniform inflation not accounted for by the basket of goods calculations. Families often required two wage earners to keep up with new expenses of home ownership, daycare, education, and child rearing costs. People stretched their finances to the limit to get into the housing market, relying on the ongoing inflation of asset prices to justify a purchase that would otherwise be unaffordable. People bought electronic items and other unneeded goods, manufactured more cheaply in developing countries; however, analysis shows that this was a very small part of the problem.[113]

---

113   Elizabeth Warren, Amelia Warren Tyagi, *The Two-Income Trap: Why Middle-Class Parents Are Going Broke*, (New York: Basic Books, 2003).

There is evidence that collapse of the system, predicted to occur as early as 1990, was prevented, first with Ponzi-like activities that were legal and tolerated because of deregulation, but finally by outright fraud.[114] After the 1990s, the only way the loan industry for housing could grow was by seeking out borrowers who previously did not qualify. Once the dynamic is allowed to operate, it will necessarily continue because any stopping will result in collapse of the system. Eventually even the regulators of the system become complicit in "turning a blind eye" to keep the party going for as long as possible. James K. Galbraith argues that, "fraud took over the financial system because it was expedient to allow it." While there are sufficient opportunities for profit in the economy fraudulent activities are not tolerated, but as resources become scarce it is more acceptable to bend the rules and fraud becomes standard practice.[115]

Borrowers who should not have qualified for loans were first encouraged to borrow, then encouraged to borrow more to meet initial obligations. Homeowners, barely staying afloat, but with house equity rising were able to meet these obligations, providing increasing profit to lending institutions.

114　In a Ponzi scheme, a plausible story for wealth creation is invented. Investors buy shares with promises of large returns. These returns are realized for the early investors from the proceeds of later investors' funding. Other investors seeing this success provide even more money for the fund. The fund grows making many people wealthy until some flaw causes a panicked withdrawal and eventual collapse of the scheme. An outright Ponzi scheme is illegal, but a financial bubble has many of the same attributes.

115　James K. Galbraith, *The End of Normal: The Great Crisis and the Future of Growth*, (New York, London, Toronto, Sydney, New Delhi: Simon & Schuster, 2015), 163.

At root, the problem relates to insufficient income. Minimum wage rates set in the sixties and seventies did not increase with inflation and therefore became lower in relative terms. In a competitive labour market, this dragged all wages down. Profits increased, enriching the investors who supplied the capital and the few who had unique and valuable skills required for production. The labour force went along with this reduction because it lost its bargaining power, to be sure, but also because it miscalculated the cost of basic needs. Private debt grew, not because there was choice towards greater consumption, but because of simple needs relative to cultural expectations and household requirements. While true that households could have scaled back consumption towards the way people lived in the 1970s, it is unlikely that this would have achieved much and it is even more difficult to imagine how a family would endure these deprivations without similar efforts from other members of a local community. Similarly, businesses had a choice of what to pay for labour, but were unable to pay more unilaterally without losing competitive advantage. The unmistakable conclusion is that the failure to provide the right cost for labour that accounts for all costs of living, both present and future, is a huge market failure. This market failure caused the economic crisis. The correct response is to increase wages at the low end of the wage scale. Raising minimum wages back to a living wage would be an effective way of doing this. Changes to the minimum wage can also push up wages for the bottom 10 percent of wage earners.[116]

116   Joseph E. Stiglitz, with Nell Abernathy, Adam Hersh, Susan Holmberg, and Mike Konczal, *Rewriting the Rules of the American Economy: An Agenda for Growth and Shared Prosperity*, (New York, London: W. W. Norton & Company, Inc., 2015), 79.

Figure 6: *Real minimum wage (United States) in 2013 dollars compared with the top 10 percent wage share. Source: Piketty.*

The more significant market failure, the failure to account for other externalities of pollution, greenhouse gas emissions, and resource depletion, is yet to come. Consumption has increased, not because of economic growth, but because a greater volume of poor quality, low cost goods have been produced. The dynamic of higher consumption enabled by higher rates of debt, was a source of economic growth but not a healthy one. Lower prices, lower quality, and increased credit compensated for lower wages, resulting in higher inequality, unsustainable economic growth, and unsustainable environmental impact.

INEQUALITY

Redistribution of wealth is justified from a moral point of view and a functional one. Aristotle believed in moderation in all things, Confucius in a humaneness towards others and a disposition to behave properly. Buddha warned of cravings for sensory delights and material possessions, maintaining that true happiness is found by training the mind to reject such cravings and to seek happiness by meditation and compassion to others. Judaism, Christianity, and Islam introduced the Golden Rule: do unto others as you would have them do unto you. Jeremy Bentham suggested that the goal of society is happiness for the greatest number of people. He noted the diminishing utility of marginal income. One hundred dollars is very useful for a poor person but adds negligible happiness to someone already rich. The United Nations has adopted the principle of human rights as a framework to meet the basic needs of everyone on the planet.

The idea that humans have basic rights is a reaction to the state of nature. Either no one has rights or everyone must have the same rights. The need for these rights is logical. Healthcare for all reduces the spread of communicable diseases. Universal education can stop the spread of superstition and foolish ideas. Redistribution is not only ethical but also economically more efficient. If the poor are helped, they become productive members of society rather than a drain. A failure to deal with the needs of the economically disadvantaged leads to a breakdown of society, conflict, crime, and poor health, that one way or the other becomes costly for society to deal with.

Rising inequality is the most important factor of lagging middle class income. The shift of wealth away from the middle class towards a small elite has been a drag on consumer demand, causing a proliferation of low cost, low quality products that wear out or become obsolete quickly. Companies like Ikea and Walmart that produce and distribute lower quality products that the more financially strapped consumer can afford have thrived in this environment. The result is increasing demand on the environment, despite lower incomes.[117]

Society will tolerate some disparity in income or in wealth as long as the system seems to be fair and everyone has a more or less equal chance of increasing income or wealth. In a more egalitarian economy, those who work hard get richer than those who are lazy. Some survive by scrounging, by cheating, or by the use of force, but mostly, society functions smoothly with a tolerable division between the wealthy and the poor. As the economy shifts to capital accumulation, being hard working or even talented is not necessarily enough. To succeed, one may also have to be highly intelligent, motivated and very organized, or just lucky. Small increments in ability can lead to huge advances in success and eventual wealth. Inherited wealth can also provide a huge head start for those born in the right family. More troubling is that growing segments of the population cannot compete at all, so that the gap between rich and poor can become unacceptably large.

Eliminating poverty is not the impossible task of making everyone rich. It is a matter of allowing everyone, rich and poor, the dignity of being productive members of society, and ensuring that everyone has a job to do, an occupation providing service to their communities. Many much poorer non-American societies maintain this requirement for their poorest citizens despite having a lower GDP per capita.

It is not reasonable to expect that all incomes in a country be equal. Nor would this be desirable. Inequality of wealth results

---

117   For more criticisms of Walmart see John Dicker, *The United States of Walmart*, (New York: The Penguin Group, 2005); see also Gordon, Laird, *The Price of a Bargain: The Quest for Cheap and the Death of Globalization*, (New York: Palgrave Macmillan, 2009).

from differentials to reward for varying skills and effort. Too much equality could slow the economy because no one could afford to hire anyone else for services required. One factor adversely affecting the present economy is that the middle class is no longer wealthy enough to hire services such as childcare, housekeeping, or home renovations.

However, too much inequality can also slow the economy. If one person owned all the wealth, all economic activity would stop. In fact, inequality was a major cause of the Great Depression in the 1930s, and was probably a major factor in the Great Recession of 2008. This was an insight of Marriner Eccles, the chairman of the Federal Reserve Board in 1934 who served for fourteen years through the depression and World War II. Eccles believed that mass production had to be accompanied by an equivalent consumption and that this implied that wealth should be more equally distributed so that people had buying power in proportion to the quantity of goods and services produced. Instead, "a giant suction pump had by 1929-30 drawn into a few hands an increasing portion of currently produced wealth…. In consequence, as in a poker game where the chips were concentrated in fewer and fewer hands, the other fellows could stay in the game only by borrowing. When their credit ran out, the game stopped."[118]

Eccles is quoted in Robert B. Reich's book *Aftershock: The Next Economy and America's Future*. Reich also describes how Henry Ford paid his workers five dollars per day—almost three times the normal wage—so that his workers could afford the cars they produced. Had the other factory owners done the same, the Great

---

118   Marriner S. Eccles, Sydney Hyman, ed. *Beckoning Frontiers: Public and Personal Recollections*, (New York: Alfred A. Knopf, 1951), 76.

Depression may have been avoided. From the 1870s to the 1930s, workers were paid far less than five dollars a day. By the 1920s, enormous wealth accumulated in fewer hands. The rich used this wealth to speculate and bid up the stock market to an unsustainable height, resulting in the inevitable crash.[119]

There is no easy answer to how equal or unequal a society should be, but the two extremes are wrong. If one person owns all the wealth, there can be no economic activity. The poker game, as Eccles said, would be over. The opposite, where everyone has equal wealth, would not work well either. If everyone were paid an equal amount regardless of how hard they worked or how talented they were, there would be no incentives for a dynamic economy.

In our present economy, those with wealth can earn, on average, a 4 to 5 percent per year return from their capital, while the economy grows by only 1 or 2 percent. The economic shocks of two world wars and the Great Depression reduced wealth inequality significantly from 1940 to 1970. Major policy shifts, including progressive income tax, more supportive social programs, and high inflation, tended to equalize wealth and make the economy much more dynamic. During the past forty years, governments have reversed many of these policies. Not only is taxation less progressive, there are even lower rates of taxes on capital, leading Warren Buffett to remark in a *New York Times* article that he pays a much lower rate of tax than his office workers, despite his much higher income. Tax on capital gain is typically only about half that on income, and the lower rate is primarily an advantage for the already wealthy. Thomas Piketty, in his monumental work *Capital in the 21ˢᵗ Century*,

---

119   As quoted in the book by Robert B. Reich, *Aftershock: The Next Economy and America's Future*, (New York: Alfred A. Knopf, 2010), 17.

has shown how wealth accumulation in most countries is now reaching levels not seen since the nineteenth century, and this trend is likely to get worse. It is likely that high concentrations of wealth contributed to the economic crisis. Low social spending and low wages enticed the economy towards easy credit as a means to keep it going. Easy credit is a quick and dirty way to stimulate a flagging economy back to health. The problem is that it creates much greater problems down the line. What we are left with now is a high concentration of wealth and a high amount of debt. The economy is still limping along on credit.

Why is redistribution necessary? Many high incomes and accumulated wealth are dependent on luck, and the reward is often disproportionate to effort. In a winner-take-all economy, slight differences in ability produce large differences in income. The second reason is that markets, by their nature, tend to drive wages down below a reasonable minimum level and above a reasonable maximum level. At the low end, the minimum wage should reflect the minimum amount required to live. If the market worked perfectly, workers would not take jobs that did not pay this level of salary. However, each individual may gain a personal advantage, to the detriment of the group as a whole, by accepting a job at a lower wage because by doing so they will get the job. In this way, the minimum wage is bid down to a lower level—a race to the bottom. Only a legislated minimum wage can stop the plunge. At the high end, hockey teams and large corporations can gain an advantage, again to the detriment of all corporations, by paying more than is reasonable for a certain star player or for a particularly good CEO. After a certain point, high salaries are an indication of status, not a reflection of value. This excessive claim on wealth is a huge distortion of the market mechanism and needs to be corrected.

Even high tax rates are not a disincentive to working hard because after a certain level of income, the benefits are positional rather than practical. People will always work to have more income than their peers, to get a bigger house, or a nicer car. The absolute level of income is of less concern.

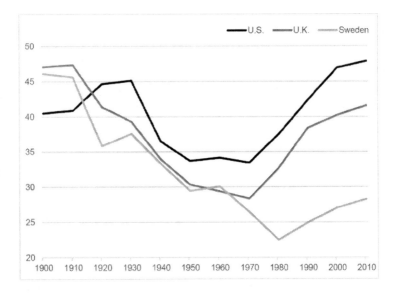

Figure 7: *Share of income (percent) going to the richest 10 percent. Source: Thomas Piketty.[120]*

From 1977 to 2007, the richest 10 percent received the benefits of three-quarters of all economic growth. The top 1 percent received nearly 60 percent. The rate of wage growth for the bottom 90 percent was less than 0.5 percent per year during this period. Piketty also notes that the internal transfer of 15 percent

---

120   Share of the top income in the total income: Europe and the USA 1900-2010, Thomas Piketty data used in *Capital in the Twenty-First Century.*

of national income from the poorest 90 percent to the richest 10 percent is nearly four times larger than the trade deficit of the United States with the rest of the world, which is often cited as one of the key contributions to the economic crisis. This internal transfer of wealth contributed to the instability of the economy in part because of "virtual stagnation of the purchasing power of the lower and middle classes in the United States, which inevitably made it more likely that modest households would take on debt...."[121] The gradual increase in inequality subtracts from the economic growth that most people see. Paul Krugman writes in a *New York Times* article that rising inequality has been a bigger drain on the income of the bottom 90 percent than the poor performance of the economy.[122] What is it like to live in an economy that doesn't grow? It is what most people have been experiencing for the past forty years.

Is there a connection between strong economic growth and a more equal society? Certainly, the experience of the United States during and just after the Second World War, and the ongoing experience of the Scandinavian countries would suggest this. Wealth concentrates when economies don't grow, and a high concentration of wealth also restricts growth by reducing the purchasing power of lower income groups. Even if ongoing economic growth fed by more consumption of the world's resources is not a good thing in the long run, a more egalitarian society is still more dynamic and more likely to pull together to solve problems

---

121   Thomas Piketty, translated by Arthur Goldhammer, *Capital in the Twenty-First Century*, (President and Fellows of Harvard College, 2014), 297.

122   Paul Krugman, "Why Inequality Matters," *New York Times*, December 15, 2013.

in creative ways. The relative success of parts of the American Economy has depended on remarkably few individuals, perhaps indicating luck rather than technique as the main contributing factor.

Governments have gone into debt equal to about one year of national income in most countries. Public ownership of capital is low because of massive movements towards privatization in the 1970s. While public debt seems high, it is dwarfed by the overall wealth in most western countries, amounting to several years of national income. Governments are in debt because of a lack of sufficient funding. Piketty has demonstrated that this problem is not likely to go away through the operation of the market. His solution is to return to progressive taxation and a tax on capital.

Is there a maximum level of taxation, above which the economy is less efficient? If the tax rate was 100 percent, there would be no incentive to do any work. If taxes were eliminated, there would be no money for infrastructure, social programs, or a safety net. In countries with low tax rates and few social programs, people become conservative about their occupations. In Korea, for example, people are afraid to quit their jobs. There are too many doctors, because it is one occupation sure to provide an income in old age.[123] In North America, tax rates are kept low in the belief that the government wastes money and that high taxation hurts the economy. Countries such as Sweden, Denmark, and Norway seem to do well with tax rates approaching 70 percent. Getting rid of waste is always a good idea, but is often used as an excuse to reduce essential services for lower income groups.

---

123   Ha-Joon Chang, *23 Things They Don't Tell You about Capitalism*, (New York, Berlin, London, Sydney: Bloomsbury Press, 2011). 222-224.

Neoliberal strategies over the past forty years have sought to roll back the welfare state. Along with deregulation and privatization, they have reduced taxes to "starve the beast."

But to achieve a decrease in the expenses of welfare, employment insurance, and pensions, the economy, and especially wages, would have to increase so that people would have the resources to save privately for the increased costs of possible ill health, unemployment, and retirement. Instead, wages have declined and there has been more, not less demand on welfare programs. Poverty rates have increased and infrastructure is crumbling. Reducing taxes has not increased economic performance as hoped; it has increased inequality and reduced the quality of public services.[124]

In summary, the cause of the economic crisis can be traced back to the misguided policies of the Reagan-Thatcher era. The proximate cause was a perfect storm of several reinforcing trends. First, wages in the US became too low relative to economic growth and growing capital requirements of households. Low taxes for the rich also starved the government of revenue for needed infrastructure and social program support. Secondly, the misguided efforts of Bill Clinton and George W. Bush sought to appease a disgruntled electorate by encouraging home ownership through encouraging banks to make loans to people that did not have the ability ever to pay them back. Thirdly, a lack of regulation of financial markets led to a dysfunctional speculation involving subprime mortgage markets. Finally, too many developing economies, most notably China, were following an export growth model pioneered by Germany and Japan. These countries kept

---

124   Michael Kumhof, Douglas Laxton, and Daniel Leigh, "To Starve or not to Starve the Beast?" *IMF Working Paper, Research Department*, September 2010.

their currency values low relative to the US dollar by, in effect, printing money. This led to significant asset inflation in North America and Europe, most notably in housing.

Reaganism and Thatcherism are long gone. Markets neutralized of their ideological status are now mere tools of the industrial economy, like the steam engine and the computer, like banks and money. Markets are not a panacea and are not appropriate in all cases. If distribution cannot be universal, markets solve the complex problem of allocating resources in a necessarily unequal manner. However, a market mechanism is not required to distribute something to everyone. This only requires the planning function of communities or governments elected by the people.[125]

125   For more information on inequality see Edward N. Wolff, *Top Heavy: The Increasing Inequality of Wealth in America and What Can Be Done About It*, (New York: The New Press, 2002); Barbara Ehrenreich, *Nickel and Dimed: On (Not) Getting By in America*, (New York: Henry Holt and Company, 2001); Robert H. Frank, *Luxury Fever: Money and Happiness in an Era of Excess*, (Princeton: Princeton University Press, 1999); Robert H. Frank, *The Darwin Economy: Liberty, Competition, and the Common Good*, (Princeton and Oxford: Princeton University Press, 2011).

TEN **FAIR DISTRIBUTION**

Imagine a marketplace where goods of every type are on display. Piles of oranges and apples, loaves of bread, and hundreds of other items sit on tables. Consumers come in with shopping carts and simply take what they need. Producers take note of which piles are dwindling the fastest and adjust their production. Such a system is obviously more efficient than a market system because there are no transaction costs—no haggling, no waiting for someone to write a receipt or to process a credit card transaction. Like a market economy, this economic system is based on self-interest and is called a commons. Not only is this the most efficient economy possible, it is also more common than a market economy. It is found within a household and within corporations. In fact, the market comprises a small proportion of all economic transactions.

If common access is so much more efficient, then why do we have markets at all? Because, for a certain class of transactions, un-monetized self-interest does not work. The system described obviously would not work for Lamborghinis. In fact, it is unlikely that any Lamborghinis would be produced. What markets do much better than the system of the commons is to determine value and thereby what is worth producing and what is not. For a certain class of transactions, markets are obviously essential and far more efficient than the only practical alternative, which is central planning and bureaucracy.

What is usually thought of as the efficiency of the market economy is actually its productivity—getting the most done with the least effort. There is no question that a market economy is productive. It is just that a great deal that is produced is not necessary. This situation is similar to many mechanical systems that do useful work, but also generate effects that are not useful or are counterproductive. We use internal combustion engines in our cars instead of electric motors even though they are only about 20 percent efficient. The incandescent bulb converts only about 2 percent of the energy consumed into useful light. We use these devices because of their productive capability, their convenience, and the availability of cheap resources. Similarly, we have gravitated towards a market economy because of its tremendous ability to produce. If our economy is to be sustainable, it is also going to have to become much more efficient at supplying the goods and services we require. We still require the extraordinary productive capacity of the free market economic engine to advance technology and provide incentives for hard work and dedication, but we also require a firm foundation of support for the whole population and a strong government that represents our communal interests and establishes the regulations to protect our environment.

THE DISTINCTION BETWEEN OPTIONAL AND ESSENTIAL

Markets are efficient for what they do best because they create local conditions of abundance. They create a local commons within conditions of overall scarcity. By setting a price, markets determine who has free access and people decide if they are interested or can afford to enter the commons. If you are very rich, you can enter a commons where diamonds can be picked at will. Without sufficient abundance, self-interest is not efficient. The advantage of markets is that scarce resources are abundant for some people, but only those with enough money and the desire to buy. The wealthy can take freely from this relative abundance according to their self-interest. Thus, it would be reasonable to assume that for the most efficient economy possible, when resources are scarce, we should fulfill basic needs with universal distribution. Markets should instead provide for diverse optional needs. Since markets will always create abundance even with scarce resources, their use should be limited.

Because of an artificial abundance within scarcity, much more is produced with a market economy. However, this increasing quantity of production does not necessarily provide benefits to society efficiently. On the one hand, market distribution is unequal. This means that the economy must produce much more than necessary to ensure that the poorest have their basic needs fulfilled. Secondly, the benefits of expanding consumption are subject to diminishing returns. As already noted, the North American economy of 1950 provided most of the benefits we have today. Our economy is now about four times the size, coming very close to demonstrating an eighty-twenty rule in which 80 percent of the benefit is achieved with 20 percent of the effort. It certainly means that ongoing growth is not going to provide much more benefit to already rich nations.

Because of additional transaction costs, markets are less efficient than distributing one to each or each taking freely. Markets can also over-produce what is not really needed, and under-produce what is badly needed, like housing for homeless people, food for the starving, and medical care for all. Markets can produce high quality, but generally cause poor quality to proliferate. An incredible range of products is produced, requiring buyer beware safeguards. On television, a few good quality shows are produced, but channels are mainly filled with hundreds of poor quality options and much time is wasted for advertising.

A serious deficiency of the unregulated free market economy is the bias towards optional production, especially when there is great inequality of wealth. Since the wealthy cannot consume any more essential items than anyone else, the opportunities for income by most of society is in providing luxury to the well off. Consumption of luxury has increased even though some essential items are inadequately supplied. Free markets, by their very nature, move away from the provision of essential items to the poor and towards the provision of luxury items for the rich. When markets distribute essential goods and services, it is almost inevitable that one company that comes to have a monopoly or a few that effectively collude in setting prices will hold the consumer to ransom. Competition often only exists by reducing quality to an unacceptable degree.

How do we solve the problems of scarcity and limit consumption? For things that are optional, a simple tax works well. People wanting to get to the centre of London, England, have several options of public transport. Therefore, if you want to discourage people from taking their cars, you only have to add a charge for doing so. This is a win-win solution. People who do not need to take a car can take public transport. Those who do will gladly pay an extra charge for the convenience of driving with less traffic congestion.

If a product or service is essential, and there is no immediately available alternative, punitive taxes do not work as well. For fossil fuel use, no ready substitute may be available to allow people to change their behaviour. In most countries, the automobile is highly subsidized and the economy has become dependent upon fuels sold at a certain price. Adding a tax merely adds another burden to an already cash strapped society and may do little to change behaviour.

TYPES OF DISTRIBUTION

Access can be free, as in the use of air and sometimes water. It can be regulated by a commons where there is an implied right of a group of people to use a certain resource that is subject to the rules and conditions of that group. Markets are really an extension of these rules and conditions, and involve many more restrictions to access and much higher transaction costs. The most restrictive access is privatization. All of these categories of access—free access, restricted common access, or private access—are equally good. They are all appropriate for certain contexts according to the abundance of the resources available. In all cases, self-interest determines the most efficient means of distribution, but in most cases restraint is required by community sanction.

For a resource that is universally required and scarce, a form of universal distribution is the fairest and most efficient method. Logically, a universal service should be more efficient than large numbers of private ones for those services that are required universally. There are many examples of well-run public services for healthcare, transportation, communication networks, the postal service, housing, scientific research, police, military, and education. The services provided are only collectively affordable, but universally required. Costs are saved because a layer of administration and transaction costs is removed, but without a market mechanism there may be waiting lists and less incentive to provide a premium service. Several countries have dealt with this deficiency by offering public and private hybrids. This is in keeping with our basic philosophy that essential services should be distributed universally for maximum efficiency but optional services of higher quality should be distributed with markets.

The choice of career is fraught with the danger of obsolescence by technology, or to outsourcing. The requirements for success are dependent on the attainment of the right skills and having the right talent as well as being willing to work hard. Being fifty-five years old and suddenly losing your job places one in a financially precarious position. At this point in life, with a household and family to support, financial needs are greater. At the same time, skills attained through long years of education and service are now out of date. As technology marches on, making necessary improvements to our lives and reducing the impact on the environment, the need to support and compensate for individual loss becomes greater. Unemployment and underemployment in the industrial world is high and getting higher. The official statistics greatly understate the problem. Not only are people having more problems finding and holding jobs, but marketing efforts to entice people to buy things are a major part of job creation rather than a pure demand.

When taxes are raised to provide more universal services, this should be compared with the associated private costs that are removed. In Canada, we may have higher taxes than in the United States, but we do not have to pay as much for healthcare out of pocket. Universal distribution of some essential services improves financial security. It removes the harsher effects of poverty and inequality by ensuring that people have at least the necessities of food, shelter, and healthcare. The welfare state is growing because financial insecurity is also growing. The possibility of financial destitution is no longer just a matter of laziness. It is now, largely, a matter of bad luck beyond anyone's control.

The default option

We know that for markets to work well there has to be choice, which is typically provided by competition between many different providers. The consumer must have a choice between many producers to ensure that the price he or she pays is accurate. If the price of one producer is too high, another will see an opening in the market and produce the goods for a lower price. However, there does not necessarily have to be competition to preserve the consumer's right to choose. For a famous rare painting, even though there is only one seller, the consumer still has perfect choice and can decide to buy or not to buy. The problem of choice only arises for those goods or services that are essential to the consumer. In this case, there must be competition to ensure fairness of price.

If a product is essential to society, the producer can charge any amount and make a high profit. The consumer has no choice, so we would say that the producer has a monopoly. With more producers, there is competition; the consumer has a choice and market forces will bring down the price of the product to an appropriate level. However, what happens to the quality of the product? The various producers will try not to compete directly with one another. They will instead try to segment the market. Some will produce a higher quality product and charge a premium price. This is acceptable because the consumer has the choice of buying the higher quality product for a higher price or the lower quality one for a lower price, forcing other producers to compete on price. These producers may reduce quality and manufacturing costs, including wages, to produce the lowest cost product for the consumer. Up to a point, this serves the consumer well. However, no limiting function of the market mechanism restricts how poor the quality of the product can be or how low the wages of the workers can be. Moreover, one company will tend to win; it will become the largest, gaining the advantage of an economy of scale, and will be able to produce the lowest cost product. Whereas the market operates efficiently for the higher optional qualities, it tends towards a monopoly for essential goods and services and may drive the quality down to an unacceptable level.

There are three functions of an economy: rationing, distribution, and allocation. The market mechanism does not ration or distribute goods efficiently. Its function is mainly to allocate—to decide who gets what and how much—not to ensure that everyone gets something or that no one gets too much. The market does not set an accurate minimum price. Market pressures drive down prices (a race to the bottom) until they are too low to provide the necessary disincentives to avoid over exploitation. The market only controls the rate of exploitation. Take fishing, for example: if all fish were caught with a rod and hook, the price per fish would reflect the effort to catch it. As there get to be fewer and fewer fish, they get harder to catch and therefore more expensive. Fewer people eat fish, and so on. Then, if someone starts using a net, fish become easier to catch and the price goes down, even though the exploitation is much more rapid. Cars get cheaper and the cost of driving gets lower, despite the fact that roads become more congested. Market pressures similarly reduce wages until they are insufficient to live on. In other words, markets fail to account for indirect costs such as depletion of fish stocks, congestion, or the true cost of living. Markets, even when they are working correctly, only set prices to find an equilibrium between supply and demand. There is never a guarantee that this price will account for future needs. When markets are not working well, further distortions occur.

With a monopoly, a large company gains exclusive control of the market and gouges the consumer with high prices. Outright monopolies are illegal, but legal action can control them to some extent. However, large corporations can also exert a kind of negative monopoly on suppliers and labour, forcing them into lower prices so that they can sell large volumes of goods much more cheaply. Called a monopsony, this provides immediate benefits to consumers because they get cheaper products, but threatens the long-term viability of the community because of low wages and the destruction of local businesses. Walmart does not keep their prices low as a service to the community. They grind their suppliers to get the lowest price because by doing so they will sell more and thereby earn more profit. Walmart does not have to pay for the resultant destruction of local businesses, community, and environment.

The market economy is undeniably useful, but it must be controlled to provide the most benefit with the least waste of resources. One way of doing this is by insisting on a default option as an alternative to excessive market choices. The default option is a craftily engineered non-market solution that provides basic minimal requirements as a regulated monopoly that can be delivered either by the state or privately. The default option prevents a tendency of the market to reduce quality in a race to the bottom effort to sell at the lowest possible price. It forces the market to focus instead on delivering optional features and improvements to the default option.

Instead of trying to ensure that sufficient competition exists in all areas of the market, governments should instead concentrate on preserving choice. The consumer should always have a choice to buy or not to buy from a private supplier. When a product is optional, this is automatic. Private markets can also provide essential goods and services with optional qualities as long as there is also a basic version available for a cheaper price. This forces producers to compete on price for optional products and optional qualities of essential products. For each essential product and service, consumers must have a choice—called the default option—that is a product or service, supplied independent of the market and with minimally acceptable qualities that is available for a nominal price. An example of this is the postal service. For a nominal fee (the price of a stamp) one can send a letter anywhere in the world. The state either owns or tightly controls this service. The price of the stamp is nominal and often does not cover the whole cost of the service. Quality of service is variable and subject to much public complaint, but the service is affordable by all and works acceptably well. For businesses and individuals that need a faster and more reliable service, there are many privately owned courier services. Because this is optional and the consumer always has the choice of the public mail service, it does not matter if one company has a monopoly. In fact, sometimes a monopoly benefits the consumer by providing a more comprehensive service than a multitude of competitors would provide.

People and businesses have gravitated towards Microsoft's computer operating system and software because of the convenience of having a common platform. Microsoft Office has become a standard mode of communication, like the English language. Anti-trust legislation and court cases have not protected the consumer as much as the default possibility of illegally copying software and open source alternatives.

The efficiency of the market economy and the freedom to choose from competing companies rarely occurs in practice. In almost every industry, one or more corporations come to dominate. The freedom to choose can still be preserved if private monopoly competes with public monopoly in the mixed economy. Public monopoly provides the lowest cost alternative—the default option—while private monopoly provides optional enhancements for a somewhat higher charge. The default option not only preserves choice, it promotes quality by setting a minimum standard.

Default income

In a similar manner, a good alternative to legislating a minimum wage is to provide a guaranteed minimum income. This is under consideration by several US states. Finland will begin a trial program of 800 Euros per month. Several Dutch cities will follow suit with similar programs. People would do work they did not enjoy if they were paid more than the default option and would do work they found personally fulfilling for less. With a default income, people could choose to work for free if the work was personally rewarding, but otherwise employers would have to pay more than the default income to get workers. Such a scheme would allow people to gain more education, start new businesses, or just be productive in other ways. Demeaning and economically inefficient welfare transfers would be eliminated.

What is the justification for this unearned income? Most shareholders of corporations do not earn their income either. The richest 1 percent of households in the United States accounted for 20 percent of business income in 1978. This rose to 49 percent in

2007, when they also took 75 percent of capital gains.[126] Perhaps we should consider all the enterprises of the world as a huge corporation and all the people as shareholders. This would give each person a right to a share of the income.

Council housing in Britain

People rarely have a viable alternative to market housing. Thus, suppliers of market housing produce a product that appears to be high quality, but has qualities that are bad for the consumer and the environment in the long run. Without the default option of reasonably priced non-market housing with qualities sufficient for the long term, the consumer has no option but to buy a house from a private developer. In markets for essential products without a viable default option, the high end is served well because it is optional, but the low to the middle is served badly because the consumer has no choice. Manufacturers compete, not by producing more efficiently, but by producing a lower quality product and making it appear to be of higher quality. Developers build market housing for the masses that is larger than necessary because adding size, like adding sugar to cereal and volume to soft drinks, costs little. Similarly, they add features of apparent quality, but exclude hidden qualities such as extra insulation, adequate ventilation, and durability. A house built in 1900 did not need many repairs for fifty years. Hardwood floors in these houses are still serviceable today, over a hundred years later. Walls made of

---

126   See Robert B. Reich, *Saving Capitalism: For the Many, Not the Few*, (New York: Alfred A. Knopf, 2015), Chapter 15 "The Rise of the Non-Working Rich."

lath and plaster were healthier and more comfortable to live with, but would cost a fortune to install today.

Housing is required universally. Therefore, governments should provide default accommodation, an abode of minimally acceptable requirements. Instead of mountains of regulations, governments or non-market institutions should create an actual product that offers the consumer the most basic requirements and a minimum level of quality at a nominal price. This forces the market to produce an equivalent product at a lower price or a better product at a higher price.

Council houses, a form of social housing in the United Kingdom, were built and operated by local councils to supply uncrowded, well-built homes at below market rents. Local councils built the first council estate in 1890 in East London. Richard Reeves stated in a BBC radio program called *Council House Blues*, "The original mission of social housing was not simply to put a roof over people's heads, but to ensure that poor people were able to remain in the mainstream of society, rather than being distanced by their poverty; and to provide a secure base upon which people could seek work."[127] By 1979, about 42 percent of the British population lived in local authority housing. In 1980, Margaret Thatcher introduced the *Right to Buy* act, which severely reduced the number of council homes. When *Right to Buy* was introduced, it was hailed as "one of the most important social revolutions of the century." Instead, as John Harris of the *Guardian* newspaper writes, "… it has led to fractured communities, the rise

---

127   Richard Reeves, "Council House Blues," *BBC Radio 4*, 26 February 2009.

of exploitative landlordism and a lack of housing so severe that some councils are now trying to buy their old homes back."[128]

Britain has provided the default option of council housing, described above, since the Second World War. This movement was successful in providing a good housing option for lower income people, but the recent insistence on a means test has degraded the communities and stigmatized the whole category of housing. Instead, the council house should be a default no frills option for affordable housing. This option is obviously appealing to poor people, but could also be a viable choice for the more affluent with different priorities.

Transportation

Transportation is another example where a default option ensures optimum quality. The default option that exists to a greater degree in urban settings is public transport, but there is also the alternative of walking or cycling. Transportation works well when there is a comprehensive and nominally priced public transport system that gives all commuters a viable alternative to the automobile. Unfortunately, this is not how the industry has developed. Instead, massive government subsidization has ensured the near universal access to the automobile, and about 8 to 10 percent of GDP is spent on highways and parking alone. In addition, each family spends from $5,000 to $10,000 per year to run their automobiles, adding another 5 to 10 percent of GDP. No market mechanism has determined that the automobile should become the primary and near universal mode of transportation in North

128   "Safe as Houses," *The Guardian*, 30 September 2008.

America, only bad planning. If people paid the full true cost of owning an automobile, its use would be restricted to the wealthy as an optional luxury. This would reduce congestion, urban sprawl, and pollution, and it would become feasible to provide a far more efficient default option of public transportation.

Interestingly, in *Political Order and Political Decay*, Francis Fukuyama notes a comparison of railroads of the late nineteenth century and the American healthcare system. Unlike most other countries, railroads in the United States were entirely the product of free market forces, for example, inefficiently supplying twenty competitive routes between St Louis and Atlanta in the 1880s. Forty years passed before the United States had a properly regulated rail system.[129] Similarly, it has taken nearly forty years to begin to reform the healthcare system in the United States.

Healthcare

Medical care is an essential service. For this reason, it requires a system of universal access. Society must make choices, however, of what types of care are essential and what are optional. Most countries have medical systems that provide universal access to some services and limited access for other optional services. Even for universal access, a nominal user fee prevents wasteful use. For medical care, the user fee should not be too high or people will avoid preventive care that may seem expensive in the short term, but will lower costs in the long term.

129   Francis Fukuyama, *Political Order and Political Decay: From the Revolution to the Globalization of Democracy*, (New York: Farrar, Straus and Giroux, 2014), 165-173.

The one obvious holdout of a universal healthcare system has been the United States, whose curious hybrid is in crisis. Ironically, the United States spends about the same proportion of GDP on publicly funded healthcare by subsidizing companies that must pay for workers' healthcare needs and by guaranteeing essential medical help to the poor. Privately funded healthcare, paradoxically, because of privately funded insurance, makes health services that should be optional almost universally accessible to the more affluent portion of society. This and the bureaucratic inefficiency of private insurance bring the total medical spending to a whopping 18 percent of GDP, nearly double that of other OECD countries.[130]

Economist Joseph Stiglitz writes in *Rewriting the Rules of the American Economy* that patients do not have medical expertise or access to price information for doing a cost benefit analysis to optimize choices of the care they need. The result is that people in the United States have poorer health outcomes, pay more for every aspect of healthcare than in other advanced economies, and "even with the big steps forward in the Affordable Care Act, 12 percent of Americans are still left without health coverage."[131]

---

130 See "America's health care crisis," *The Economist*, January 28, 2006, 24-26. OECD refers to Organisation for Economic Co-operation and Development. It is an international economic organisation of 34 countries, founded in 1961 to stimulate economic progress and world trade.

131 Joseph E. Stiglitz, with Nell Abernathy, Adam Hersh, Susan Holmberg, and Mike Konczal, *Rewriting the Rules of the American Economy: An Agenda for Growth and Shared Prosperity*, (New York, London: W. W. Norton & Company, Inc., 2015), 158-160.

CORPORATIONS

Corporations function as a commons from within. While conducting business, salaried members of a corporation freely use the resources owned by the corporation without the need of financial negotiation. Large corporations wield a non-democratic power in society that can rival the power of a democratic government. Corporations use this power to establish monopolies by influencing government with campaign contributions, by lobbying government to remove regulations that would prevent monopolies from forming, and by buying smaller companies that sell a similar product or service. Walmart, Microsoft, Facebook, Google, and Amazon have all established monopolies that control a huge proportion of the economy. This market domination allows these corporations to reduce wages, increase prices, or destroy competition.

Network effects ensure that new so-called platform monopolies are even more disruptive to the economy. With the new ride-sharing service Uber, drivers want to join the network with the most customers, and customers are drawn to the network with the most drivers. Uber currently has competition from Lyft but ultimately, experts predict, only one platform will remain. Meanwhile the traditional taxi share of the market will shrink to almost nothing.[132] Similar network effects ensure the dominance of Amazon, Google, and Facebook in their respective markets. This is fine as long as these corporations abide by Google's motto "don't be evil," but what guarantees does society have that these corporations will

---

132   "Business travellers have all but abandoned taxis," *The Economist*, June 14, 2016.

continue to have a positive influence on our lives?[133] While taxi
drivers' businesses are destroyed, more Uber drivers are employed
but often earning less than minimum wage. Civilizations have
learned that although the best government is a dictatorship, as
long as the right dictator is in charge, democracies are far safer
and result in a more equitable division of power if set up correctly.
With some corporations becoming the size of countries, is it not
time to consider a democratic means of controlling them? Several
options already exist.

The goal for conventional corporations is to maximize profits
to benefit the shareholders. A benefit corporation is a for-profit
company that is set up to maximize the benefits for workers,
community, and the environment as well as shareholders. As of
2014, twenty-seven American states allow companies to incorporate in this way. At this time, there are 165 companies in 121
industries so certified.[134] James Surowiecki, author of *The Wisdom
of Crowds*, points out that although benefit corporations are a
recent phenomenon, the idea of balancing purpose and profit
may be a return to a model that American companies once followed. Henry Ford, for example, preferred to build better cars and
increase wages rather than just to increase shareholder value.[135]

---

133   For the negative effects of platform monopolies that are already occur-
       ring see Douglas Rushkoff, *Throwing Rocks at the Google Bus: How
       Growth Became the Enemy of Prosperity*, (New York: Penguin, 2016).

134   See Robert B. Reich, *Saving Capitalism: For the Many, Not the Few*,
       (New York: Alfred A. Knopf, 2015), Chapter 21 "Reinventing the Cor-
       poration"; Peter Barnes, *Capitalism 3.0: A Guide to Reclaiming the Com-
       mons*, (San Francisco: Berrett-Koehler Publisher, Inc., 2006).

135   James Surowiecki, "Companies with Benefits," *The New Yorker*, August
       4, 2014.

Co-operatives are competitive institutions within the market economy. They are democratically run corporations providing goods and services at cost without requiring profit for shareholders. This means that workers can be given higher salaries and more attention can be given to ecological and social concerns.

According to the International Co-operative Alliance (ICA), the Co-operative movement brings together over one billion people around the world and positively affects the livelihood of nearly three billion.[136] In France, 21,000 co-ops employ 3.5 percent of the active working population. Ninety-one percent of Japanese farmers belong to an agricultural co-op. Forty percent of Canadians belong to at least one co-op. Worldwide, co-ops account for 4.3 percent of GDP, but comprise 20 percent of the economy in New Zealand and up to 30 percent in Northern Italy.

Some people are ideologically opposed to co-operatives. In a country of high inequality, members of society are in a perpetual quest to achieve wealth with entrepreneurial ventures. Venture capitalists are less likely to invest in co-operatives and co-ops do not provide a long-term reward for the founders. In the United States there are 30,000 co-operatives providing two million jobs, but this accounts for only 1 percent of GDP.

Markets do not work for large comprehensive systems of essential service because it is impossible to eliminate monopolies, there is inefficient duplication of services, and competing private companies do not have the same economy of scale as government. I argue that the welfare state is both an inevitable and essential component of industrialization, and that it can distribute certain goods and services that are universally required,

136   www.ica.coop.

far more efficiently than markets. The reason that markets fail is that they are sometimes used for the wrong purpose. In Part Four, I suggest that markets can be used to ration if the economy is two-dimensional.

And thus the native hue of resolution
Is sicklied o'er with the pale cast of thought,
And enterprises of great pitch and moment
With this regard their currents turn awry
And lose the name of action. Soft you now,
The fair Ophelia! Nymph, in thy orisons
Be all my sins remember'd.

—William Shakespeare, Hamlet

PART FOUR EXTERNAL COSTS

And thus the quest to end global warming
Is tainted with selfish individualism,
And green enterprises of great importance
With this regard their currents turn awry
And lose the name of action. Soft you now,
Sweet Gaia! Mother Earth, hear our prayers;
Please forgive us all our sins.

ELEVEN RATIONING WITH MARKETS

Contrary to popular belief, there is nothing very accurate about the price set by a market. In competitive markets, prices tend towards the minimum that can be charged. Even then, if there is an accurate price based on cost of production and profits, producers will often discount future costs or will not accurately account for all costs. In addition, they will not account for external costs at all. Competitive markets will therefore tend to be deflationary with new businesses often failing or society as a whole bearing the added cost. Consumers get a good deal, but wages may also be driven too low to sustain the cycle of production and consumption. On the other hand, if the producer has the advantage because of no competition, they will charge the highest price possible. The market price is a balance between supply and demand—what someone is willing to pay. An accurate price is the cost of production plus a profit to account for the risk of investment. The right price for labour is the amount required to cover living expenses plus an amount to cover abilities and the time and money invested in human capital. What someone is willing to pay for a product or service is not necessarily the price required to meet production or labour costs. What producers are willing to pay for labour does not necessarily account for the costs of living. The relationship is also circular. If labour is underfunded, then consumers will not be willing to pay as much for products. Less revenue for what is produced will result in less investment and lower wages.

Markets do not set accurate prices in absolute terms or account for non-commercial costs. The cost of labour does not account for the social cost of someone not working. The cost of fish does not account for the relative scarcity of fish caused by over-fishing. The cost of oil does not account for the pollution it causes and the fact that it is a limited resource. Conventional money only provides the ability to ration in relative terms. If a product is scarce, the price determines who can afford to buy it. There is no rationing in the sense of saving some for a rainy day or of restricting the supply of remaining resources.

A relatively small proportion of the world's population is responsible for the majority of all environmental impact. Inevitably, poor economies now using few resources will grow and adopt consumption patterns similar to rich economies. Technology may help, but people will not change habits and adopt new technologies without a combination of incentives and restrictions. To make the changes we require it will be necessary for people to modulate and control their levels of consumption. The private sector must be encouraged to develop and deploy new and more resource efficient technologies. And governments must create legislation to regulate and control consumption. Voluntary methods to reduce consumption have clearly failed to make the slightest reduction of impact.

While effective regulations can reduce environmental impact, carbon taxes, or a cap-and-trade system are the main contenders for a market based approach to reducing the external cost of greenhouse gas emissions. The specified carbon tax is a price paid per tonne of greenhouse gases generated. The most upstream energy producers pay the carbon tax rather than downstream energy users. A cap-and-trade system sets a cap on the total amount of greenhouse gases that can be emitted. Emission credits are then auctioned off to the biggest emitters. Analysis shows that the two alternatives are effectively equivalent.[137] Both the carbon tax and the tradable credits result in a price put on a tonne of carbon dioxide. The difference is in the uncertainty that is necessarily part of each system. With a carbon tax, there is great uncertainty of what the price on carbon should be to achieve the right amount of reduction. Because of political pressures, there is a great danger that the price will be set too low. Oil prices are sensitive to demand. If a carbon tax added to the cost of oil reduces demand, then the underlying price will come down, partially negating the effect of the tax. With a cap-and-trade scheme, the right amount of reduction is set as a cap, but the price of carbon, which is set by the market by trading credits, and the effect on the economy, are both uncertain. Both systems are politically difficult to implement.

On July 17, 2014, Australia repealed their carbon tax after only two years, for political reasons. Even though the tax was working well to reduce emissions and had a negligible effect on the economy, it caused much discontent. Energy prices did go up,

---

137   See Lawrence H. Goulder and Andrew R. Schein, "Carbon Taxes Versus Cap and Trade: A Critical Review," *Climate Change Economics*, Vol. 4, No. 3 (2013).

but mainly due to investments in infrastructure. The added costs affected lower income groups more, making the tax unpopular and a divisive election issue.[138] In British Columbia, the carbon tax in place since 2008 has fared better. Less than half of the population oppose the tax but the opposition is concentrated in middle and low-income, older, male, and rural groups.[139] A further problem is that the much-touted reductions in emissions may be partly because of an increase in cross border shopping. A notable feature of the carbon tax is that it does not work well without international commitments.

Consumers pay more for energy, food and all manufactured goods because of the carbon tax. The tax burden is relatively higher with low-income households, which are also less able to make the investments to avoid the tax. Governments, however, can offset these costs by using the revenue collected to reduce other taxes. In this way, the economic impact of a carbon tax should be minimal. Governments use the extra revenue to reduce other less efficient taxes. However, such a neutral response will not provide a beneficial effect on the environment. To reduce emissions, businesses will have to look for ways to avoid the tax by investing in greener technology. Consumers will also have to avoid the higher upfront costs by making appropriate investments such as more solar panels or an electric car. Governments can also aid in the process by using the revenue collected for research and development or infrastructure investments rather than tax reduction. In this way,

---

138   Julia Baird, "A Carbon Tax's Ignoble End: Why Tony Abbott Axed Australia's Carbon Tax," *New York Times*, July 24, 2014.

139   Brian C. Murray and Nicholas Rivers, "British Columbia's Revenue-Neutral Carbon Tax: A Review of the Latest 'Grand Experiment,'" *Environmental Policy*, 19.

the carbon tax does add cost, but society gains an environmental dividend.[140]

It is easier to implement a carbon tax upstream on the major emitters, the producers of energy, rather than downstream. By controlling a handful of major companies, emissions from the whole economy can be reduced through a straightforward action of the market mechanism. The problem I see is a lack of feedback for companies down the line and especially for the ultimate consumer. The consumer sees products that cost more, but receives little information as to why. And even if a credit is received as compensation for higher prices, the connection is difficult to make. This lack of feedback not only causes political resistance to a carbon tax, but may also impair its function. The carbon tax and cap-and-trade systems act on the supply side of production. In the next section, I would like to suggest a different method of tackling environmental impact that works on the demand side: the ultimate consumer.

TWO-DIMENSIONAL CURRENCY

Our economy presents few motivations for sustainable solutions. Problems of unemployment, poverty, and financial insecurity drive financial decision making more than threats of global warming, pollution, or resource scarcity. Our lack of action on these matters is not for lack of caring, but due to a lack of economic accounting. An environmental austerity, though clearly

---

140   Don Fullerton, Gilbert E. Metcalf, "Environmental Taxes and the Double-Dividend Hypothesis: Did You Really Expect Something for Nothing?" *Chicago-Kent Law Review*, Vol. 73, no. 1 (1998), 221-256.

warranted, does not register in our economic calculus. This is because we do not pay directly for the use of resources we use or the damage we inflict on the environment. Instead, we pay a resource rent for items that we consume based on who owns them and how they are modified by capital. We strive to reduce labour costs and complain of unemployment, but ignore resource costs that could be reduced with more labour. When we talk of the economic cost of tackling climate change, we are not talking about resource cost, because surely it would cost less in resource terms to reduce the rate of global warming.

A large part of this resource rent is a purely economic rent: that which is charged over and above what should be the true market value. In a broader sense, resource rent is what we pay to each other for services rendered independent of the resources we use or the damage we inflict on the environment. The price of labour is also a rent for the use of the body's energy, skills, and knowledge. The problem with resource rent is that the value tends to dwarf resource costs. Rental costs expand with the inflation of the money supply and are the biggest part of our budget. For this reason, the economic incentive to reduce impact on the environment is just not there. The amount of money saved by turning off a light, recycling, or not using plastic bags for your shopping is insignificant compared to the rents we pay.

The use of markets stimulates production. Rather than ration, markets stimulate overconsumption. Most manufactured goods are over-produced to such a degree that they appear cheap compared to the high fixed costs people have to pay for land, food, and essential services. Over-production occurs because of excess production capacity in the world including a high amount of underused labour. Wages are down as other rents and costs have increased, but because a television or a smartphone is so cheap in relative terms, consumers have little incentive not to buy. There are few signals in the free market economy that would suggest a curb on consumption. On the contrary, goods of every description are produced in vast quantities before there is even a demand expressed. People are encouraged to buy first at the full retail cost, and then at continuously discounted rates that may not even cover the actual cost of production. Because of high capital costs and low production costs at volume, the marginal cost of production is low and much that is produced is not necessary.

With our one-dimensional monetary system, our economy functions like a house with only one source of heat. In such a house, if you want to have hot water you must heat the whole house, even in summer. If you want ice, you have to reduce the temperature of all the rooms to below freezing. Similarly, in our economy, because everyone needs to work, we have to encourage continuous growth of the economy regardless of what we need.

What changes would we have to make to have the same versatility in our economy as is found in an average house? I propose that the answer is in the design of our currency systems. Our measures of wealth and income confuse real resource wealth with claims on that resource wealth—environmental cost versus environmental rent. For the most part, the economy considers resources to be free and environmental impact to be without cost.

We have this problem because there is nothing in our economic system to measure environmental impact. Different categories of value are amalgamated into a single value, the selling price, which is determined by balancing the cost of supply with a willingness of a consumer to pay, or demand. When we buy food, we do not know if the high cost is because it came from some faraway place, or if it simply reflects the high cost of local labour. A high cost can reflect a high capital investment or a high economic rent charged because of a lack of any competition. Rents dominate value in our economy and obscure the cost of resources consumed. The problem is that the amount of rent we pay does not correlate in any way with environmental impact. Our current monetary system is one-dimensional. If we add external costs to the market cost to provide a composite cost (by adding a carbon tax, for example), the consumer is confused and is not able to tell if the cost of the product signifies a high quality product with a low external cost or a low quality product with a high external cost. Our economic system rations only according to wealth, demanding a relative sacrifice of the many in favour of the few, as opposed to an absolute sacrifice of all.

I propose a two-dimensional currency (TDC) to represent separate dimensions of value. One dimension, the same as conventional money now, would represent environmental rent, while the other would represent environmental cost. The consumer does not have a ready alternative to the use of fossil fuels, but many choices exist for the car he or she buys or the source of the fuel. Similarly, there are choices that are more or less environmentally friendly for food, electronics products, and forestry products. Food can be organic and locally grown or imported; it can be beef requiring more land, or sustainably harvested fish. Forestry products can be sustainably produced soft woods or exotic hardwoods that take hundreds of years to grow. Electronics products can be durable or designed to become obsolete quickly. The way to influence choice is with a monetary system that not only determines value in conventional terms, but also values in social and environmental terms—in other words, a two-dimensional currency.

Instead of applying a carbon tax to primary sources, tax should be applied to what is ultimately consumed. One convenient measure of environmental impact is the amount of greenhouse gas or equivalents embodied in the product or service. This is a reasonable simplification because most products or services causing high emissions of greenhouse gases also tend to have high levels of other environmental impacts. Data for greenhouse gas emissions measured in carbon dioxide equivalents (CO_2E) is readily available from various sources.

As with the carbon tax, taxation would be used to limit consumption. Furthermore, this limit would be reduced by a set amount each year. People will find ways to reduce emissions to avoid paying extra tax. People will be more motivated to find functional and technological efficiencies. Companies producing the products required will be highly motivated to develop new technologies to meet expected demands. People will reduce consumption through a combination of using less by eliminating wasteful consumption and by utilizing better technology that they will be more motivated to buy. Most importantly, it is easily possible to set up the system as a progressive consumption tax. Consumers pay no tax for an average level of consumption, but a progressively higher rate as consumption increases. Whereas the carbon tax negatively affects the poor, requiring compensation with tax rebates, the TDC system has a negative effect mainly on the rich who are better able to afford it.

Consumers will search for ways to reduce impact with minimal or no cost. They will do this by taking a hard look at what they really need. They will eliminate consumption of goods and services with a low benefit to impact ratio. The benefit of a larger house relative to its added environmental impact, for example, is low, while the benefit of a well-designed, smaller house to its impact is high. Ultimately, businesses will also be motivated to find and implement new technologies for reduced greenhouse gas emissions because that will be where the biggest markets are.

COMPARISONS WITH CARBON TAX ALTERNATIVES

There is widespread agreement that adding a price to carbon is a good idea. However, there remains considerable political resistance to this idea. There is a danger that the price set will be too low, international agreements will come too late, and political pressure will lead to exemptions of major industries, thereby reducing the effectiveness of the tax. I believe that applying the tax to the demand side rather than the supply side as a two-dimensional currency will have advantages over supply-side alternatives. In summary:

- The TDC system is equivalent to a progressive consumption tax. Because below average consumption is untaxed, higher income groups are affected much more than lower income groups.

- The TDC provides more feedback to consumers. Consumers will search for ways to reduce impact with minimal or no cost.

- Fossil fuels will come to have less value as alternative sources of energy become available. Market clearing effects will motivate more consumption even with a high carbon tax in place. The TDC, however, will add a high-level cost with higher taxation regardless of the lower market value.

- If the TDC replaces other unpopular consumption taxes, consumers will be less likely to object to the new tax. Lobby groups representing special interests will have less reason to oppose it.

- Whereas a carbon tax must be international to be fully effective, the TDC system can be implemented at a local level and then gradually expanded. If there already is a carbon tax, the TDC system could provide feedback to consumers and provide a means for governments to determine rebates.

- Imported goods from countries that do not have a carbon tax will not require a tariff because the carbon content will be accounted for in the TDC system. However, goods from countries with a carbon tax will have a higher price because of the embedded carbon tax. A rebate could be issued to compensate for this or exporting countries could apply an equivalent subsidy when exporting to countries with a TDC system. This would eliminate the need for complex trade sanctions against countries without any form of carbon tax. Export oriented countries with a TDC system instead of a carbon tax could place an export tariff on exported goods equal to the carbon tax that other countries pay in order to comply with international agreements.

- Countries whose economies are based on fossil fuel production are understandably reluctant to implement a carbon tax. With a TDC system, countries producing oil would not have to add a carbon tax if exporting to another country with a TDC system.

The system could work with voluntary compliance, especially for the first few years. Governments could gradually introduce and increase tax rates as required to meet target levels of consumption. The consumer, though encouraged to ration, would be free to make trade-offs: continue eating beef while cutting down air travel; drive an SUV, but live in a smaller house. Companies would compete on price, quality, and environmental impact.

In Part Two, I provided many examples of complementary currencies used to utilize labour resources efficiently. Are there also examples of an alternative currency that regulates resource use? Cuba provides an interesting case study.

THE USE OF CURRENCY FOR RATIONING IN CUBA

In 1990, the economy of the Soviet Union collapsed. Oil production dropped nearly 50 percent from 1988 to 1995, from 12 million barrels to 7 million. This drop in production seriously affected the economies of North Korea and Cuba. Subsidized oil supplies to North Korea dropped 90 percent in a two-year period. Elites preserved the military and a political status quo by imposing a severe austerity on the general population, resulting in the starvation of 600 thousand to 1 million people, or 3 to 5 percent of the population. At the same time, Cuba faced a similar oil supply shock, but in contrast was able to adapt and scale back the economy with a highly effective program of rationing that preserved the prosperity of the people. The poor in North Korea continue to endure frequent food shortages.

Cuba is an interesting country from an environmental point of view. Having a GDP per capita of less than $5,000, it is a very poor country, but in many ways, it has levels of prosperity equivalent or even exceeding many richer countries. Life expectancy is 77.7 years, compared to 78.4 in the United States; infant mortality is 4.8 per 1,000 births, compared to 6.06 in the US. The obesity rate is only 11.8 percent. The average amount of education is eighteen years and literacy is almost universal. Despite low

GDP, there is virtually no actual poverty or unemployment. On the environmental side, Cuba generates only one seventh of the greenhouse gas emissions per capita that are generated by the United States.

From 1989 to 1993, after the collapse of the Soviet Union, the Cuban economy shrank by 35 percent. Fidel Castro responded with pragmatic economic reforms. He allowed farmers markets, licensed family businesses such as restaurants, and legalized the American dollar. When the Soviet Union collapsed, Cuba's economic system, dependent on subsidized trade, went into freefall. Fossil fuels to power tractors and for fertilizers and pesticides were unavailable. Daily energy intake fell from 2,889 calories to 1,863. During the so-called Special Period, the economy was transformed. There was a total breakdown of industrial and agricultural sectors. Refineries and factories were forced to close, putting millions out of work. Agriculture became labour intensive and organic practices were introduced. Fidel Castro encouraged foreign investment in hotels, nickel mines, telecoms, and oil exploration to earn foreign currency. Cuba had to adapt to severe shortages of oil, medicine, and food.

Despite a lack of medical supplies, a humanitarian catastrophe was averted after the crisis because the Cuban government maintained a high level of support for their healthcare system. Today, Cuba has 6.4 doctors and 5.9 hospital beds per 1,000 people, compared to 2.67 and 3.1 in the United States.

In agriculture, a reduction of fossil fuel-based fertilizer from 1.3 million tonnes to 160,000 tonnes was made possible with ecological practices including organic fertilizers, the use of oxen, mixed cropping, and biological pest control. Urban gardens and farms increased yields of fruits and vegetables. Large state farms were redistributed to thousands of farmers' co-operatives and leased to private farmers. A four-fold increase in vegetable production was achieved from 1994 to 1999 by using agro-ecological methods without agrochemicals. The daily per capita energy supply increased to 3,200 calories by 2007. Cuba was able to transform its food production in just a decade to become a world leader in low-energy food production. In Cuba, it now takes ten to twenty calories of mostly renewable energy to produce a calorie of food. In the United States, a calorie of industrial organic lettuce takes sixty calories of fossil fuels alone.[141]

Schools, health clinics, and social centres were powered by solar panels. In 2005, 9.4 million compact fluorescent bulbs were distributed to homes and businesses to replace nearly all incandescent bulbs. Millions of inefficient electrical appliances including fans, refrigerators, air conditioners, televisions, and electric motors were replaced. Three and a half million rice-cookers and three million pressure-cookers were distributed to encourage cooking with electricity instead of kerosene. People were allowed to use 100 kilowatt-hours per month at a cheap rate, but then a tariff was added to discourage excessive consumption. Cubans use on average 85 percent less electricity and generate 86 percent less carbon dioxide per capita than the United States.[142]

From 1993 to 2004, the Cuban currency was split between the peso for staples and non-luxury items and the US dollar for tourism and luxury goods. Since 2004, the US dollar could not be traded, but had to be converted to the convertible peso pegged at

---

141   Chris Turner, *The Geography of Hope: A Tour of the World We Need*, (Toronto: Vintage Canada, 2007), 277.

142   Pat Murphy and Faith Morgan, "Cuba: Lessons from a Forced Decline," in Eric Assadourian and Prugh, Project Directors, World Watch Institute, *State of the World 2013: Is Sustainability Still Possible?* (Washington, Covelo, London: Island Press, 2013) chapter 30.

$1.08 US dollars and subject to a 10 percent surcharge for conversion. A salary of 400 to 700 non-convertible peso covers basic needs of food and shelter. For further income, Cubans have other businesses on the side such as shoe mending and taxi services. Hard currency from abroad finances an informal capital-based economy to which just two thirds of Cubans have access.[143]

Instead of a complementary currency for local communities as an alternative to the national currency, the hard international currency is a complement to the national Cuban currency that represents scarce internationally received resources.

Circumstance has forced Cuba, a poor socialist country widely criticized for the lack of free market principles in its economy, to adopt a labour-based economy with low resource consumption. However, it consistently scores reasonably high on the Human Development Index, ranking forty-eighth in the world. Development has been constrained by limited resources and lack of development aid. It has nonetheless done very well with healthcare and education. The prevalence of HIV is nearly zero. The average unemployment rate from 1996 to 2005 is only 1.9 percent. The economy is not ideal, but has been forced by circumstance towards a highly sustainable model.

What Cuba has done well, more because of limited options than by design, is to achieve the right degree of capitalization, and the right balance between capitalized mechanical production and production by means of labour. They have achieved an economy that in many ways is more sustainable than most other developed countries. Its citizens have a high amount of common wealth relative to limited resources. Less than 10 percent of Cubans have

143   Dale Allen Pfeiffer, *Eating fossil fuels: Oil, Food and the Coming Crisis in Agriculture*, (Gabriola Island: New Society Publishers, 2006).

private cars. Average housing space per person is only 150 square feet, compared to 800 for the United States, but the average Cuban does not have to worry about healthcare or the costs of education. They are not weighed down with debt and few have to worry about going hungry or being homeless.

The experience of Cuba provides an example of what happens when there is a drastic reduction of capital available in an economy and a serious shortage of fossil fuels. The experience shows that the economy can survive and maintain similar levels of prosperity by expanding the local labour-based economy and with an alternate currency that restricts the use of resources. A local currency encourages a more thorough exploitation of local resources including labour. It formalizes a natural response to a shortage of international capital. What occurred in Cuba was a shortage of capital brought about by an ongoing American embargo and the sudden reduction of Soviet aid. Although the effect was traumatic, the response clearly shows that local resources were previously underused. They were able to transform an economy that was dependent on imported oil to one that could produce sufficient food with local labour. Local resources were utilized in a more thorough and sustainable way. The limited amount of US dollars in the economy has prevented over exploitation of resources.

CONCLUSION

If there is high unemployment, employing some people to break windows and another group of people to repair them has some merit, but surely, there would be other things to do that would be more useful. The broken window story, written by Frédéric Bastiat in 1807, was used by Austrian economists to demonstrate, by its absurdity, the wrongness of Keynesian stimulus of the economy:

> Have you ever witnessed the anger of the good shopkeeper, James
> Goodfellow, when his careless son has happened to break a pane
> of glass? If you have been present at such a scene, you will most
> assuredly bear witness to the fact that every one of the spectators,
> were there even thirty of them, by common consent apparently,
> offered the unfortunate owner this invariable consolation—"It
> is an ill wind that blows nobody good. Everybody must live,
> and what would become of the glaziers if panes of glass were
> never broken?[144]

If a window is broken and then repaired, it means that other
services that may be required will be left undone. This is true, but
in an economy of high unemployment, doing something may
indeed be better than doing nothing. Keynes himself suggested
burying bags of cash and hiring people to find them. There is
another interpretation of the parable, however: breaking windows
is a form of environmental destruction and a waste of resources.

As noted in Chapter Six, economists have long proclaimed
that the Luddites of the nineteenth century were wrong to try
to stop technological change to preserve their jobs. Jobs would
disappear, but others would emerge and everyone would be
better off. But even economists now believe that everyone must
continue mindless consumption (much like breaking windows)
for a healthy economy. If new technology that destroys jobs does
not harm the economy, then new technology or frugal habits
that reduce consumption will not harm the economy either. In
this way, creative destruction is equivalent to creative reduction.
Instead of producing useless products, we should consider doing

144   Bastiat, Frédéric (1850). Wikisource link to "That Which Is Seen, and
       That Which Is Not Seen" [original French: Ce qu'on voit et ce qu'on ne
       voit pas]. Translated by Patrick James.

more that is useful such as provide housing for the poor or build better infrastructure.

As product quality improves, corporations will sell fewer products, but product cost and profit margins will increase. As environmental impact is rationed, people will search for ways to lessen it. This will lead to higher costs as local, non-specialized, higher quality production will cost more than high volume, low quality imported goods.

Consider an article of furniture from Ikea made in a highly automated process out of materials that break down and become unappealing in a short time. Alternatively, single artisans could produce furniture that lasts indefinitely. The cost per year is comparable, but involves much higher upfront costs. Such a strategy could involve economic growth, lower impact on the environment, and more employment.

Corporations can grow by producing better technology and charging more. The economy grows because consumers pay a premium for the better technology above the actual cost. People consume less, but they pay more for what they do consume. This is the reverse of what is happening in our economy: corporations earn higher profits by increasing volume; prices come down, leading to even higher consumption. During the past forty years, wages for CEOs increased for no valid reason (rent seeking), real estate increased in value for no reason, but a lot of goods and services decreased in price because they were produced in higher volumes in China or because wages were arbitrarily kept low.

If the economy moves towards lower consumption, prices will naturally increase. Otherwise, companies will not be able to stay in business. Higher prices may be interpreted as inflationary, but should not be if quality improvements are taken into account.

Reducing impact will require innovation and this will cause the economy to grow. Economic growth cannot reduce environmental impact, but by adding the right discipline of rationing, reducing environmental impact can cause the economy to grow. There is now ample money in the economy to adequately fund social programs and invest in new technologies. Governments are starved for cash, not because of a shortage of resources in the world, but because the rich 1 percent have simply not paid their fair share of taxes. Higher taxation and more investment in infrastructure by governments will also cause the economy to grow. At the same time, more welfare spending will increase prosperity by reducing poverty and increasing financial security.

Investment will move decisively to greener initiatives. The economy will continue to grow even more than now, but gradually as consumption continues to decrease, growth will slow and the measure of GDP will become an irrelevant and archaic measure of the twentieth century. We will become interested in other measures of prosperity.

In the final chapter, I consider the likelihood that we will succeed. The following is a summary of what we need to do:

- We need accurate accounting of the ecological inputs of everything we do. We need to measure how much we are consuming and what our resource efficiency is. We need to use this information to measure, monitor, and regulate resource use.

- We need to decouple labour from the economy such that capital growth is not required for reducing unemployment. Reducing unemployment with capital growth is an inefficient use of resources if people already have enough of everything.

- We need to base prosperity on the fulfillment of needs and financial security instead of a gross measure of consumption. Improvements in quality of service will increase levels of prosperity far more effectively than growth in consumption.

- We need to reduce inequality of wealth. People can emerge from poverty more efficiently by redistributing wealth than by growing the economy.

- We need to eliminate unnecessary production of products and stop producing products that people do not need or only want because of elaborate marketing pressures.

- We need to reduce positional overconsumption and exaggerated expectations of size and amount. Instead, make quality of production and quality of service a measure of status.

- In general, we need to produce better products that last longer and that we can repair when they break down. Instead of design for recycling, we need design for durability and design for repair-ability. Instead of reduce, reuse, and recycle, we need reduce, reuse, and repair.

I am irrationally optimistic.

TWELVE RATIONAL PESSIMISM

The constant effort towards population, which is found to act even in the most vicious societies, increases the number of people before the means of subsistence are increased.

—Thomas Malthus

I hate to side with the optimists because the pessimists are probably right to be pessimistic and the optimists are probably hopelessly naïve. However, I am optimistic that things could turn out well if we all started being a bit more pessimistic about how things could turn out if we do nothing.

Matt Ridley, the self-proclaimed rational optimist who writes regularly for *The Times* and *The Wall Street Journal*, bases his beliefs on the undeniable improvements to people's lives over the past 10,000 years. He feels that these improvements, rapidly accelerating for the past 200 years, suggest that it is rational to expect more improvements in the future. In his book, *The Rational Optimist*, he argues that pessimism in general is not rational because it has failed to predict the future so many times in the past. Instead, he predicts that the pace of innovation will increase and living standards will improve to unimagined heights. He argues that although such optimism is unfashionable, it is actually more realistic than pessimism.[145]

In other words, Ridley feels it is more rational to be optimistic. Optimism may be accurate more often than not, but it is hardly rational. When Thomas Malthus made his famous prognosis for the future of humankind, given the knowledge he had available to him, his pessimism was entirely rational. He could not have known that Justus von Liebig would found the science of soil nutrients in the 1840s, that Gregor Mendel would discover modern genetics in the 1860s, or that Fritz Haber and Carl Bosch would invent the Haber-Bosch process to get nitrogen fertilizers out of the air in the 1950s. Optimism is usually irrational because it is based on a leap of faith that an opportunity will present itself at some point in the future. And, yes, it often does. It may be reasonable for social commentators like Ridley to be optimistic about our future based on our accomplishments, but we should note that scientists, engineers, and inventors who are pessimistic and dissatisfied about some aspect of the present are the ones that make these changes happen.

The Limits to Growth (LTG), when published in 1972, was an immense success, selling twelve million copies in more than thirty languages. The message was clear and resonated with many people: we are consuming too much and overtaxing the earth's resources. Understandably, available resources and subsequent developments of technology were underestimated.

---

145   Matt Ridley, *The Rational Optimist: How Prosperity Evolves*, (London: Harper Collins, 2010), 352.

However, critics have attacked and ridiculed the publication unfairly, many perpetuating a myth that a depletion of oil was predicted for 1992, and other minerals even sooner. So maligned is the publication that it is worth setting the record straight. The source of the misconception is found in Table Four of the second chapter. In the table listing several resources, there are three columns of data with three hypothetical assumptions: in column three, extraction of known reserves continues at a constant rate; in column five, extraction increases at an exponential rate; and in column six, extraction increases as in column five, but reserves also increase by five times. The so-called prediction of resource depletion by the end of the twentieth century is based on the data found in column five. The assumptions and simple calculations in the table are arbitrary and have nothing to do with the World3 computer simulation used in the LTG study.[146] Literally thousands of articles used this misreading of the text to condemn the book. Bjorn Lomborg, already relegating the book to "the dustbin of history" in 2009, continues in a Foreign Affairs article in 2012 that, "it is not too great an exaggeration to say that this one book helped send the world down a path of worrying obsessively about misguided remedies for minor problems while ignoring much greater concerns and sensible ways of dealing with them."[147]

---

146   Donella Meadows, Jorgen Randers, and Dennis Meadows, *The Limits to Growth: A Report for the Club of Rome's Project on the Predicament of Mankind,* (New York: Universe Books, 1972), 55-65.

147   Bjorn Lomborg, "Environmental Alarmism, Then and Now," *Foreign Affairs,* 2012.

LTG used a complex computer simulation called World3 to test various scenarios of future resource use, population increase, technological development, and growth of industrial output. No collapse of civilization was predicted for the end of the twentieth century; what the authors stated in the introduction was that if present trends of world population, industrialization, pollution, food production, and resource depletion continued, a limit to growth would be reached within the next hundred years.[148]

William Nordhaus did an in depth analysis of the study in 1992. He charged that the LTG study had underestimated new reserves, technological progress, and the possibility for substitution. Using other sources and analysis, he concluded that a scarcity of resources including energy, minerals, and the cost of greenhouse gas and pollution mitigation would only reduce world growth by 19.4 percent from 1980 to 2050, or about a third of a percent per year. He suggested that only five to ten dollars per tonne of CO_2 would be justified to combat climate change. In contrast, he suggests in *The Climate Casino*, written in 2012, that twenty-five dollars per tonne is required for 2015, rising to fifty-three dollars per tonne in 2030, and ninety-three dollars in 2040, to keep average global temperature rise below 2.5 degrees Celsius.[149]

Recent analysis suggests that the LTG scenarios are reasonably accurate. Ecologists Charles Hall and John Day suggest that LTG predictions made in 1972 are reasonably close to

---

148   Donella Meadows, Jorgen Randers, and Dennis Meadows, *The Limits to Growth: A Report for the Club of Rome's Project on the Predicament of Mankind*, (New York: Universe Books, 1972), 23.

149   William Nordhaus, *The Climate Casino: Risk, Uncertainty, and Economics for a Warming World*, (New Haven & London: Yale University Press, 2013), Chapter 19.

actual data for 2008.[150] A study conducted by the Melbourne Sustainable Society Institute comparing original projections from LTG to historical data also indicates that, so far, the business as usual projections are close enough to reject the notion that their scenarios are "spectacularly wrong" as Lomborg also asserts in the 2012 article.[151]

It is also not reasonable to reject an analysis because of a failure to anticipate technological progress. If the purpose of the LTG study is to provide a warning in order to stimulate appropriate action, then adding investment for technological progress is one such action appropriate for avoiding the economic collapse predicted. Ignoring facts and the consensus of many scientists seems to be the height of irrationality. Often a rational pessimism encourages the changes and the drives to innovation that cause the predictions to turn out wrong. Many of the outcomes that have turned out positive such as the recovery of the ozone layer, the control of acid rain or reduced pollution in American cities have come about because of, not in spite of, a rational pessimism at the time. It does make sense to be optimistic, not because there are no serious problems to solve, but rather because we do have an excellent record of accomplishment.

Lomborg, who wrote the much disputed and hugely controversial book called *The Skeptical Environmentalist*,[152] is not only optimistic about our future but also strangely pessimistic about

150   Charles A. S. Hall and John W. Day, Jr., "Revisiting the Limits to Growth after Peak Oil," *American Scientist*, Volume 97 (2009), 230-237.

151   G. Turner, "Is Global Collapse Imminent?" *Melbourne Sustainable Society Institute, The University of Melbourne*, MSSI Research Paper No. 4, (2014).

152   Bjorn Lomborg, *The Skeptical Environmentalist: Measuring the Real State of the World*, (Cambridge: Cambridge University Press, 1998).

current science and our ability to get along without fossil fuels. Shortly after publication of the book in 2002, *Scientific American* published essays by several scientists claiming that Lomborg misrepresented scientific evidence and scientific opinion. In 2003, The Danish Committee on Scientific Dishonesty cited the book for fabrication of data, selective discarding of unwanted results, deliberately misleading use of statistical methods, and distorted interpretation of conclusions. Since 2004, Kare Fog, a Danish biologist, has maintained a website documenting page-by-page errors in *The Skeptical Environmentalist*. Howard Friel has written a book called *The Lomborg Deception*.

Initially, major publications uncritically supported *The Skeptical Environmentalist*. *The New York Times*, tallying over 3,000 footnotes, declared the book a substantial work of analysis. *The Wall Street Journal* similarly declared the book superbly documented. *The Economist* weighed in with "This is one of the most valuable books on public policy—not merely on environmental policy—to have been written for the intelligent general reader in the past ten years…. *The Skeptical Environmentalist* is a triumph."[153] In short, the message was exactly what many people, tired of dire warnings from environmentalists, wanted to hear. *It is not too great an exaggeration* to say that *The Skeptical Environmentalist* and other books written by Lomborg may have caused policy makers to be unduly complacent about pressing environmental problems, resulting in a significant delay to action.

The climate change debate is reminiscent of the long struggle to prove beyond the shadow of a doubt that cigarette smoking

---

153   "Doomsday Postponed," *The Economist*, September 6, 2001.

was the leading cause of lung cancer. Climate change deniers have certain characteristics of which we should be aware. They tend to be older, meaning that global warming will not affect them as much.[154] They are often on the right of the political spectrum. In the United States, they tend to vote Republican.[155] They are committed to a high carbon lifestyle and live in the country or on the outskirts of cities where lot sizes and houses can be large. In short, they are people who, because of the resources they have access to and the lifestyles they lead, cannot imagine that there could be a problem.

It is difficult to counter the partisan divide, where conservatives reject the science of climate change simply because it has become a liberal cause. William Nordhaus notes in *Climate Casino* that many conservative economists including Martin Feldstein, chief economist to Ronald Reagan, Michael Boskin, chief economist to George H. W. Bush, Greg Mankiw, chief economist to George W. Bush, Kevin Hassett of the American Enterprise Institute, Arthur Laffer of Laffer curve fame, George Schultz, economist in the Reagan administration, and Gary Becker, a Nobel Prize-winning Chicago School economist, all favour a carbon tax as the most efficient way of dealing with global warming.[156] Ronald Reagan himself stated:

---

154   A recent Gallop poll indicates that only 18 percent of senior citizens are concerned that global warming will affect their lives. Well over 40 percent of younger age groups believe it will. http://www.gallup.com/poll/167879/not-global-warming-serious-threat.aspx.

155   "Special Report: Climate Change, Public Opinion," *The Economist*, November 28, 2015. In 2013, 70 percent of Democratic voters accepted the likelihood of anthropogenic climate change, while only 19 percent of Republicans did.

156   William Nordhaus, *The Climate Casino: Risk, Uncertainty, and Econom-*

If we've learned any lessons during the past few decades, perhaps the most important is that preservation of our environment is not a partisan challenge; it's common sense. Our physical health, our social happiness, and our economic well-being will be sustained only by all of us working in partnership as thoughtful, effective stewards of our natural resources.[157]

Reagan not only embraced the 1987 Montreal Protocol to phase out ozone-depleting substances, but was also highly committed to using US leadership to address global warming.[158] Republicans stubbornly refusing to accept the science will find themselves clearly on the wrong side of history.

If the economy is running at full capacity, barely providing the goods and services required, any diversion to fight a war, build infrastructure for solar energy or public transportation, eliminate disease, or combat poverty, would have an opportunity cost that would have to be evaluated. This is the justification given for not dealing with climate change offered by Bjorn Lomborg and the Copenhagen Consensus. Lomborg and many economists evidently believe that solving problems of the world is a zero-sum game. If we spend all our money on fighting climate change, we will not be able to stop the spread of HIV and AIDS, reduce malnutrition and hunger, control and treat

---

ics for a Warming World, (New Haven & London: Yale University Press, 2013), 314.

157   From a speech given by Ronald Reagan at 1:40 pm, July 11, 1984 on Theodore Roosevelt Island before signing the Annual Report of the Council on Environmental Quality.

158   Memorandum from Frederick M. Bernthal, United States Department of State, Assistant Secretary of State for Oceans and International Environmental and Scientific Affairs, Washington, DC 20520, February 9, 1989.

malaria, or conduct research into new agricultural methods. [159]
This is like saying (in 1965) that the great effort to land a man
on the moon would interfere with our ability to develop new
technologies. In fact, the very opposite was the case. Hundreds
of spin-offs resulted from the space program, affecting robotics,
computer hardware and software, nanotechnology, aeronautics,
transportation and healthcare industries. The Apollo program
spurred the development of companies such as Intel and the
emergence of Silicon Valley. The need to cut down weight
and power consumption led to the invention of the integrated
circuit, and ultimately to laptops and smartphones.

The cost of climate change mitigation has been estimated
to be between 0.5 and 2 percent of GDP per year.[160] However,
the cost of mortality from outdoor air pollution alone is almost
4 percent of GDP in the United States and over 10 percent of
GDP in China.[161] It should also be noted that this climate change
mitigation is a cost added to GDP, and therefore contributes to
economic growth. If people have to give up an equivalent amount
of goods and services they consume, the size of the economy is
unchanged, but giving up this amount of consumption is not

159   Bjorn Lomborg, *How to Spend $75 Billion to Make the World a Better Place*, (Copenhagen Consensus Center, 2013). The Copenhagen Consensus considered some 32 possible interventions, with most being far more cost effective than trying to reduce climate change.

160   James Rydge. "Implementing Effective Carbon Pricing, Contributing paper for Seizing the Global Opportunity: Partnerships for Better Growth and a Better Climate." *New Climate Economy*, London and Washington, DC. (2015), Available at: http://newclimateeconomy.report/misc/working-papers/.

161   "The New Climate Economy Report," *New Climate Economy*, 2014.

necessarily the same as giving up an equal amount of prosperity if environmental benefits are taken into account.

The world as a whole has excess production capacity. Most production in developing countries is intended for export to rich countries, so it is likely that the added costs for tackling climate change will improve developing economies. In summary, rich countries may have to give up consumption they do not really need and poor countries will give up opportunities to export more goods the world really does not need, but economic growth can be maintained along with the cost of climate change mitigation.

Looking to the future, populations are going to keep growing and resources will become more expensive to access. Technology will become more advanced and at an accelerating rate. The world economy will also keep on growing for quite a while. There is a possibility that we can alter tragic trajectories with the right encouragement. There are signs that people want to consume less. Homes are getting smaller, and the centre of cities denser. People are opting for experiences rather than amassing material possessions. Smaller spaces require less furniture and have less room for things. People are driving less, cycling more, and taking advantage of increased public transportation in cities. These trends, encouraging as they may be, will not lead to a solution to our problems without some large-scale efforts.

In the coming century, we face numerous challenges that will not be solved simply by being more optimistic. The apparent solutions to the environmental crisis advocated by environmental groups and exploited by green-minded corporations are either inadequate, unlikely to help in a timely manner, or are even counterproductive. Although actions such as recycling, driving smaller cars, and making more sustainable and greener buying choices are an admirable first step, they are unlikely to have much of an effect even if this behaviour becomes more widespread.[162]

REDUCING IMPACT

While we will continue to use the market mechanism as a useful tool, we must also recognize its limitations. The huge marketing industry exists mainly because of the focus on consumption that is part of our dysfunctional economy. These efforts at the most benign level inform us of new choices, but also support an advertising industry that encourages the use of products that are health and planet destroying, without regard for healthy and sustainable choices.

Although the rise of civilization and the corresponding sophistication of science and technology are impressive, what we have achieved in evolutionary terms is no different from any primitive organism. We have simply evolved and adapted to exploit our environment in the most thorough way possible so that our population can grow. However, like bacteria in a petri dish, we have not found a way to be in equilibrium with our environment. Civilization must come to some form of resolution. It must recognize the constraints of nature. Society must recognize the difference between what is optional and what is essential, and must make the hard choices that determine this division. The perfect economy does not happen by itself. It requires planning and design according to logical principles. Reducing impact is going

---

162   For an optimistic, but more realistic assessment of the state of the world see Ramez Naam, *The Infinite Resource: The Power of Ideas on a Finite Planet*, (Hanover and London: University Press of New England, 2013).

to take a comprehensive and concerted effort. We can reduce consumption while still increasing prosperity, but we must redefine prosperity to include:

- Good quality nutritious food in sufficient quantity

- Housing that protects from the elements and provides good air quality

- Access to good quality medical care that reduces infant mortality, controls infectious diseases, and ensures high life expectancy

- Access to good quality education

- The provision of opportunities for mobility, communication, and economic transactions

- Less negative stress that results in high crime rates, suicides, and mental disorders

- Employment opportunities and low inequality to ensure that prosperity is well distributed

- More leisure time

There is a wealth of information providing measures of environmental impact (EI). Impacts are expressed as "footprints" or in terms of the number of hectares of land per person required for a given lifestyle contrasted with what is available. The carbon footprint (CF) is the amount of carbon dioxide and other gases equivalent in terms of global warming effect (CO_2E) that a person is responsible for producing. The CF for most people in developed countries is a bit more than half of total EI. It is possible to calculate the exact environmental impact of every single product and service we consume with techniques of life cycle analysis (LCA).[163]

In 2009, Johan Rockstrom and several Earth Systems scientists compiled a list of nine planetary boundaries including greenhouse gases, ocean acidification, ozone depletion, nitrogen and phosphorous buildup, fresh water limits, land use change, biodiversity loss, aerosol loading and chemical pollution. We are already surpassing three of these limits. The buildup of greenhouse gases is the most serious of these boundaries because it may lead to undesirable climate change.

Daniel Coleman, in his book *Ecological Intelligence*, calls for ecological transparency to provide consumers with complete information regarding the environmental impact of the products they buy. Eventually it will be possible to devise a rating system that considers all environmental, health, and social impacts.[164] GoodGuide, founded in 2007, already provides a rating of one to ten for 250,000 consumer products based on health, environment, and social impacts. Research indicates that such disclosure does influence consumer choice. Roughly, 10 percent of consumers will pay more for products that have ecological or ethical virtue. However, those who are indifferent outnumber those who care by two or three to one.[165] This leaves a sizable majority of about two-thirds that lie between the two

---

163   LCA is a comprehensive, internationally standardized tool (ISO 14040 and ISO 14044) for quantifying emissions, resource consumption, and environmental impacts associated with production of all goods and services.

164   Daniel Coleman, *Ecological Intelligence: How Knowing the Hidden Impacts of What we Buy can Change Everything*, (New York: Broadway Books, 2009), 79.

165   Ibid, 120.

extremes—caring about ethical choices as long as the choice is easy and it does not cost much more. Only a few consumers believe that these eco-qualities justify a higher price. The minority includes those that are affluent enough to afford it and those that see the overall tragedy-of-the-commons-like consequences of buying a product of low ecological quality. I fear that such transparency, although helpful, will not be enough to influence the buying choices of the majority of shoppers to the degree necessary to make a difference.

In the previous chapter, I suggested the TDC system as a means to limit environmental impact by using greenhouse gas emissions as a means of quantification. The advantage of this system is that the information is readily available and the system is directly comparable to a demand-side carbon tax. Greenhouse gas emissions are directly associated with climate change, ocean acidification, and land use changes. Food production, responsible for a quarter to a third of all greenhouse gas emissions worldwide, also requires the most water. Fossil fuel use responsible for most greenhouse gases is a direct factor with most of the remaining planetary boundaries.

Although apparently more complex, the TDC system may be easier to implement than a carbon tax. Extensive data is collected on the internet of the buying habits of consumers. Credit card companies and banks record all financial transactions. As the economy becomes more cashless, collecting data on greenhouse gas emissions associated with every purchase will become straightforward. Many companies now routinely calculate the carbon footprint of the products and services they produce.

Greenhouse gas emissions per capita vary in each country, but tend to be substantially higher in higher income countries and much higher in North America. Ideally, the measure would be based on goods and services consumed rather than produced.

Table 3: *Measuring environmental impact.*

	Examples	kg CO_2E	g CO_2E/kWh
Per capita greenhouse gas emissions produced per year[166]	Canada	24,600	
	US	18,500	
	UK	8,600	
	China	7,900	
	World	6,800	
Per capita greenhouse gas emissions consumed per year including exports and imports[167]	Canada emissions reduced by 5 percent	24,000	
	US emissions increased by 12 percent	21,000	
	UK emissions increased by 46 percent	13,000	
	China emissions reduced by 22 percent	6,000	
Greenhouse gas emissions per kilowatt-hour of electricity consumed[168]	Iceland		0.2
	Canada		196
	US		586
	India		1,800

166   Based on 2012 data from World Resources Institute.
167   Based on 2012 data from World Resources Institute and 2004 data from Steven J. Davis and Ken Caldeira, "Consumption-based accounting of CO_2 emissions," *PNAS*, March 23, 2010, vol. 107, no. 12, 5687–5692. The PNAS analysis only includes carbon dioxide.
168   Based on data from Matthew Brander et al., "Electricity-specific emission factors for grid electricity," *Ecometrica*, August 2011.

A study by Steven J. Davis and Ken Caldeira indicates that if imports and exports were accounted for, the usual figures given for European consumption would be 46 percent higher, and for the United States 12 percent higher. Comparable figures for China would be 22 percent lower and for Canada 5 percent lower.[169]

Environmental impact can be broken down into six categories of consumption: food, transportation, personal products, residential, private corporations, and public services. Only the first four are accountable to personal choice. For the six categories, let us assume that 20,000 kilograms of carbon dioxide equivalents represents an average level of consumption, and a starting point for a carbon budget. This is less than current levels of consumption in North America and Australia, but considerably more than average levels in Europe. The tables provide examples of the products and services we use and typical values for their associated emissions. The goal should be to reduce emissions by roughly 1,000 kilograms in the first year and 5 percent of the total thereafter. This task will become progressively easier as more energy is derived from electricity from solar sources. Greenhouse gas emissions per kilowatt-hour of electricity are only 0.2 grams for Iceland where electricity is produced geothermally, but 1,800 grams for India where electricity is produced by burning coal.

169   Steven J. Davis and Ken Caldeira, "Consumption-based accounting of CO_2 emissions," *PNAS*, March 23, 2010, vol. 107, no. 12, 5687–5692. Although there is a great deal of information on the internet on greenhouse gas emissions of various sources, it is conflicting and unreliable at this point. The analysis of Davis and Caldeira, for example, is based on 2004 data that only includes emissions from carbon dioxide. I have used their percentages and applied them to recent data that includes CO_2E emissions.

CATEGORY ONE: FOOD

The average diet consists of about 2,700 calories (3,500 if you include what is wasted). If you obtained these calories exclusively by eating beef, it could result in about 10,000 kilograms of carbon dioxide equivalents, about half the carbon budget.

Table 4: *For an average diet of 2,700 calories, the suggested limit is 3,000 kg CO_2E.*[170]

	Examples	kg CO_2E
Includes	Carbon dioxide from fossil fuel use for energy and fertilizer production	
	Methane from beef and rice production	
	Nitrous oxide	
	Deforestation	
	Retail outlets including transport and refrigeration	
Emissions per year for a diet of 2,700 calories	If your diet consisted of only beef (4 to 25 kg/kg CO_2E; 13 kg/kg average)	10,000
	If your diet consisted of only tomatoes (0.4 to 50 kg/kg CO_2E; 9.1 kg/kg average)	50,000
	If your diet consisted of only rice	3,000
	If your diet consisted of only bananas	800
Typical emissions per year	Packaging	500

---

170   Based on data from Mike Berners-Lee, *How Bad are Bananas? The Carbon Footprint of Everything*, (Vancouver, Toronto, Berkeley: Greystone Books, 2011).

Food production includes greenhouse gas emissions from converting old growth forests to agricultural land, methane gas from beef and rice production, nitrous oxide from fertilizer, and carbon dioxide from the fossil fuels required for agriculture, transport, and retail outlets. Packaging is a significant fraction of emissions, but helps to minimize food spoilage.

The Paleolithic diet currently in vogue may be the most natural ideal for the way we have evolved over hundreds of thousands of years, but it is not practical for the number of people living on the planet. People have also been relatively healthy on the traditional agricultural diet that has developed over thousands of years. The one diet we can agree is very unhealthy is the one developed over the past hundred years: the industrial diet of refined sugars and carbohydrates. This diet causes obesity, diabetes, bad teeth, and many other diseases of modern civilization. The green revolution in agriculture has succeeded in producing more than enough food for the seven billion people in the world today. However, it depends on unsustainable practices that deplete the soil of nutrients and cause damage to the environment because of the extensive use of pesticides. Unsustainable consumption of fossil fuels makes the huge productivity of the modern agricultural sector possible. Moreover, the empty calories of highly processed cheap foods derived from a few engineered grains has caused malnutrition in poor countries due to the lack of micronutrients that would be included in traditional diets. Even in rich countries, the relative cheapness of empty calories has caused an obesity epidemic.

By 2050, we may have to feed ten billion people. Studies of organic farming have suggested that yields are too low to compete with conventional farming practices. Less impact per acre is not an advantage if we have to clear more forests to feed the world. However, a meta-analysis of 115 studies comparing organic and conventional farming by University of California researchers found that the difference is much lower than previously thought, and that certain practices could further reduce this gap to only about 8 percent.[171] Conventional agricultural practices can also improve a great deal to become more sustainable. Techniques of advanced precision agriculture that minimize water, fertilizer, and pesticide use, not only increase yields, but also minimize impact on the environment. Imported food can sometimes have a lower impact than locally produced food because shipping cost, depending on the method used, can be a small proportion of total impact. Consumer preferences to eat meat as incomes rise may mean that farming practices that are even more intensive may be required. All of this is conjecture, however. A measure of impact on the TDC scale using techniques of life cycle analysis is required to determine what the environmental cost of that head of lettuce actually is.

Although using grains to produce meat is wasteful, this does not mean that we all have to become vegetarians. We have evolved over hundreds of thousands of years to eat meat. The industrial production of grains is causing many of our problems. The increase in land productivity is only possible with copious amounts of fossil fuels for fertilizers and pesticides, high water consumption, and less variety of food crops. This results in lower quality food and negative impacts on the environment. Eliminating the consumption of beef in favour of more production of grains simply enlarges this problem. The elimination of manure from animals increases reliance on artificial fertilizers derived from fossil fuels.

---

171   L. C. Ponisio, L. K. M'Gonigle, K. C. Mace, J. Palomino, P. de Valpine, C. Kremen, "Diversification practices reduce organic to conventional yield gap," Proc. R. Soc. B 282: 20141396. http://dx.doi.org/10.1098/rspb.2014.1396., 2015

A better approach is to get back to balanced methods of agriculture that incorporate mixed farming methods. Meat from animals grass fed on marginal land rather than grain is healthier, uses less water, and does not displace food crops.[172]

There seems to be a moral preference to farm land-based animals and to hunt fish. However, it is possible to harvest sustainably many wild animals that exist in large populations including kangaroos, deer, reindeer, and rabbits. Fish farming done the right way could be sustainable. Insects provide another large protein source already exploited in many parts of the world. A further possibility is to grow meat from muscle cells without harming a living animal. This is a long way from commercialization, but is technically feasible.

The use of more labour rather than fossil fuels reduces unemployment and increases resource use efficiency. This would allow us to grow a greater variety of food with higher levels of nutrition. Agro-ecological practices mimic nature by integrating crops and livestock with the environment. Growing crops such as maize, wheat, sorghum, millet, and vegetables alongside trees can double or even triple yields. The trees provide shade, improve the availability of water, prevent soil erosion, and add nitrogen.[173] Farmers in Japan use ducks instead of pesticides for pest and weed control. The droppings provide nutrients and the ducks provide another source of protein.

---

172   Grass fed beef grown on marginal land can have an impact as low as 4 kg. per $kgCO_2E$ compared with a high of 25 kg. and the world average of 13 kg.

173   Danielle Nierenberg, "Agriculture: Growing Food—Solutio*n*s," in Eric Assadourian and Prugh, Project Directors, World Watch Institute, *State of the World 2013: Is Sustainability Still Possible?* (Washington, Covelo, London: Island Press, 2013), Chapter 17.

CATEGORY TWO: NON-BUSINESS USE PRODUCTS

The embodied greenhouse emissions of a product should be calculated according to its expected useful life. For example, over a ten year period, the embodied emissions of a television are 15 to 20 kilograms per year depending on type and size. For computers, the figure is 100 to 150 kilograms per year over a two to five year period, depending on durability—laptops have a lower life expectancy—and size. Watching television for about four hours per day typically generates 150 kilograms per year, but varies greatly according to the source of the electricity. Using a computer for four hours a day and surfing the internet, requiring servers and networks, could generate 100 to 300 kilograms per year. In contrast, a daily newspaper may generate 100 to 150 kilograms per year.

The average person buys about 10 kilograms of clothing per year. The carbon footprint varies from a low of about 50 kilograms per year for synthetic clothing and 500 kilograms for cotton. Cotton displaces food crops and requires large amounts of water and pesticides to grow. In contrast, hemp requires no fertilizers or pesticides and has a low carbon footprint. The consumption of clothing has been increasing in recent decades because of low prices and frequent changes in fashion. Getting back to wearing clothing that is more durable or by choosing more sustainable alternatives to cotton can reduce emissions substantially.

Table 5: *For non-business use products and services, the suggested limit is 2,000 kg CO_2E.*[174]

	Examples	kg CO_2E
Includes	Energy for manufacture and shipping	
	Industrial processes	
	Retail outlets, not including administration	
	Computers, smartphones, televisions, and other electronics	
	Paper, inks, and other consumables	
	Sports equipment including snowmobiles, jet skis, and bicycles	
	Clothing, soft goods, and personal products	
Embodied emissions per year	Television per year (over 10 years)	15-20
	Computer per year (over 5 years)	100-150
	Clothing used per year	50-500
Emissions from use per year	Watching television (32 inch LCD) 4 hours per day	150
	Daily newspaper	100-150
	Laundry	175
	Computer use 4 hour per day	50-250
	Servers and networks	50

The natural industriousness of people threatened with the loss of income results in a continual search for the creation of some useful service or product. Inventors and innovators try to exploit a small niche in the market. In almost all cases the success of these

---

174   Based on data from Mike Berners-Lee, *How Bad are Bananas? The Carbon Footprint of Everything*, (Vancouver, Toronto, Berkeley: Greystone Books, 2011).

ventures is dependent not only on coming up with a winning design, but also a concerted marketing effort to convince enough people that what they have been doing perfectly well without for years and years is now worth having. Products constantly improve, but new products are also constantly introduced. Many of these products are of questionable merit—using valuable resources, adding more pollution to the environment and ending up in the landfill. I am sure that if you added up all the useless production that provides much of the necessary employment for manufacturing, marketing and sales, you would come up with a high proportion of the economy that is not doing anything very worthwhile. Companies provide services such as holiday resorts for pets, and plastic toys to help sell tasteless and innutritious fast food meals to children. To the unemployed and the underemployed should be added the uselessly employed plus a large proportion of the financial industry that helps to fund many of these useless ventures.

McDonough and Braungart remind us that the design of products should be effective instead of just efficient, that instead of producing less waste (less bad, in their terms), products should be designed for no waste. Instead of recycling, which usually means down-cycling, materials should be up-cycled to become techno-nutrients for other products, or made up of materials that can decompose and become bio-nutrients.[175]

Consumer choice and industrial design can have a big influence. Choices of better quality and less fashion inspired, more timeless styles and managing with fewer products could help, as well as design for repair and replacement of worn parts, or even,

---

175   William McDonough and Michael Braungart, *Cradle to Cradle: Remaking the Way We Make Things*, (New York: North Point Press, 2002), 105-109.

in the case of electronic products, completely new technologies replaced in a more durable chassis.

Marketing pressures to increase sales have induced manufacturers to create cheaper products. Added features that make a product more compelling at the point of sale often increase complexity and shorten the life of a product. Consumer products have become less sustainable during the last thirty years. In garage sales, you can find many products designed and manufactured in the 1950s that are still serviceable today. The use of durable materials, simple technologies, and replaceable parts ensured a long life.

Some of the early kettles manufactured from 1956 to the mid-1970s by Russell Hobbs are still in service. The ruggedness of these kettles, which typically lasted over twenty years, was amazing. The modern electric kettle, in contrast, lasts an average of only 3.5 years. Many break down in as little as two years.

Using an electric kettle has a significant impact on the environment. Ninety-seven percent of households in Britain own an electric kettle. New features such as illuminated water levels, keep-warm capabilities, water temperature selectors, and larger capacities often mean that kettles are less energy efficient than in the past. Electric kettles account for about 18 percent of all domestic cooking energy costs. Using an electric kettle is, however, far more energy efficient than heating water on a stove.

Recently, consumer demand for green products has prompted manufacturers to make changes. Some sustainable design characteristics are more marketable than others. The use of recycled materials and low energy consumption are obvious characteristics of a "green" product. It makes sense for materials used to be recyclable, sustainably harvested, and non-toxic. Products should also be designed so that different materials can be easily separated and recycled. There are other standard principles of good design that can be even more effective in creating a sustainable product:

- Create simple products: the greenest product is one not thrown away. All products, no matter how green, take energy and resources to produce and contribute to the growth of landfills when thrown away. A well-designed product will have a longer life. Simple and timeless design statements will make it less likely that a product will go out of fashion.

- Reduce the product's weight, footprint, and overall size: Reducing the footprint of a product has several advantages from a sustainability perspective. Space on countertops and in desks, pockets, and backpacks is at a premium. One of the main reasons for throwing away an otherwise useful product is to get a new one that takes up less space. Large bulky products take up more room in shipping containers and warehouses. Products larger than necessary have a tendency to look old fashioned very quickly. Reducing the weight of a product reduces the energy required for shipping.

- Use durable materials and durable technologies: Always design a product for a long useful life. Even products that become obsolete because of changing technologies can often remain useful for longer in the second hand market or for use in developing countries.

Most metals are extracted from ore using large amounts of energy and other resources such as water. China produces 95 percent of the world's rare earth metals; Brazil, 90 percent of niobium; and South Africa 79 percent of rhodium. Aluminum, iron, silicon, and titanium are abundant, whereas indium, silver, and some rare earth metals are scarce. There is only enough indium in confirmed sources for about fifteen years at current rates of consumption. On the other hand, there are untapped riches in urban landfills. As virgin ores become scarce and more expensive to access, these currently uneconomic sources will become viable. Landfills in the United States contain enough steel to build 11,000 Golden Gate Bridges. A circular economy— one that recycles all resources and treats them as finite assets— will ensure that resource shortages will not be an impediment to developing needed infrastructure and cleaner sources of energy in the future.[176]

Approximately 10 percent of the 270 million tonnes of plastic produced every year makes its way to oceans directly from coastal areas and via streams and rivers. A large proportion of this is from single use plastic products including plastic bags, food containers, and lids for beverages. The harm that this does to oceans and aquatic life is far beyond that measured by the embodied greenhouse gases in the material itself. The solution is simple, but seldom applied: reusable products.

Private property is convenient, a luxury for the affluent, and more efficient for increasing production, but it is less efficient in terms of conserving and sharing resources. Many people can own property rather than just a few. It would be more efficient in resource terms for a group of neighbours in a suburb to share a lawnmower, rather than for each to own one separately. The reason

---

176   Gary Gardner, "Conserving Nonrenewable Resources," in Eric Assa-
        dourian and Prugh, Project Directors, World Watch Institute, *State of
        the World 2013: Is Sustainability Still Possible?* (Washington, Covelo,
        London: Island Press, 2013), Chapter 9.

we like private ownership rather than sharing is for convenience and time efficiency, not resource efficiency.

CATEGORY THREE: PERSONAL TRANSPORTATION

Embodied emissions from an automobile range from 600 to 1,500 kilograms per year, depending on whether it is a small gasoline powered car or a large electric vehicle. Based on travel distance of 15,000 kilometres per year, a car with a single occupant can generate anywhere from 3,000 to 12,000 kilograms of greenhouse gases—the latter, a gas-guzzling SUV. The same distance by train generates about 1,400 kilograms per passenger, and by bus, 750 kilograms. One trans-Atlantic flight and the return generate about 5,000 kilograms of greenhouse gas. Depending on how the electricity is generated, an electric car's impact can be almost zero if the electricity comes from low carbon sources. There is little advantage to an electric car if the electricity is produced by burning coal.

People use a certain amount of energy whether they are exercising or not and a certain amount of exercise is required to maintain health. The energy required for a distance of less than about ten kilometres per day is therefore included in the standard diet of 2,700 calories. Unless distances are long, walking or cycling, as a person's only form of exercise, generate no extra greenhouse gases. For longer distances, the energy required can be made up with some extra carbohydrates with a low carbon footprint.

Table 6: *For personal transportation, the suggested limit is 5,000 kg CO_2E.*[177]

	Examples	kg CO_2E
Includes	Energy used	
	Vehicles including automobiles, airplanes, and ships	
	Retail outlets, transport	
Embodied emissions per year	Conventional automobile (200,000 km)	600-900
	Electric car (200,000 km)	1,000-1,400
	Bicycle (10 years)	80
Emissions from travel of 15,000 km per year	By conventional car (one passenger per car)	3,000-12,000
	By electric car (depending on source of electricity)	0-4,500
	By train	1,400-2,500
	By bus	300
	One trans-Atlantic flight and return (15,000 km)	5,000
	Walking or cycling less than 10 km per day	0
	Walking or cycling 40 km per day (15,000 km)	800

Significant reductions in impact are possible with the right consumer choices. Smaller and lighter cars, electric propulsion, and more efficient fuel economy can help a great deal, but shifts to public transportation can be even more effective.

Carbon emissions from ground transportation are a source that could easily be reduced except for the general appeal of the

177 Based on data from Mike Berners-Lee, *How Bad are Bananas? The Carbon Footprint of Everything*, (Vancouver, Toronto, Berkeley: Greystone Books, 2011); Shrinkthatfootprint.com "Shades of Green: Electric Cars' Emissions Around the Globe;" *BRANZ study report 150.*

automobile. The automobile is highly subsidized and extraordinarily expensive in environmental terms. It is also so popular that the massive infrastructure of multilane expressways, bridges, and tunnels that now exist are all hopelessly congested. Despite the overall inefficiency of this system, it is unlikely that a comprehensive system of public transport involving trains and buses could ever be set up to compete with it. Ground transport accounts for roughly 20 percent of all carbon emissions. Although fuel-efficient hyper-cars, having a tenth of the environmental impact of conventional cars, could be made with existing technology, the automobile industry is notoriously slow and reluctant to respond in this fashion. An interesting but discouraging statistic is that the average gas mileage in the United States is currently 20.8 miles per gallon. In 1988, it was 22.1. In 1908, the Model T Ford, an average car at the time, achieved 25 miles per gallon.[178]

Buses could utilize existing infrastructure and move people far more efficiently than automobiles. At an average speed of 100 kilometres per hour, 1,200 kilometres of the M25 motorway in Britain could accommodate only 19,000 passengers in automobiles, without congestion. Alternatively, coaches could provide transport for up to 260,000 passengers over the same distance.[179] What may help save the planet are driverless cars and small buses programmed for multiple stops. The technology for this is close and could eventually rival the convenience of the private car. Imagine a smartphone app where you call for transportation. In a few minutes, a driverless car or a small bus comes and picks you up. A comprehensive system like Google Maps determines the most

---

178178 George Monbiot, *Heat: How to Stop the Planet From Burning*, (Random House LLC, Mar 19, 2009), 155-156.
179 Ibid, 150.

efficient routes, dynamically eliminating waits and congestion. People working from home, virtual meetings, and home delivery could also reduce the amount of travelling required. Better cycling and walking infrastructure, less affected by automobile noise and pollution, would help to reduce emissions.

The one area of transportation that will be the most difficult to improve is long distance international air travel. The environmental cost of getting halfway around the world in a few hours is enormous and there is little reason to believe than much can be done technologically, now or in the future, to change this. To meet our target of sustainability, the luxury of frequent plane journeys to faraway places will have to be sharply curtailed. High-speed trains are not much better and require huge capital costs to set up. Some may consider this a significant loss of prosperity, but one way to counteract this is with an increase in leisure time. With more time on our hands, other opportunities for long distance travel are possible, without involving the same degree of fossil fuel use. For example, airships suspended by hydrogen with an airspeed of around 130 kilometres per hour could get from London to New York in forty-three hours.[180] The experience could be cheaper in environmental terms, but otherwise comparable to a cruise or a scenic train journey.

CATEGORY FOUR: RESIDENTIAL

For the American average of 77 square metres per person (800 square feet per person) and a house that lasts thirty-five years, the average embodied emissions per person works out to about 1,100

---

180   Ibid, 186.

kilograms per year. If the space requirements could be reduced to about 30 square metres per person—more typical in Europe— and houses could last 100 years, the carbon footprint could be reduced to 300 kilograms per year. Energy used typically results in emissions of about 1,600 kilograms per year, but this in theory could be reduced to zero with energy efficient construction and on-site generation of geothermal or solar-based power.

Table 7: *For residential, the suggested limit is 5,000 kg CO₂E.[181]*

	Examples	kg CO_2E
Includes	Energy for heating and cooling	
	Building and landscaping	
	Interior furnishings	
	Household appliances	
Embodied emissions per year	House that lasts 35 years (77 m²/person)	1,100
	High rise apartment that lasts 100 years (30 m²/person)	300
	Vinyl floor covering (77 m²/person)	400
	Large appliance	20
Emissions per year	Energy used (77 m²/person)	1,600
	Energy used (30 m²/person)	600
	Washing dishes (dishwasher)	150
	Washing dishes (by hand)	700

The built environment represents a missed opportunity on a massive scale when it comes to solving the problems of the

---

181   Data from Roger Hitchin, "Embodied Carbon and Building Services," *CIBSE Research Report 9* (2013). A typical house embodies 500 kg/m², a high rise about 1,000 kg/m². The energy used is based on 21 kg/m².

environment. Although buildings in North America use almost half of all energy consumed, they could be built, at little extra cost, to consume practically no energy. Making houses significantly smaller and of higher quality so that they last much longer would dramatically reduce the amount of resources consumed. The reason they are not is due to a lack of appropriate regulation and the wrong market incentives. Builders will add granite countertops to kitchens to help sell a unit, but if they can remove a feature not apparent at the point of sale, it is more money in their pocket.

The Passivhaus, developed in Germany in the 1980s, has had a slow uptake in the market despite costing less than 10 percent more than conventional construction—the cost of more expensive features is offset by less need for a heating or cooling system. Buildings so constructed would cost more in the short term, but considerably less over the life of the building. Proper regulation could have made a big difference. Simple changes to building codes would add many useful and energy saving features such as heat recovery ventilation, extra insulation, and means of optimizing solar gain. Unfortunately, existing housing stock cannot be replaced overnight, so upgrades and the replacement of fossil fuel energy sources with those derived from solar will be required.

CATEGORY FIVE: PRIVATE, CORPORATE AND NON-GOVERNMENT ORGANIZATIONS

Almost everyone in an advanced industrialized country has a second home—the office where they work. The average twenty square metres per person results in about 400 kilograms per year of embodied greenhouse gas emissions in the building and operating energy of 1,800 kilograms per year, assuming office buildings last fifty years. If space per person could be reduced to ten square metres, and buildings could last 100 years, the embodied carbon dioxide and equivalents could be reduced by 75 percent. As with houses, there is no reason why office buildings could not be built to require very little energy for heating and cooling, and energy required could be easily supplied with solar sources.

Table 8: *For private, corporate and non-government organizations, the suggested limit is 2,000 kg CO_2E.*[182]

	Examples	kg CO_2E
Includes	Energy for heating and cooling	
	Transportation	
	Buildings, equipment, and infrastructure	
	Film industry and theatres	
	Data storage, internet, social networking	
	Other consumption by businesses	
Embodied emissions per year	Office that lasts 50 years (20 m²/person)	400
	Office that lasts 100 years (10 m²/person)	100
Emissions per year	Operational energy (20 m²/person)	1,800

Whereas an eco-efficient building minimizes energy and water use by making windows smaller and reducing ventilation, an eco-effective building creates its own energy, recycles water used, and collects rainwater. The building is designed to maximize

---

182   Data from Roger Hitchin, "Embodied Carbon and Building Services," *CIBSE Research Report 9* (2013).

natural airflows and natural light. A layer of native grasses covers the roof.[183]

CATEGORY SIX: PUBLIC SERVICES

Growth in infrastructure is the primary reason that developing countries like China and India are achieving double-digit growth. The cost of the infrastructure, created in the short term, should be mortgaged over its life. The size of the economy should be determined by an equation to reflect current consumption plus the cost of maintenance of current infrastructure plus the yearly cost of infrastructure created. Thought of in this way, the economic growth in developing countries would be negligible because they have so little pre-existing infrastructure to maintain and repair. In the developed countries, we can aim to reduce consumption and use this slack in the economy to produce more infrastructure for more efficient transportation networks, and more efficient energy systems with solar sources rather than non-renewable resources.

183   See McDonough's design for the Ford Motor Company in William McDonough and Michael Braungart, *Cradle to Cradle: Remaking the Way We Make Things*, (New York: North Point Press, 2002), 157-165.

Table 9: *For public services, the suggested limit is 2,000 kg CO_2E.* [184]

	Examples	kg CO_2E
Includes	Energy used	
	Buildings	
	Infrastructure including roads, railways, and airports	
	Hospitals and universities	
Embodied emissions per year	Office that lasts 50 years (20 m²/person)	400
	Office that lasts 100 years (10 m²/person)	100
Emissions per year	Typical school or university per student over 20 years	1,400

ENERGY

Even with some form of advanced nuclear power, it is unlikely that we will have limitless amounts of energy available for the next twenty or thirty years. The use of all energy including fossil fuels, solar, wind, nuclear, hydro and bio-fuels all have some impact on the environment. The transition from fossil fuels to these other forms is going to require massive investment and a considerable draw on resources. This means we should strive to increase efficiency and reduce all energy consumption as much as possible.

---

184   Based on data from Mike Berners-Lee, *How Bad are Bananas? The Carbon Footprint of Everything*, (Vancouver, Toronto, Berkeley: Greystone Books, 2011); Roger Hitchin, "Embodied Carbon and Building Services," *CIBSE Research Report 9* (2013).

Off-the-shelf conservation measures, including efficient lighting, heating, cooling, and more insulated and energy efficient windows, could reduce energy consumption by 23 percent with a lower investment.[185] Solar energy costs have come down dramatically since 2008 and can now compete with conventional sources. Offshore wind and wave power combined with high voltage DC lines could supply a large amount of power from faraway and distributed sources. DC lines are more expensive than AC lines for short distances but do not get much more expensive for much longer distances.[186] Wind speeds increase by one metre per second for every 100 kilometres from shore. Solar energy is abundant in desserts. The combination of wind farms and natural gas powered generators needed when the wind is not blowing but offset with carbon capture could easily replace coal-fired generators. Heat pumps can be used to extract heat from ground sources or even from sewage produced by cities. Micro generation systems comprised of solar panels, windmills, and hydrogen fuel cells could all be linked together in an energy internet to provide a very resilient form of power for domestic needs.[187]

---

185   T. W. Murphy, Jr., "Beyond Fossil Fuels: Assessing Energy Alternatives," in Eric Assadourian and Prugh, Project Directors, World Watch Institute, *State of the World 2013: Is Sustainability Still Possible?* (Washington, Covelo, London: Island Press, 2013), Chapter 15.

186   George Monbiot, *Heat: How to Stop the Planet From Burning*, (Random House LLC, Mar 19, 2009), 104-105.

187   See Jeremy Rifkin, *The Third Industrial Revolution: How Lateral Power is Transforming Energy, The Economy, and the World*, (New York: Palgrave Macmillan, 2011).

Figure 8: *The exhaust stacks, transformed into public art, light up at night at Vancouver's False Creek Energy Centre.*[188]

Using a food crop to make biofuels makes no sense, especially if it takes more energy to produce the fuel than the resulting fuel can provide. However, biofuels made from sugarcane already supply about a third of fuel requirements in Brazil. Biofuels made from sugarcane have a high-energy return on investment (EROI)

---

188   The first big wastewater heat-recovery system in North America is in Vancouver, British Columbia. It provides 70 percent of energy needs to homes and businesses in the Olympic Village originally built for the 2010 Winter Olympics on a former industrial waterfront site. Photo supplied by the City of Vancouver.

and are practically carbon neutral. Growing the sugarcane absorbs the carbon generated from burning the fuel. Sugarcane also requires so little land to grow that it does not significantly impair food production.[189]

Abundant energy is available from solar sources. The intermittent nature of the supply requires expensive energy storage solutions. William McDonough and Michael Braungart have suggested a novel approach for energy storage in their second book *The Upcycle*. Excess and intermittent energy from solar or wind power could be used to power multi-tiered greenhouses with LED lights. The growing plants would act as the battery for storing energy.[190] Taking this idea further, there could be two electricity grids. One grid would have priority to deliver a constant supply of energy. It would be augmented with fossil fuels when required. Excess energy would go into a second grid for powering LEDs in greenhouses, charging batteries in electric cars, heating hot water, and other uses where intermittent power is not a problem. The second grid would sell energy at a lower price, providing an incentive to use it rather than the more expensive constant supply grid.

189   Jens Ulltveit-Moe, "Glimpse 10-3: Rich on Biofuels" in Jorgen Randers, *2052: A Global Forecast for the next Forty Years*, (White River Junction, Vermont: Chelsea Green Publishing, 2012), Chapter 10.

190   William McDonough and Michael Braungart, *The Upcycle: Beyond Sustainability—Designing for Abundance*, (New York: North Point Press, 2013), 140-142.

IN CONCLUSION

Rising populations, resource depletion, increasing pollution, and technological change indicate that in all probability our economy cannot stay the same as it is now. The poor design of the economy is the main reason that appropriate action to combat global warming has been delayed for decades. It is possible this is merely a short transition period from scarcity to real abundance. In future, abundant energy from solar sources can produce unlimited amounts of fresh water from saltwater in oceans. If pollution can be eliminated there will be few limits on the production of goods and services. This is in contrast to the opening phases of the industrial revolution. Abundant fossil fuels created a fake abundance—a richness of technologically created wealth but with an unacknowledged cost, borrowed from our present and our children's future. The economy will resolve itself and find an equilibrium positive for society if governments take decisive action now to limit the overconsumption of resources that threaten this future. It is important to restructure our economy to ration and more fairly distribute available resources. A supply-side carbon tax makes sense but has not worked well. I argue that a demand-side carbon tax, with the help of a Two-Dimensional Currency, although more complex to implement, is well within the capabilities of current technologies, and will receive less political resistance.

The overarching premise of this book is that reducing consumption need not reduce prosperity. This is because overconsumption has many obvious costs including pollution, degradation of the environment, and global warming, as well as less obvious ones of increased stress, over-choice, reduced social capital, and economic insecurity. It has become relatively easy for the economy to produce enough for basic needs and most wants as well. Disconnect occurs because people have to do work that has sufficient value to buy the things they need. Higher productivity and lower consumption can lead to higher unemployment.

Rising unemployment is not new. It has been an ongoing side effect of increasing technological development, beginning with agriculture and increasing with ongoing industrialization. However, unemployment is a political problem. People may run out of employment opportunities in which they can receive sufficient income, but there will always be things to do that are a benefit to society. Full employment, if that is necessary, is a matter of changing the structure of the economy to reflect the new realities of increasing capitalization. This can be done by substituting a free exchange for labour, possibly with the help of alternative time-based currencies, or by increasing socialization such that a new leisure economy, as suggested in Part Two, could expand to fill the void.

I have demonstrated how individual actions may be rational in aggregate (the wisdom of crowds), but sometimes have a tendency to be irrational (the prisoner's dilemma or the tragedy of the commons). The means to counteract the negative tendency is obviously through agreements, regulation, and the building of trust within communities. The self-serving logic of the prisoner's dilemma is also a factor in world problems. Any country moving unilaterally to reduce emissions of greenhouse gases will bear tremendous cost without achieving significant benefit. The solution to global warming, more than any other problem in history, requires international cooperation. Without international agreements—the Paris Agreement in 2015 is a good start—the result will be a tragedy of the commons on a large scale. The solution is to form new international agencies or give more power to existing ones like the United Nations. We saw in Chapter Eight that both the individual acting alone and profit-oriented corporations are

unlikely to institute the broad changes required. Without sufficient power residing in government, the economy will degenerate
to corporate control or a libertarian survival of the fittest. Small
powerful governments could do the job, but are likely to be more
authoritarian. Instead, we need a sufficiently large, decentralized,
and more democratized government organized by communities,
and supported and challenged by many groups of individuals that
can integrate and work together towards a common goal. Citizens
must band together to solve local problems and to influence governments at an international level. Governments must become
bigger and more democratic, but without becoming bogged down
with populist contradictions. Leadership should be centralized
and decisive, but accountable to the people. We need more argument and discussion, but also larger, more encompassing international organizations with real power to make decisions.

There is no sense that the present distribution of wealth in the
world is fair or justified. The four hundred or so individuals in the
United States with wealth equal to that of 185 million individuals at
the bottom of the scale have not earned their wealth in any meaningful way. Rather, they have become rich as a snowball captures snow,
with an ever increasing, geometrically derived efficacy, resulting in
a profound loss of economic efficiency in society as a whole. Their
undeserved claim on wealth has also resulted in a concentration of
power and the ability to control corporations and influence governments. However, individuals such as Bill Gates, Warren Buffett, and
many others are sympathetic or at least unopposed to more equality
in the world. Philanthropy of a scale rivalling the robber baron era is
fully under way. These well-meaning individuals could be far more
effective and make a significant mark for posterity by accumulating
valuable resources and donating them to the public trust. There are
fossil fuels worth twenty-one trillion dollars that should remain in
the ground. The purchase of some of these to become a part of the

public domain, like the national parks from previous ages of wealth, would be a far greater legacy than the many acts of charity that serve only to lessen the immediate effects of poverty without any long-term improvements. Consumption will have to increase to reduce poverty in the world, but such increases should be concentrated on the poor.

Let us pretend that China is actually two countries—urban China and rural China. Urban China is a rich country with advanced technology and a growing economy quite similar to other industrialized nations. Rural China is a very poor country. Urban China is expending a major effort, a large proportion of its GDP, in developing infrastructure to bring Rural China out of poverty. Now imagine that the rest of the rich world does the same thing for poorer countries. The world's economy would suddenly also have double-digit growth as it adds infrastructure, housing and economic development for billions of people. At the same time, infrastructure to reduce climate change and limit consumption would be improved. This sounds like another fairy tale, but it is what China is already doing in Africa and parts of South America. China is becoming the saviour of the developing world by buying, controlling, and developing their resources, providing jobs, and reducing poverty.[191]

Mathis Wackernagel, co-creator of the ecological footprint concept, predicts "resource constraints will produce social upsets way before producing ecological collapse." China's leaders have been preparing for these resource constraints for decades. They have "limited their population growth, reforested devastated areas, and carefully managed urbanization pressures." Their ultimate goal is "a self-sufficient China—a continuation of the age-old

---

191   Dambisa F. Moyo, *Winner Take All: China's Race for Resources and What it Means for the World*, (New York: Basic Books, 2012).

Middle Kingdom." Economic growth is a means of keeping its population motivated and loyal, but it also has the biggest bio-capacity deficit of all nations: over two Chinas are required to support current domestic demand. The difference between China and other nations is that China is aware of the problem and is "... putting considerable efforts into building a national resource base and an economy based on domestic consumption rather than on resource-intensive exports to the rich world."[192]

The laissez-faire market-based system has undoubtedly shown some advantages over the years in terms of technological innovations and the ability to harness a wide range of talents to achieve remarkable advances in technology, science, and medicine. China's state-led approach has been successful in orchestrating dramatic economic growth and reducing poverty. It has also avoided many of the pitfalls leading to the current recession. Europe, with its blended approach, has many of the advantages of the US system but retains much higher social responsibility. The Scandinavian countries have shown that a big welfare state is compatible with high living standards. Cuba emerges, unexpectedly, as a promising prototype of sustainable development. It has not produced any smartphones, but advances have been made in agriculture that may have more impact in the end.

The process of creative destruction caused by new technologies has destroyed jobs while creating only lower paying entrepreneurial activity. The digital economy in particular is responsible for destroying secure well-paid professions such as graphic design, journalism, and retail, while at the same time making possible

---

192   Mathis Wackernagel, "Glimpse 6-3: *The Race to Lose Last*" in Jorgen Randers, *2052: A Global Forecast for the next Forty Years*, (White River Junction, Vermont: Chelsea Green Publishing, 2012), Chapter 6.

internet based alternatives that in most cases do not pay well. More work is being done, but without the rewards that have previously created a strong middle class culture.

This type of economy has been described by some as winner-take-all. Small differences in performance result in huge rewards. A more serious concern is that these differences do not necessarily reflect an objective measure of quality. The bestselling popstar is hardly the best singer or the best musician. Blockbuster movies based on comic book heroes hardly represent a pinnacle of high drama. Scott Timberg writes in the provocatively titled book *Culture Crash: The Killing of the Creative Class*, "With the cultural and psychological triumph of the market, we've lost the very language by which we might express the worth of things."[193] In the market, value is determined by gross measures of popularity. Popularity is influenced by a herd mentality that often succumbs to what is familiar and pleasant, or conversely, to what is new and glaring. Corporations have been complicit in creating these values and have profited mightily from them. Value is also distorted by power. The financial industry as a whole seems to receive rewards out of proportion to its contribution to society. For this reason, governments need to step in to level the playing field. Without this intervention and support, the quality of our culture will continue to suffer.

My prediction of a new leisure economy in Part Two is based on the idea that unemployment is caused by a concentration of wealth. There is plenty of money in the economy but it is concentrated on unproductive assets such as real estate. Only capital and labour can create wealth, but if only a few own all capital and all wealth, then labour will sit idle and no one will be able to afford to

---

193   Scott Timberg, *Culture Crash: The Killing of the Creative Class*, (New Haven and London: Yale University Press, 2015), 249.

buy what is produced. On the other hand, society is going to gain if people work, if they create works of art, write novels, play music, or build furniture. If wealth is more distributed, and through the power of the market, people will create their own jobs based on arts, crafts, leisure, personal development, and healthcare.

Increasing capitalization results in fewer jobs. More welfare payments, guaranteed income, and more support by the state will allow individuals to concentrate on less productive but more fulfilling occupations. Higher food prices, ongoing requirements to increase yields per acre, and the failure of capitalized farming methods to increase land productivity sustainably could result in a return to a more labour intensive agriculture. I conceive the new leisure economy as a combination of hobby and occupation embracing productive crafts, live entertainment, and household based production. These labour-based occupations will augment ongoing capital-based production.

Our economy has been based on producing as much as possible while using as little labour as possible. In recent years, this has meant lower quality products and unsustainable use of resources. Creative reduction is required to reduce unneeded production. How do we work to increase wealth while at the same time reducing consumption? By increasing the quality of what we produce with better design. By design, we can produce products that are more durable, that are more useful, that do not become obsolete, and that are forever beautiful. By design, we can choose materials that can be sustainably harvested or are already available as technical nutrients. By design, we can choose technologies that more efficiently utilize available energy sources that are less damaging to the environment. By design, we choose materials that are less toxic to ourselves. As consumers, we can use less and be happier with what we have. By rationing appropriately, what is

scarce on Earth, we can ensure that wealth defined by our satisfaction can increase indefinitely.

ACKNOWLEDGEMENTS

This book, like all worthwhile projects, has turned out to be far more work than I could ever have imagined. I received much help and support from family and friends. I especially want to thank my wife Jackie for poring over many successive versions to improve understanding and continuity. I benefited enormously from comments and support from Nancy Butler, Mel Maxon, Durk deVries, Simon Bentz, Richard Fearn, and Alex Feldman, who all saw early drafts of the manuscript. In particular, I would like to thank Jacek Kaim who read not just one, but two early versions, providing extensive written feedback, and Christopher Fukushima who read and corrected the final draft. Julie Fukushima and Monica Feldman both made invaluable suggestions for layout and general appearance of the text. I would also like to thank the editors and staff at FriesenPress who used considerable skill in designing the book cover, editing, and publishing the book.

INDEX

computer simulation: growth,
28, 64-65, 244-245;
climate, 17, 50, 127
conditional cash transfers, 114
Confucius, 191
consumerism, 30, 73
consumption: conspicuous,
125; in Cuba, 233-237;
local, 166-167; overcon-
sumption, 12-13, 32, 146,
186, 227-228, 241, 280;
reducing, 71, 75, 81, 173,
223, 230, 238, 253, 280,
286; resource, 9, 15, 20,
31, 44, 68-72, 78, 197; tax,
230-231, wasteful, 10, 154
cooperation, 108, 156-175, 281
co-operatives, co-ops, 219, 234
corporation, 30, 50, 80, 85,
108, 133-141, 149, 168,
170-171, 182, 195, 201,
209, 211-212, 217-218,
239, 251, 257, 281-282,
285; benefit, 217-219
corporatism, 128-155
council housing, 212-214
craft brewers, 122
crash, 2008, 6, 124,
145, 185-193
creative destruction,
74-81, 238, 284

creative reduction, 81, 238,
286; less is more, 81
credit cards, 55, 172, 201, 255
Cuba, 40, 233-237, 284
cultural degradation, 58-59

debt, 64, 71, 74, 116, 119, 132,
142, 144-146, 148, 178,
180-190, 195, 197-198, 237
default option, 207-215
deficit, 144, 180; trade, 197;
bio-capacity, 284
deflation, 144, 222
deforestation, 67-68,
124-125, 258-259
dematerialized economy, 70
democracy, 36, 62, 86, 131,
143, 149, 159, 168; and
corporations, 134, 136,
139; survival of, 35-36
Denmark, 144, 151-
153, 174, 198
deregulation, 142, 182,
188, 198-199
design, 1-6, 12, 14, 16, 32, 113,
229, 230, 241, 252, 274,
286-287; industrial, 1, 4,
14, 263-266; of currency,
102, 228; of the economy,
5-6, 12, 31, 175, 280
design thinking, 1-6

developing countries, 5, 38, 63,
  66, 68, 72, 109, 116, 129,
  170, 184-187, 251, 266, 275
Diamond, Jared, 8, 124-125
dot-com, 184-185
double income, 30, 183

Easter Island, see Rapa Nui
Eccles, Mariner, 193-194
eco-efficiency, 29
ecological footprint,
  see footprint
ecology, 25
eco-money, Eco Money
  Network, 102
economic growth: benefits of,
  62-63; decoupling, 66-70;
  exponential, 28, 149;
  hedonic factors, 69-70;
  limits to, 28-30; Peter
  Victor and computer
  generated growth scenarios,
  64-65; rates relative to
  development, 63-64
efficiency: economic, 11-12,
  72, 75, 282; energy, 276-
  277; labour, 15, 31, 38, 73,
  88, 149; market, 19, 202,
  206, 211, 216; of common
  ownership, 167; produc-
  tion, 15, 16, 21, 81, 89;
  resource, 10, 16, 21, 31,

73, 76, 80, 104, 112, 174,
  233, 240, 261; technology,
  11, 81; time, 54, 268
Einstein, Albert, 4-5, 177
electric kettle, 265
empire, 110-111, 130
end of history, 168
endocrine, 49
energy: from food, 113, 234-
  235, 268; from fossil fuels,
  15-16, 28, 67, 88, 224-231;
  human, 76, 113, 268; renewable, 276-279; solar, 67, 225,
  235, 249, 257, 272-280
England, 39, 157, 204
essential production as opposed
  to optional, 31, 66, 77,
  87-90, 93, 97, 111, 113-114,
  154-155, 203-216, 252
estrogen mimicking chemi-
  cals, see chemicals
Europe, 14, 26-27, 32, 46,
  68, 114, 118, 126, 131,
  143, 145, 152, 170, 185,
  200, 257, 272, 284
European currency (Euro), 100
external costs, 12, 15, 19-20,
  31, 65, 72, 150, 172,
  186, 221, 222, 229
externalities, 175, 190
extreme capitalization, 105-126

Germany, 3, 67, 130,
143, 145, 199, 273
global warming, 7, 13, 19, 21,
23, 31-32, 38, 50, 56, 79,
109, 112-113, 115, 140,
173, 186, 221, 226-227,
248-249, 253, 280-281
globalization, 74, 130, 182
gold standard, 145
golden rule, 191
golden years, 14
Google, 139, 152, 217, 270
Gordon, Robert J., 119-120
government, 124-126,
129-155, 159-164
Great Depression, 14, 96,
130-133, 134, 143, 145,
147, 150, 178, 185-190
greenhouse gas emissions, 7, 20,
38, 64-65, 71, 115, 190, 224,
254-255, 281; by transportation, 268; cost of, 245;
embodied, 229-230, 262,
267; of buildings, 273-274;
of food, 255, 259; of products, 262; per capita, 234,
255-256, 273; per kilowatt
hour of electricity, 256-257
Great Transformation,
The, see Polanyi
Greenland ice sheet, 51

Gross Domestic Consumption,
41, 43, 72-73
Gross Domestic Product,
15, 30, 58, 63-64, 71-72
111-112, 121, 145, 147-153,
184-185, 214, 216, 240,
283; and quality, 71-74;
co-ops share of, 219; cost
of climate change, 250; of
Cuba, 233-234; per capita,
36, 40-41, 67-70, 192-193

Haber-Bosch process, 243
happiness, 31, 37, 61, 138,
191; measure of, 42-44
Hayek, F. A., 179; *The Road*
to Serfdom, 179-180
HDI, see Human
Development Index
healthcare, 31, 41, 58-59,
72-73, 90, 96, 98, 123, 146,
149, 236-237, 250, 286;
universal, 40-41, 100, 113,
132, 150-154, 191, 205-207;
in Cuba, 234-237; in the
US, 141, 148, 184, 215-216
high-density industrial
countries, 68
Hitler, Adolf, 145; *Mein*
Kampf, 140
Hobsbawm, Eric J., 106, 170

hormone-disrupting chemi-
cals, see chemicals
Hubbert, Marion King, 28
Human Condition, The,
see Arendt
Human Development
Index, 236
hyperinflation, 174

illegal drug industry, 108, 116
IMF, see International
Monetary Fund
income: average, 42; default,
211-212; distribution of,
58-60; growth in, 15; low
to high income countries,
47, 64, 235; single versus
double, 30-31, 92, 100,
183; per capita, 35-37
indium, 267
individualism, 19, 125, 169, 221
industrial design, see
design, industrial
industrialization, 16-17, 18,
21, 36, 46, 52, 56, 57, 89,
104-105, 117, 119-121,
130-131, 137, 142-144,
150, 163-166, 219, 245,
281; of agriculture, 110
industrial revolution, 27,
32, 46, 50, 52, 85, 88-89,
94, 95, 128, 280

inequality 15, 25, 59-61, 73-74,
125, 130, 141-142, 150, 154,
174, 184, 207, 241, 253; and
redistribution, 190-200; and
the 1 percent, 37-38, 59-60,
196, 211, 240; extremes of
wealth and poverty 204
inflation, 73, 98, 181-185, 189,
194, 200, 227, 239; of assets,
14, 183, 187; non-uniform,
187; of rewards, 14, 71
International Monetary
Fund, 170, 174
International Organization
for Standardization, 171
international trade, see trade
Internet, 42, 45, 100, 107,
121, 140, 143, 150, 255,
262, 274, 277, 284-285
Ireland, 144
Islam, 191
ISO, see International
Organization
for Standardization
Ithaca HOURS, 101

Japan, 40, 51, 67, 101, 130, 151,
182, 185, 199, 219, 261
Jevons paradox, 10-11
Jevons, William Stanley,
see Jevons paradox
Judaism, 191

manufacturing, 63, 109-111,
116, 119, 121-124, 128,
143, 184, 208, 264
marginal cost, 228
market: based economy, 19-20,
87, 98-100, 104, 122-124,
131-134, 143, 150, 154, 168,
172, 201-204, 209, 219,
227-228, 284; clearing, 231;
efficiency, 18-19, 203-204,
211; failures, 176-200;
farmers, 234; financial,
199; mechanism, 14, 195,
200, 206, 208, 214, 226,
252; stock, 119, 184, 194
Marx, Karl, 84
Maya kings, 124-125
meat, 25; eating, 56, 260-261
Mein Kampf, see Hitler
Mendel, Gregor, 243
methane, 51, 258-259
Microsoft, 139, 152, 210, 217
Mies van der Rohe, Ludwig, 81
migraine headaches, 46
missing middle, 169
monopoly, 204, 207-211;
platform, 217-218
monopsony, 209
morality, 18, 158-160, 170-171
Mussolini, Benito, 128

Nationalization, 96
Nayahan Banjar, 103
Nazism, 130, 134
neoliberalism, neoliberal,
18, 108, 141, 170, 199
neurological disorders, 49
New Deal, 133, 147, 178
Newton, Isaac, 176-177
Nordhaus, William, 245;
Climate Casino, 51, 245, 248
Nordic countries, 152
North America, 14, 27, 30, 32,
46, 71-72, 89, 93, 118, 122,
168, 178, 180, 182, 198,
200, 203, 255, 257, 273
North Korea, 233
nuclear arms race, 41, 159

OAPEC, see Organization
of Arab Petroleum
Exporting Countries
open source, 100, 210
optional as opposed to essential
production, see essential
organic, 102, 125, 229;
agriculture, 234-235, 259
Organization of Arab
Petroleum Exporting
Countries, 29
Orwell, George, 140
outsourcing, 109, 116, 119-
120, 130, 142, 182, 206

quality: measuring, 71-74,
285; of air, 46, 60-61, 70,
253; of culture, 58-59; of
food, 55-57, 79, 253, 260;
of housing, 70, 79, 93,
212-213, 273; of life, 11,
14, 36-37, 47, 60, 72, 93,
109, 115; of medical care,
253; of products, 10-12, 16,
37, 57-58, 60, 70, 73, 76,
79, 93, 105, 172, 190-191,
204, 207-209, 211, 229,
239, 264, 286; of service,
10, 199, 206, 210, 241
quantitative easing, 145, 147

race to the bottom, 159,
172, 195, 208, 209
Rapa Nui, 24
Rapanui, 8, 125
rational optimism, 242-243
rational pessimism, 242-286
rationing: in Cuba, 233-237;
resources, 72, 75; with
markets, 222-241
Reagan, Ronald, 170,
180, 199, 248-249
Reaganism, 200
reciprocity, 84
redistribution, 84, 190-191, 195
regional expression, 166

regulation, 15, 18-19, 50, 65-66,
125, 155, 157, 161, 170-173,
179-180, 183, 187, 199, 202,
213, 217, 224, 273, 281
rent: economic, 227-228;
environmental, 228-229;
resource, 227; seeking, 239
resource: depletion, 5, 65, 80,
112, 150, 175, 190, 244-245,
280; limited, 12, 17-18, 26,
30, 75, 86, 88, 236, 268;
scarcity, 19-20, 61, 67, 73,
80, 98-99, 104, 113-116,
124, 129-130, 203, 226, 245;
unlimited, 12, 28, 92, 149
Ricardo, David, 160, 162
rich world, 74, 129,
184, 283-284
Ridley, Matt, 242-243
right wing: policies, 170,
182; economics, 96
Road to Serfdom, The, see Hayek
Roaring Twenties, 118
Roman Empire, 26, 88
Roosevelt, Franklin D., 178
rules, 160-161, 171, 188, 205
Rupiah, 103

Sachs, Jeffrey D., 9, 12, 35,
38, 56, 63-64, 153
Scandinavian, 153, 197, 284
scarcity, 175, 203-204, 223, 226

Schumacher, E.F., *Small
is Beautiful*, 29
Schumpeter, Joseph
Alois, 75-76, 81
science, 2, 6, 17, 88, 122,
243, 252, 284; of global
warming, 246-249
scientific analysis, 3-5
Second World War, see
World War II
self-interest, 18-19, 98, 134,
170-171, 173, 176, 187,
201-203, 205; and laissez-
faire, 156-161, 175
self-provisioning, 96
singularity, 109
*Skeptical Environmentalist,
The*, see Lomborg
slavery, 116
smallpox, 27
smartphone, 120, 124, 227, 250
Smith, Adam, 18, 33, 59, 134,
158-161, 169-170, 176;
The Wealth of Nations, 159
Small is Beautiful,
see Schumacher
social capital, 94, 168-169, 280
socialization, 54, 107-108,
130, 151, 182, 281
South Korea, 67
Soviet Union, 15, 116, 131-132,
164, 168-169, 233-234

special theory of relativity, 177
specialization, 2, 78; and comparative advantage, 161-168
sperm counts, 49
Stiglitz, Joseph E.,
8-9, 189, 216
sustainability, 30, 112,
167, 266, 271
sustainable develop-
ment, 29, 35, 284

TDC, see two-dimen-
sional currency
technology: as ideology, 140;
benefits of, 69, 88; change
of, 5, 141, 238, 271, 280-
281; displaces labour, 17, 77,
80, 110, 118, 128-130, 238;
disruptive, 120; efficiency
of, 11-12, 76, 80-81, 223,
230; emerging, 120, 122;
household, 52; improve-
ments, 37, 39, 45, 61, 70,
109, 239; labour-based,
112; labour saving, 112;
pollution reducing, 36
Thatcher, Margaret, 170,
179-180, 199-200, 213
Thatcherism, 200
thyroid, 49
time: free, 52, 100, 110;
leisure, 52-55, 65, 253

Victor, Peter, see eco-
nomic growth
volatile organic compounds, 48
VOCs, see volatile
organic compounds

Wackernagel, Mathis, 283-
284; see also footprint
wage: growth, 101, 133, 181,
196, 199; labour, 89, 97;
living, 112-114, 189; of
CEOs, 239; minimum, 57,
170, 184, 189-190, 195,
211, 218; reductions, 106,
109, 142, 144-145, 217
Washington Consensus, 144
Wealth of Nations,
The, see Smith
welfare state, 18, 99-100,
107, 122, 128-155,
199, 207, 219, 284
winner-take-all, 166, 195
wisdom of crowds, 158, 281
work, labour and action,
see labour
World War I, 118,
130, 133, 134
World War II, 119, 126,
130-131, 133, 143, 178,
181, 193, 167, 214

ABOUT THE AUTHOR

Michael O'Shea Photography

Herb Bentz is an industrial designer and a founding partner at Form3 Design (form3.com), a company in Vancouver, Canada that has a strong commitment to the design of ecologically sustainable products. He holds degrees in science, architecture, and industrial design.

CPSIA information can be obtained
at www.ICGtesting.com
Printed in the USA
LVOW11*1909181216
517850LV00001B/2/P